The
Quest
for Mind

Second Edition

The Quest for Mind

Piaget, Lévi-Strauss,
and the Structuralist
Movement

Howard Gardner

The University of Chicago Press
Chicago and London

The University of Chicago Press, Chicago 60637
The University of Chicago Press, Ltd., London

© 1972, 1981 by Howard Gardner
All rights reserved. Published 1973
Second edition 1981
Printed in the United States of America

88 87 86 85 84 83 82 81   1 2 3 4 5

Library of Congress Cataloging in Publication Data
Gardner, Howard
The quest for mind.
Includes index.
1. Structuralism. 2. Piaget, Jean, 1896–1980.
3. Lévi-Strauss, Claude. I. Title.
B841.4.G37 1981   300′.1   81-11391
AACR2
ISBN 0-226-28331-3
ISBN 0-226-28332-1 (pbk.)

For Judy

Contents

Acknowledgments

Grateful acknowledgment is made to the following for permission to use the material indicated:

Philosophical Library, Inc., for material from H. Bergson, *An Introduction to Metaphysics*, Littlefield Adams, New Jersey, 1965.

William Morrow and Co., for material from M. Mead, *Sex and Temperament in Three Primitive Societies*, William Morrow, New York, 1955.

Harper and Row, Publishers, for material from C. Lévi-Strauss, *The Raw and the Cooked*, Harper and Row, New York, 1969.

Simon and Schuster, Inc., for material from *Knowledge Among Men*, Simon and Schuster, New York, 1966.

W. W. Norton and Co., for material from J. B. Watson, *Behaviorism*, New York, 1930; J. Piaget, *The Origins of Intelligence*, New York, 1963.

Basic Books, Inc., Publishers, for material from J. Piaget, *Structuralism*, translated and edited by Chaninah Maschler, Basic Books, Inc., Publishers, New York, 1970; from B. Inhelder and J. Piaget, *The Growth of Logical Thinking from Childhood to Adolescence: An Essay on the Construction of Formal Operational Structures*, translated by Anne Parsons and Stanley Milgram, Basic Books, Inc., Publishers, New York, 1958; from J. Piaget, *The Construction of Reality in the Child*, translated by Margaret Cook, Basic Books, Inc., Publishers, New York, 1954.

The New York Times, for material from "There Are No Superior Societies," S. de Gramont, *The New York Times Magazine*, 1968, Copyright by *The New York Times*. Reprinted by permission.

Dover Publications, for reproduction of a figure (p 225) from *Primitive Art* by F. Boas, Dover Publications, New York, 1955.

E. P. Dutton and Co., Inc., for material from Bronislaw Malinowski, *Argonauts of the Western Pacific*, New York, 1964. Published by E. P. Dutton and Co., and used with their permission.

Humanities Press, Inc., and Routledge and Kegan Paul for material from J. Piaget, *Judgment and Reasoning in the Child*, Littlefield Adams, New Jersey, 1964; J. Piaget, *The Child's Conception of the World*, Littlefield Adams, New Jersey, 1965; J. Piaget, *Language and Thought of the Child*, World Publishing Co., Cleveland, 1963.

University of Chicago Press and George Weidenfeld and Nicholson Ltd., for material from C. Lévi-Strauss, *The Savage Mind*, University of Chicago Press, Chicago, 1966.

Georges Borchardt, Inc., for material from C. Lévi-Strauss, *Tristes Tropiques*, Atheneum, New York, 1964.

The Free Press, Macmillan Co., and Routledge and Kegan Paul, for material from M. Mauss, *The Gift*, W. W. Norton, New York, 1967.

Professor Roman Jakobson for material from his book *Child Language Aphasia and Phonological Universals*, Mouton, The Hague, 1968.

The New York Academy of Sciences and Professor Edmund Leach, for material and a diagram adapted from E. Leach, "Lévi-Strauss in the Garden of Eden," *Transactions of the New York Academy of Sciences*, Series II, Vol. XXIII, No. 4.

Social Research (New York), for material adapted from "Piaget and Lévi-Strauss: The Quest for Mind," Vol. 37 (1970), 348–65.

Semiotica and Mouton and Co., Publishers (The Hague), for material adapted from "The Structural Analysis of Protocols and Myths," Vol. 5 (1972), 31–57.

The Human Context (London), for material adapted from "Structure and Development," 1972, in press.

Preface to the Second Edition

As a student of the social sciences in the later 1960's, I became convinced that Jean Piaget and Claude Lévi-Strauss were embarked on parallel scientific enterprises and that their work represented the most significant recent innovation in the sciences of man. These convictions ultimately led to the publication in 1973 of *The Quest for Mind*. In this introduction to structuralism I sought, through a focus on the writings of Piaget and Lévi-Strauss, to lay out the principal tenets of that novel approach to the study of behavior and culture.

Reissuance of *The Quest for Mind* gives me a welcome chance to reflect on the particular niche that it may originally have occupied and on the book's possible usefulness today. The passage of a decade since its writing also offers an opportunity to describe recent events in the structuralist movement and to review the scholarly efforts of Lévi-Strauss since the publication of *Mythologiques* and of Piaget during the last decade of his inspiring life. Most of my comments on the past ten years in structuralism will be found in the Afterword; I restrict myself here to some remarks about the place of this book in the literature of the movement.

When *The Quest for Mind* was written, little was known in the United States about structuralism. In particular, the role of this largely French-inspired movement within the social sciences was unclear. The works of Piaget and Lévi-Strauss were not well understood and had yet to be related to one another. Nor was it clear (at least to me) how great the claims (and implications) of Noam Chomsky's work would be for the social sciences.

While "structuralism" is still by no means a household word in this country and my book remains more of a "brief" on the movement's behalf than a description of a consensus, the work of its leading practitioners is now much more familiar. Many of its assumptions and techniques have been taken over by workers throughout the social sciences—sometimes with credit, sometimes in ignorance (or even in scorn) of the contributions of individuals like Piaget and Lévi-Strauss. But even when a structuralist debt is directly acknowledged, I think that the pathbreaking contributions of Piaget and Lévi-Strauss are often not sufficiently appreciated. *The Quest for Mind* can continue to serve a function to the extent that it brings their seminal work to the attention of the public.

The passage of a decade has clarified what this book is, as well as what it is not. At the time of its initial publication, several critics felt that I was simply introducing to the American public the latest in a series of Gallic intellectual fads. True, for many structuralism was a fad, but one that had already passed by 1970. And since that time, so many literary fads have swept through Paris that it would take several books merely to chronicle them. It must be emphasized, then, that *The Quest for Mind* treats a structuralist approach to the social sciences, an intellectual movement which, far from being faddishly accessible, continues to challenge serious scholars. In contrast, *Quest* touches only incidentally on structuralism in literature.

I see now with greater clarity that it was their complementary interests in the "core" of mind that first attracted me to the works of Piaget and Lévi-Strauss, singly and jointly. Piaget conceived the mind in terms of its scientific orientation; Lévi-Strauss was attracted to the mind because of its sensory and aesthetic dimensions. Their works of the past decade have revealed these contrasting conceptions of mind with ever greater force.

As I (among others) had anticipated, structuralism as a *distinctive* force in the social sciences was spent by the middle 1970's. Nearly everyone who had once used the term, except perhaps Piaget, explicitly rejected the title of structuralist. Even Lévi-Strauss, in effect its originator, abandoned the label when he saw how loosely it was being bandied about. There were also less transitory reasons to question the term "structuralism." The structural models first developed by Ferdinand de Saussure and Roman Jakobson were criticized extensively, and the formal models advanced by first generation structuralists were seen as outmoded, even, at times, by the practitioners themselves. In place of the emphasis on structures, current efforts in the social sciences have been directed increasingly at questions of process.

Labels come and go, but contributions last. I believe that the works of the original structuralist writers, and, in particular, of Lévi-Strauss and Piaget have proved to be of genuine and lasting importance. If I were writing the book today, I would add Chomsky to this group, for reasons sketched in the Afterword. My feeling is that while recent social scientists have in impressive ways gone beyond the first generation structuralists, they have not infrequently done so at the cost of ignoring both the compelling phenomena and the broad vision that first attracted me, with so many others, to the works of Piaget and Lévi-Strauss. Making sure that their contributions—like those of Freud and Marx, and Weber and Durkheim—are not forgotten in the rush to the newest fad, the most complex technology, the latest "paradigm," is for me the principal reason for re-presenting *The Quest for Mind* to the public today.

I have been helped by numerous individuals in the preparation of the two editions of this book. Special thanks are due Noam Chomsky, Tom Considine, Hans Furth, Judy Gardner, Howard Gruber, Barbara Leondar, William Lohman, Dan Okrent, Mel Rosenthal, Peter Rivière, and Ellen Winner. I am especially indebted to Professors Lévi-Strauss and Piaget themselves, who encouraged this project from its inception, took time to discuss a number of perplexing issues with me, and have continued to inspire me in my work.

Cambridge, Massachusetts
May 1981

I A New Approach to the Social Sciences

1 A New Development in the Social Sciences

*Ideas are a system complete within us, like any of
the kingdoms of Nature—a sort of flora whose
iconography will one day be traced out by a man
of genius, whom the world will call a lunatic.*

—BALZAC*

Computer simulation, psychotherapy, industrial relations
boards, economic planning, teaching machines, public
polling, and advertising have become such accepted parts
of modern life that the recency of these phenomena is
sometimes forgotten. One is tempted to conclude that the
social sciences sprang up full-grown during the Enlightenment and have always been accepted by the larger society.
In fact, however, it was only during the last century that
specific disciplines dealing with human activity and institutions arose and that investigators came to think of themselves as psychologists, economists, sociologists, anthropologists, or, more broadly, as social scientists. Furthermore,
since it customarily takes a generation or so for theory to
be translated into practice, current public thinking and
present-day social institutions reflect the theory of some
decades ago. Thus, behaviorism and psychoanalytic theory

* All references will be found in the Notes Section in the back of the
book.

3

dominate most people's views on human psychology; writers like B. F. Skinner, Herbert Marcuse, and Norman O. Brown are hailed as utopian prophets, even though the theories on which their projections are based are now out-dated in the eyes of many contemporary social scientists. Given the widespread application of social-scientific theory, and this "cultural gap" between theory and practice, a new development in the social sciences looms important for those interested in the shape of the future.

A new school of social science might be expected to rely heavily upon modern mathematics, neurophysiological and biochemical breakthroughs, and high-speed computers and precise measuring instruments. Surprisingly, however, the most innovative group of social scientists—the structuralists—for the most part spurn such sources and tools. Instead, they seek insights about behavior and thoughts from such seemingly unlikely sources as kinship relations among primitive groups, hundreds of myths about food and fire, the casual remarks of children engaged in solving a puzzle, the minute differences between two imitations of the same model. Initially the structuralist proceeds in a common-sense manner, simply observing and describing what he sees; but he subsequently proceeds to employ powerful formal models and to draw remarkable and unexpected conclusions about the significance of the phenomena investigated. The flavor of structuralism can perhaps be most readily conveyed by listing a few of the questions which have preoccupied its adherents:

(1) A five-year-old child is given two mounds and asked to make sure they have equal amounts of clay. When the child has patted the balls to his satisfaction, an experimenter takes one and rolls it until it assumes the shape of a sausage. He asks the child, "Is there more clay in the ball over there, in the sausage over here, or do they both have the same amount of clay?" Only an extraordinary five-year-old will declare that the ball and sausage have the

same amount of clay. Most commonly, children of this age will note that the sausage is longer and conclude that it contains more to eat or to play with. An eight-year-old child, however, will typically think the question silly, because anyone knows the ball and the sausage have, and will always have, the same amount of clay. The psychologist Jean Piaget has sought to determine how this enhanced understanding in the older child has come about.

(2) Eight-month-old infants the world over will babble the gamut of possible sounds, many of which never appear in the language of the surrounding culture. Within a few months, however, this variegated babbling will have ceased, and children will begin to utter a small set of sounds purposefully and regularly. In many parts of the world, the first discernible words will be "mama" and "papa." The linguist Roman Jakobson has offered an explanation of "Why Mama and Papa?"

(3) It is a common practice in Western society to give names to domestic animals. One might think that naming practices in these domains are purely random; but a closer study has revealed striking regularities. For example, pet birds receive names which could also be given to humans (Pierre, Donald, Jacqueline), while dogs are given names (Fido, Spot, Pluto) which would never be found on a birth certificate. The French anthropologist Claude Lévi-Strauss has introduced a fascinating hypothesis to explain these practices.

(4) Unless the Bible is viewed as the Word of God, or the random concatenation of disparate myths, some explanation is required for a number of parallel themes in the stories of the Creation, the Garden of Eden, and the clash between Cain and Abel. The English anthropologist Edmund Leach has applied structuralist methods in a provocative exegesis of the opening chapters of the Bible.

In trying to unravel puzzles like these, the structurally-oriented social scientist typically models himself after a natural scientist. For example, the biologist intent on elucidating the makeup of the human organism artificially divides the body into various systems—the nervous system, vascular system, muscular system, and so on. All appreciate that this is merely a convention but, for pedagogical and conceptual reasons, a useful and perhaps necessary one. Similarly, in investigating the makeup of the external world, the chemist and physicist search for basic units— atoms, electrons, subatomic particles, as well as larger components, like cells or molecules—in the hope that they can build up from these units to more and more complex phenomena. All these scientists may be said to be searching for the structural components, and the underlying structure, of the physical or biological world; they do so by seeking units which they can see (like cells) or which, though invisible, can in some sense be said to have a physical existence (like atoms) . The social scientist, by contrast, deals with behavior, with institutions, with thoughts, beliefs, fears, dreams. At various times, it has been claimed that these do not exist and therefore should not be studied, or, alternatively, that they do exist and are as physical as cells or crystals. The structuralists subscribe to neither view. They believe that behavior and institutions do have a structure, and not merely in a trivial or metaphorical sense, but that this structure will never be visible or tangible; nonetheless, that it is incumbent upon the investigator to ferret it out and to map its dimensions, in clear, preferably formal or mathematical language. Whatever the complex phenomenon under investigation—a child interpreting a proverb, the exchange of women between social groups, the rhyme scheme of a fourteenth-century sonnet— the structuralist treats it like a foreign language which must be deciphered; through careful observation, and the performance of appropriate experiments, he determines the basic "words" or units, the syntax, and the meaning of the foreign behavior, and describes it in terms which other scientists can comprehend. In addition, he adopts procedures which can be followed independently by other scientists, thereby avoiding a classic pitfall of earlier times—a set of brilliant ideas flowing from the pen of one or another scientist, which can be admired but not carried further by the next generation of thinkers.

The burgeoning of the social sciences, and the founding of the new school of structuralism, can be traced to a variety of causes, ranging from a desire to apply methods of the natural sciences to questions traditionally posed by philosophers, to a need for more effective means of aiding the mentally sick and the culturally disadvantaged. An especially potent stimulus came from the pioneering works of specific researchers—innovative thinkers like Freud and Marx—who imposed a convincing organizational framework upon great areas of data that had been confusing and somewhat overwhelming, and thus showed that a comprehensive theory of behavior or society was possible. Freud's demonstration that mental illness and mental health are of a piece, that much of thought is unconscious, that events of early childhood exercise a determining influence on subsequent behavior, may have initially shocked his contemporaries; but with the passage of time and the accumulation of evidence, it became clear that here was a theory which could account for many aspects of individual conduct. Similarly, Marx's analysis of the development of capitalism, the role of economic factors in social and political history, the nature of the class structure and the class struggle itself, initially aroused strong opposition; still, these ideas eventually altered the thinking and the direction of research of social scientists, because this orientation promised a viable approach to the nature and evolution of human institutions. The dramatic and revolutionary sweep of these men's ideas, coupled with the devoted labors and elaborations of their followers, did much to spur both interest and progress in the social sciences. And, before much more time had elapsed, the conceptions of Marx and Freud had been assimilated by educated persons generally, even as they left lasting imprints upon social, cultural, and political institutions throughout the world.

Another impetus to progress in the social sciences came from the adoption of more sophisticated methods of research and more appropriate models of behavior. The original generation of social scientists, whose work will be described in the next chapter, were often keen observers and careful describers; but their work usually lacked systematic coherence and experimental rigor, thereby precluding the possibility of followthrough by other scientists. In addition, the first social scientists, when seeking models or analogies for the phenomena they were investigating, naturally gravitated to quite simple devices: they regarded the reflex arc as a model for behavior, a patch of light as a model for external stimulation, a tool as a model for a social institution, or biological cell as the model for a society. The primitive nature of these analogies seriously limited the scope of their investigations, either by directing their attention to trivial problems or by constraining them to forced and oversimplified explanations of complex phenomena. Only as social scientists were able to make more appropriate uses of examples and methods from the "harder" sciences, only when they chose models more closely suited to the phenomena they sought to elucidate, did further breakthroughs in this difficult area of study become possible.

In the last few decades, owing in large part to the efforts of a small group, working in relative isolation from their contemporaries and, indeed, from one another, structuralism has developed as a new approach in the social sciences, one which holds promise for the non-distorted and non-simplified study of human behavior and institutions, and which any trained investigator should be able to apply. To be sure, the terms "structure," "structuralism," and "structuralist" are of long-standing use among scholars and have already well permeated the popular consciousness. Yet it must at once be added that my estimate here of the value and importance of the contemporary structuralist movement is open to dispute; the present work should be viewed as a brief in support of its claims, rather than as an account of what is already believed by all reasonable social scientists.

Accompanying the recent interest in the structuralist approach and in the writings of Piaget and Lévi-Strauss has come a spate of books, articles, and mass-media presentations on "the mind of man," "cognitive development," "the world of the child," "the life of primitive man." Anyone who has examined these sources will have at least some general notion of what structuralism is about—although he is quite unlikely to have acquired a firm grasp of the movement's methods and implications. Ignorance about structuralism abounds because writers have characterized the methods used instead of demonstrating them; named three dozen structuralists, but described none in any detail; assumed ignorance on the audience's part about current findings, but omniscience concerning the past history of psychology and anthropology. As a result, book-collecting in the human sciences and the dropping of hyphenated French names are on the ascendancy, while comprehension and critical understanding lag behind. By focusing in depth on the most seminal figures in the structuralist camp, this book seeks to repair the existing imbalance.

At this juncture, it is tempting (if not obligatory) to offer a capsule definition of the subject. Yet, having just castigated others for espousing the glib formula or the misleading catch phrase, I do not wish to contribute further to misapprehensions about structuralism. The fact is, I think, that it is not possible to define the movement with any precision, any more than it is to delineate clearly a field called social psychology or behavioral genetics. Writers have tended to apply the term "structuralism" either to a hopelessly vague field of literary analysis, to all contemporary French intellectual thought which is not avowedly existentialist, or to the writings of any and all scholars and critics who call themselves structuralists. Certainly none of these approaches is wholly satisfactory. Add to the confusion that no two structuralists, not even Lévi-Strauss and Piaget, define "structure" in the same way, and one wonders why the term has not been publicly banned or appropriated by Newspeak.

My own solution has been as follows: With very occasional lapses, I am restricting the term "structuralism" to certain common themes and approaches found in the writings of a small group of men, chief among them Lévi-Strauss, Piaget, Edmund Leach, and Roman Jakobson. I am at the same time claiming that these common elements have given rise to a new movement or paradigm in the social sciences which may (and perhaps should) be called structuralism. I have postponed until Chapter 5 any attempt at an overall definition, preferring initially—in line with my view of structuralism as a method or approach, rather than a given doctrine or body of beliefs—to illustrate what structuralism is by showing how it is done. For the present, it is hoped that the few examples given above will provide enough of a foretaste of the structuralist approach to guide and sustain the reader as he is led toward the ultimate goal through what may seem to be somewhat remote pathways.

The structuralists are distinguished first and foremost by their ardent, powerfully held conviction that there is structure underlying all human behavior and mental functioning, and by their belief that this structure can be discovered through orderly analysis, that it has cohesiveness and meaning, and that structures have generality (otherwise there would be as many structures as behaviors, and little point in spelling them out). I hope that readers who follow the argument to its conclusion will be able, not merely to evaluate the legitimacy of these assumptions in the abstract, but to use them to make their own structural analyses concerning questions of interest to them. This would be the best possible proof of the utility of structuralism.

Recent findings in chemistry, physics, and other "hard" disciplines can be cogently described without mentioning names; but such a state of affairs has not yet been realized in the social sciences. In attempting to describe structuralist research, one is faced with a choice: either overlook the vast differences among theorists and pretend that a consensus exists, or concentrate upon a few central figures and disregard the more peripheral contributors. Because I believe their achievements to be of signal importance for the social sciences, ranking with those of Freud, Marx, and Weber, I have chosen to deal at length with the writings of Jean Piaget and Claude Lévi-Strauss. In their lives and works, these men throw into sharp relief the central themes of structuralism, so that a thoughtful analysis of their contributions should help illuminate the works of their colleagues as well. And, more generally, a detailed consideration of the work of one or two leading practitioners seems to me the best way to convey understanding of any new method. The reader's immersion in the researches of Piaget and Lévi-Strauss will, it is hoped, enable him to develop an intuitive sense of the nature of structuralism, and he should then be better able to cope with my more formal analysis, and my efforts to reconcile conflicts in the views of these two thinkers.

Structuralism is controversial, in part because it involves a rejection of earlier approaches in the social sciences, and in part because it has certain peculiarly French characteristics which make it seem strange, even exotic, to many people of Anglo-Saxon culture. Any assessment of the movement, therefore, is necessarily incomplete without an understanding of its origins, the background out of which it has emerged, and of the competing paradigms against which it puts forward its own claims. For this reason, the discussion here will begin with a description of the intellectual tradition into which both Piaget and Lévi-Strauss were born, and a thumbnail history of the disciplines to which they were later to make such substantial contributions.

It is in both the importance of the questions it tackles and the sophistication of its analytical tools that structuralism represents a major advance in the social sciences. Unfortunately, in an introductory work it is not possible to discuss in detail the formal procedures and models, the mathematical and logical formulations, which Lévi-Strauss, Piaget, and others sometimes use; and in any case I am not equipped to do so. Regrettably, part of structuralism's power must be taken on faith in this book. But I hope at least to provide some indication of what structural analysis based on logical principles can yield. Furthermore, there is no need for the reader to feel in awe of the mathematical foundations of structuralism; indeed, the movement has been subjected to strong criticism for its overreliance on or even misuse of formalisms, and I myself feel that many insights are more effectively presented without the mathematics and that some of the formal analysis is metaphorical and suggestive rather than precise and necessary. At any rate, even if the reader lacks the technical knowledge to evaluate structuralist techniques critically, he can and should judge whether the problems studied by structuralists are significant and whether the solutions offered are meaningful and revealing.

Various differences in method and orientation exist between the two men under consideration. For example, Piaget uses a structural-developmental approach in which he seeks to account for phenomena, such as the conservation of liquids, through an examination of the processes whereby they unfold over time; Lévi-Strauss prefers an "agenetic" structural approach, treating phenomena like naming practices in different cultures, which date from different periods and have separate histories, as if they all existed at the present time under similar circumstances.

Nonetheless, there are certain broad themes which have come to dominate the thinking of both men. Among these are the effect of the language a person uses on the nature and quality of his thought processes; the origins and development of the moral code and religious beliefs of a given social group; the affinities and differences among thought processes of children, animals, primitives, the mentally ill, and normal Western adults; the appropriateness of certain "root metaphors" of action or perception as a description of the fundamental essence of thought; the relative validity of the developmental and the agenetic, or nonhistorical, approach. In the chapters that follow, I shall review the solutions which each man has proposed for these problems and then offer my own thoughts on how a rapprochement between outstanding differences of opinion might be brought about. Perhaps the proposed synthesis can also serve as a point of departure for an integration of the structural and developmental approaches to human nature.

Two assumptions mark the structuralist enterprise overall. One is the belief that through careful examination of groups which, like children or primitives, differ from the contemporary Western adult, new light can be cast on the whole of human experience; the second is the faith that what is distinctive about human beliefs, development, and institutions is a reflection of the fundamental nature of human thought, and hence, the biological structure of the "human mind."* Such a view of the mind as central to behavior and institutions is controversial, but it is deeply ingrained in the background of both Piaget and Lévi-Strauss, and forms a point of departure for their theorizing.

---

* The quotation marks are my way of indicating my strong reservations about such a concept as the "human mind," implying as it does a mind-body dichotomy, a dualistic view of human nature that I reject. For present purposes, however, it has seemed expedient to use the term, and I have done so throughout.

Whether right or wrong, the quest for mind is an exciting and, potentially, an enormously fruitful enterprise. Like the Cartesian intellectual tradition out of which it emerges, this quest has already yielded powerful insights into the questions which currently intrigue social scientists and have always fascinated thoughtful individuals.

2 The French Intellectual Tradition and the Roots of Structuralism: A Structural-Developmental Analysis

As to the opinions which are truly and wholly mine, I offer no apology for them as new—persuaded as I am that if their reasons be well considered, they will be found to be so simple and so conformed to common sense as to appear less extraordinary and less paradoxical than any others which can be held on the same subjects.

—DESCARTES

I do not see that I should ever conclude anything from these various sense perceptions concerning things outside of ourselves, unless the mind has carefully and maturely examined them. For it seems to me that it is the business of the mind alone, and not of the being composed of mind and body, to decide the truth of such matters.

—DESCARTES

Few schoolboys today have ever read a line of the Federalist papers or of Jefferson's writings, let alone the philosophical writings of Locke or Montesquieu which formed the basis for American political thought. Nevertheless, there is a sense in which the Founding Fathers have been "read" by Americans of all ages; such articles of faith as

the essential equality of all men, the right to possess property and pursue happiness, the need for checks and balances within a constitutional system, have for so long been
"in the air" that they form a natural and effortlessly acquired set of beliefs for most inhabitants of our country.
Somewhat more subtle, but equally pervasive, is the conviction that every man should have the right to make a new
life for himself, unburdened by old religious or political
tradition; as self-fulfillment is most likely to be found in an
environment bereft of constraints, the opportunity to develop in a new, relatively fluid milieu (like a frontier
territory) becomes particularly attractive. For, just as
immutable laws, an entrenched hierarchical social order,
and rigid religious and social mores can restrict a person's
range of choice and preordain his eventual fate, so life in
a nontraditional society can foster development and pro-
ductivity. This set of beliefs, part and parcel of one's birth-
right as an American, extends into the scientific realm,
where Americans have challenged the view that man's
mind and his development are determined by a fixed genetic endowment or by parental social status. Instead, they
hold that men can evolve in as many different ways as there
are diverse settings—indeed, man is best viewed as a reflection of those pressures and models present in his own environment. These forces, and not the biological heritage, are
the prime determinants of man's development and his
eventual status in life.

Even as young Americans (and often young Britons)
have effortlessly imbibed such ideas, French youths have
similarly picked up another set of unconscious attitudes
which inevitably color their views on man and society.
(I am using the term "French" broadly, to include such
outposts of French culture as Western Switzerland and
Belgium.) As members of a culture which has existed for
many centuries, has few means for nonviolent change, and
is dominated by the lingering effects of past events, they
place greater emphasis on the traditions of their society

and are far less sanguine about the possibilities for environmental change or novel human development. Such ideas, presumably assimilated years ago by the youthful Piaget and Lévi-Strauss, constitute an important part of the heritage of structuralism. Because they are less well known to those outside Continental circles, these elements of the Gallic tradition will require some elaboration here.

1. THE FRENCH INTELLECTUAL TRADITION

Since the time of René Descartes, the most influential philosopher in French intellectual history, French thinkers have been fascinated with the "human mind." Descartes saw the mind as an entity apart from the rest of the person; mechanical and biological functions were carried on by the body, while language, reasoning, and originality were reflections of unique mental powers possessed by the mind or soul. This dualistic approach to human nature has been severely criticized since his time, but Descartes' belief that the mind should be studied on its own, that it can be examined separately from the more animal-like aspects of human beings, has persisted in the academies and salons of his country.

Many other Cartesian views and biases have exhibited comparable longevity: the conviction that inspection of one's own mind is the primary route to truth; the denigration of humanistic philosophy and the arts, accompanied by an exaltation of logical-mathematical and geometrical reasoning; the belief that animals lack mind and hence are incapable of generative, creative thought; affirmation of the central role of human language in understanding and thought; the aspiration to unify all knowledge; an abiding preoccupation with the essence of human nature. Less acceptable have been Descartes' ignorance of social and cultural factors; his peculiar proof of the existence of God; his rejection of sense data; his lack of interest in the way skills and abilities are acquired; his failure to consider historical trends. In any event, it is hardly overstating Descartes' importance to assert that the primary concern of French thinkers in the succeeding centuries has been, on the one hand, to refine and elaborate those of his ideas they found most compelling and, on the other, to modify or sift out those tenets which seemed less palatable.

There is perhaps only one other figure in French intellectual history whose influence is at all comparable to that of Descartes: the Genevan philosopher Jean Jacques Rousseau. Often writing in opposition to the Cartesians, and to Enlightenment counterparts like Voltaire, Rousseau took pains to stress the very aspects of human nature which Descartes had overlooked or disdained. Where Descartes had concentrated on the rational and logical aspects of human cognition, Rousseau emphasized the affective, sentimental, and emotional portions of the human psyche. Where Descartes was content to focus on the individual, and, indeed, on one particular Frenchman, Rousseau took into account the range of human societies, exhibiting special empathy with peoples from the remote past and on distant shores. And where Descartes' interest was restricted to the mature thought and action of the developed adult, a principal treatise of Rousseau's concerned the education of the naïve child.

Rousseau also introduced a number of concerns which had not occupied Descartes. He was fascinated by the question of society's influence upon "natural" or "savage man" and attempted to devise idealized models of the State of Nature and the Social Contract. Rousseau knew these models were inevitably conjectural, but felt it vital "to know closely a state which no longer exists, which may never have existed, and which probably will never exist," in order to make plausible extrapolations about the current plight of mankind. First he reduced man and society to first principles (man is free in the State of Nature); then he performed hypothetical experiments upon these models and principles (let us see what happens when one man becomes dominant in this State). Rousseau intuitively anticipated certain themes which were to concern future generations: the relationship between Nature and Culture; the possible differences between primitive and civilized man, the respective psychologies of child and adult; the pivotal nature of private property, power relationships among men, the general will of a community; the perception of sensible qualities. Because of his perspicacity and his passionate insights he has been hailed by some, including Claude Lévi-Strauss, as the first scientific student of human nature.

Yet, despite his many divergencies, Rousseau demonstrated appreciable loyalty to Cartesian canons. He joined in the condemnation of earlier philosophy and the learned academies; he concurred in the centrality of man and the essential differences between man and beast; he underscored the importance of language; he continued to rely on his own introspection and to ponder the place of mind in human nature. Rousseau, then, stands in the French tradition as a crucial antipode to the seminal Descartes: antagonist and revisionist on some issues, supporter and amplifier on a number of others. Between their respective positions those of the remaining contributors to the tradition can be plotted, with certain themes and issues recurring inexorably, others oscillating in emphasis from the Cartesian to the Rousseauian pole.

One enduring facet of the French tradition concerns the status of empirical evidence—that is, the relative weight attached to systematic observation and measurement of phenomena by oneself and others. Descartes, of course, had little interest in such observation, preferring to rely on introspection, his own pure, unaided ratiocination; and Rousseau, though paying lip service to explorers, scientists, and historians, also deemed his own sentiments and inner promptings the surest guide to truth. This "conceit" is very difficult for those outside the tradition to accept; the necessity of achieving consensus within a community of scientists, for example, has long been an article of faith in the Anglo-Saxon world. Yet the tendency to turn inward, even in the face of contradictory observations by others, has persisted among the French, and is found even today in many writings. All the same, among those interested in anthropology, psychology, and sociology, there has been a slow but steady movement toward empiricism. In the course of the nineteenth and twentieth centuries, systematic data collection has been embraced, scientific institutions have been set up, the value attached to one's own perceptions has been minimized in favor of consensual agreement among scholars investigating related phenomena. To be sure, this progress has been less rapid or decisive than in other intellectual circles and one encounters regressions toward a more solipsistic interpretation of phenomena; the sacrosanctity of one's own observations remains a latent leitmotif of French thought. Yet the overall trend toward empiricism seems inexorable.

A number of leading participants in the development of the luminous French intellectual tradition have made major contributions to the emergence of the social sciences as an autonomous field of study—in particular, Claude Henri Saint-Simon, Auguste Comte, and Émile Durkheim. Comte and Saint-Simon made encyclopedic efforts to cull and collate all knowledge about the range of human societies and activities. Like Spencer in England and Hegel in Germany, however, they tended to view their own society as the culmination of social evolution, hardly considering that other groups might have reached comparable levels of development or possess equal integrity. Moreover, although they strongly espoused a positivistic approach—i.e., dealing only with immediate, observable, material entities—they tended to fall back on unsupported philosophical speculation in their own work. As Comte boasted:

The progress I have achieved has procured for me a certain authority; and my conceptions are now sufficiently matured. I am entitled, therefore, to proceed with the same freedom and rapidity as my principal ancestors, Aristotle, Descartes, and Leibniz, who confined themselves to a definite expression of their views, leaving the verification and development of them to the public.

Durkheim's work represented a definite advance over that of the founding sociologists, for he practiced careful methods of data accumulation, employed statistical controls, and embraced a less parochial view of the relation of his society to others around the world. Durkheim appreciated the important role played by feelings of solidarity, religion, and morality within a social group; in splendidly paradoxical fashion, he used hard-nosed empirical methods to document conclusions which ran counter to positivist orthodoxy. For example, he was able to show that suicide rates, which had generally been interpreted as the sum of individual decisions by isolated actors, could more adequately be accounted for as a reflection of the mores of the culture in which a person lived; given the dominant religion of a society, one could predict its suicide rate. Rather than stemming from individual neuroses, suicide reflected the degree of social integration in a group. Similarly, Durkheim was able to draw upon the legal system, the economic forces and the division of labor in a society in order to demonstrate the nature and degree of social solidarity found therein. Norms and social solidarity, hitherto thought to be abstract or even metaphysical entities, were demonstrable social facts, as specifiable and accessible to study as individual actions or physical objects. Almost singlehandedly, Durkheim conferred upon French social science a coherence which it had theretofore lacked; yet his reluctance to consider psychological factors and his failure to devise formal, testable models of social processes imposed a certain one-sidedness and circularity upon his formulations which it was left to succeeding generations to correct.

Another French thinker of Durkheim's time represents, from one point of view, a regressive influence; and yet Henri Bergson exercised such a powerful hold over youth in the early part of the present century that he cannot be ignored. A mathematician and Cartesian philosopher by training, an artist and metaphysician by inclination, Bergson immersed himself in the sciences of his era, only to emerge with a devastating critique of the limitations of scientific knowledge. He contrasted the intellect to the intuition, regarding the intuition as a natural way of reacting and understanding, the intellect as a labored form of cognition suited only to narrowly focused scientific investigation. Philosophers and scientists had paid too exclusive attention to the intellect; Bergson proposed to demonstrate the limitations of science and the creative power of intuition. He called special attention to the flux and flow of reality—the aspect of experience which he felt was central—and deplored the "isolated, cinematographic" approach of science, which worked instead with discrete moments of time and substituted symbols for the ongoing, unceasing continuity of life:

If one looks a little more closely at each of these states, noticing that it varies, asking how it could endure if it did not change, the understanding hastens to replace it by a series of short states, which in their turn break up if necessary and so forth, ad infinitum. But how can we help seeing that the essence of duration is to flow, and that the fixed placed side by side with the fixed will never constitute anything which has duration. It is not the "states," simple snapshots we have taken . . . along the course of change, that are real; on the contrary, it is flux, the continuity of transition, it is change itself that is real.

Bergson, in sum, hurled a challenge at the masters of the French tradition: recognize the limits of rational and scientific inquiry, its incapacity to illuminate central aspects of human experience; and attempt to grasp in an intuitive way the innermost qualities of life itself.

Bergson's position may be viewed as reactionary, in that it ran counter to the increasing reliance upon empiricism and the increasing faith in science; and yet, he was touching upon many of the same antirationalist themes which had recurred periodically in French thought, most memorably in Rousseau. Furthermore, a remarkable number of themes which were articles of faith for Descartes are preserved with little change in Bergson's writings: the nonmechanical nature of mind; the centrality of language in human society; the disdain for earlier philosophical efforts; the desire to unify all knowledge; the reliance on logical exposition; the perpetual fascination with the nature of human intelligence and mental functioning. Thus, despite his opposition to the general thrust of Cartesian thought, Bergson carried forward many of its cardinal precepts, and couched even his critique of it in terms acceptable to its practitioners.

We see, then, that while there is certainly movement and change within the French intellectual tradition, many of its central tenets have remained more or less fixed and unchallenged since the early seventeenth century. Whenever such regularities can be discerned in a given system, a structural analysis becomes possible. To give the reader, therefore, a kind of foretaste of structuralist methodology, I propose to make here just such an analysis of the French intellectual tradition, as it has been presented (very sketchily, to be sure) above. Naturally, the method will seem somewhat strange at first, and the analysis in need of further explication. Nonetheless, the experiment seems worth pursuing, if only because structuralism should be applicable to most any domain, including its own history. For similar reasons, I shall undertake, later in this chapter, a developmental analysis of social-scientific thought in general, in the hope of giving the reader at least partial familiarity with developmental methods even as these are brought to bear upon their own genesis.

The structural analyst confronted with a given subject area, or "domain," first attempts to isolate those factors within it which have remained constant. These he views as "outside time," "given," "perpetually present," hence *synchronic*—in the present case, those elements that constitute the essence of the French intellectual tradition. Next, the analyst incorporates temporal considerations, searching for factors which change with time, which are subject to historical pressures and therefore *diachronic*. These diachronic aspects, in turn, may be of two sorts: those which move solely in one direction over the course of time and so are referred to as *irreversible*; and those which seem to shift from one pole to another and back again and so are considered to be *reversible*.

After this brief introduction to terminology, let me now present in tabular form a structural model of the French intellectual tradition:

A STRUCTURAL ANALYSIS OF THE FRENCH
INTELLECTUAL TRADITION

Synchronic Elements (always present from 1650 to 1900)	interest in mind; detached objectivity; desire to synthesize all knowledge; special status of human beings; unique properties of language; interest in, but disdain for, previous philosophy; respect for mathematical (logical) thinking
Diachronic Elements, Reversible (alternate in importance from 1650 to 1900)	primary interest: in the individual/in society primary interest: in French culture/in the variety of world cultures primary interest: in logical-mathematical thought /in the affective life and aesthetic aspects of thought
Diachronic Elements, Irreversible (of increasing importance from 1650 to 1900)	interest in findings of modern science rejection of introspection search for empirical data and confirmation

What insight, if any, can such a structural analysis yield? First of all, it represents a radical, and yet revealing, simplification of a vast amount of information—here, of the leading themes in the history of modern French thought. The themes are organized in such a way that their changes or continuities can readily be seen: some remain unchanged, others oscillate in importance, still others steadily increase or decrease in significance during the given period. Once such a set of coordinates has been laid out, it also becomes possible to compare thinkers and to note their predominant biases. Thus, Bergson and Rousseau can both be seen to have emphasized the affective and aesthetic aspects of mental functioning; yet they differ, in that Rousseau was relatively more interested in the diverse cultures of the world, and in society in general, while Bergson directed his attention to the individual within French civilization. A more detailed version of this chart might also indicate whether those diachronic features which are reversible tend to change at the same time, or at different moments in history. For example, one could determine from such an analysis whether a shift from interest in the individual to interest in society has tended to accompany a shift from interest in logical/ mathematical reasoning to an interest in affective and aesthetic thought; or whether, instead, these shifts have always occurred at different times, independent of one another. Finally, one could make similar structural analyses of other intellectual traditions and thereby determine whether themes which were synchronic in one culture were necessarily synchronic in others as well. And so on.

The most dramatic property of a structural analysis is the possibility it offers for deducing the existence of hitherto-undiscovered phenomena; if structuralist principles are legitimate and if the analysis is properly carried out, the analyst should be able to anticipate the shape of future events. From this perspective, the above analysis is of some interest. Had a structural analysis of French

thought been made in the year 1900, one could have predicted with some confidence that a brilliant young social
scientist would be interested in questions of the mind;
that he would adopt empirical methods and spurn introspective techniques; and that he was equally likely to
focus on individual or societal factors, primitive culture
or his own culture, logical-mathematical or affective-
aesthetic thought. Finally, he would probably continue to
display, in one form or another, certain staples of the
tradition: a critique of earlier philosophy, an interest in
human/animal differences, an aspiration to synthesize all
scientific knowledge, an emphasis on the power of language, and a desire to account for the nature of thought.
Of course, the present analysis *is* being made with the
benefit of hindsight; yet it is at least conceivable that a
prescient analyst at the turn of the century, equipped with
structural tools, could have predicted the advent of thinkers like Piaget and Lévi-Strauss.

While a purely structural analysis ordinarily assumes
that all relevant factors are present in some form throughout the period and across the domain being investigated,
a developmental analysis is predicated on the assumption
that higher levels of organization may evolve which could
not have been predicted simply from knowledge of earlier
events. The history of scientific disciplines has not been
subjected to extensive developmental analysis (although
the writings of Piaget, Foucault, Kuhn, and certain other
historians of science do contain hints of such an approach).
Nonetheless, in the belief that it will at least provide some
insight into its methodology, and with the hope that it
will complement our structural analysis of the French
tradition, I will attempt below a developmental analysis
of the history of modern social-scientific thought.

Although interest in the nature of man antedates recorded history, and speculation about a science of man
was rife during the Enlightenment, it was only in the

latter part of the nineteenth century that empirical investigations concerning human nature and experience were definitively launched. Perhaps Darwin's conclusive determination of man's place within a naturalistically explicable evolutionary process helped to legitimize a science of man. After *The Origin of Species* was published in 1859, theological objections to a study of human nature gradually lost their potency.

Data collection and theoretical formulations about man took numerous forms, of course, ranging from neurophysiological investigations of spinal reflexes to psychophysical investigations of the threshold of pain perception. The strand of investigation to be explored here may be broadly termed "social science" and may be defined as the effort to increase understanding of man's behavior, his mental processes, his relations with other men, his position in various cultures, his social institutions. Two countries, especially, became noted as centers for the social sciences: Germany, for the investigation of human psychological processes; England, for the exploration of the behaviors, customs, and ideas of diverse groups of people.

2. EARLY INVESTIGATIONS IN PSYCHOLOGY

In Leipzig in the late 1870's, Wilhelm Wundt, a philosopher of enormous breadth, located an old, unused auditorium which he could use for demonstrations and experiments. Soon afterwards, he opened what is generally deemed the first laboratory for psychological experimentation, and through a combination of zeal, diligence, and entrepreneurship, he successfully preached the gospel of psychology to the rest of the learned world. In this laboratory Wundt and his students conducted scores of studies of human sensory capacities—perception of space, time, memory, attention, reaction time, and other topics which were shortly to become the mainstay of the science of psychology. They relied heavily on introspection—systematic self-observation—in their search for the basic elements of psychology; and they came to believe that atomistic sensations (of light, sound, smell, etc.) were associated together to compose human perceptions. Many students from Western Europe and overseas came to study in this laboratory, in order to use its instruments, learn its methods, and rub elbows with the "great man." Those who returned to America tended to retain more of Wundt's methodology than of his overarching philosophy, and America became, within thirty years, the principal center for experimental psychological research, while a more philosophical approach tended to prevail in Western Europe, particularly France.

As Wundt's ideas and methods invaded the United States, heated debates about the respective merits of introspection or controlled investigations, the examination of consciousness or the study of conduct, "philosophical" or "biological" psychology, dominated the field. After some years of fierce debate about the "true" mission of psychology, the upper hand was gained by those suspicious of philosophizing, consciousness, and introspection, and committed to controlled methods of experimentation, fine-grained explanations of behavior, and a flexible view of human nature. Thus Wundt's experimental methodology triumphed, even as his faith in introspection and his interest in consciousness were forgotten. The emergence of "behaviorism" reflected a widespread belief among Americans in the controlling power of the environment, reflecting, perhaps, the unique history of the country. The behaviorist cause was considerably buoyed by the powerful and effective propagandizing of John Watson, famed for his boast:

> Give me a dozen healthy infants well-formed and my own specified world to bring them up in, and I'll guarantee to take any one of them at random and train him to become any type of specialist I might select—doctor, lawyer, artist, merchant-

chief, and, yes, even beggar man and thief, regardless of his talents, penchants, tendencies, abilities, vocations, and race of his ancestors.

With the victory of Watson and his like-minded contemporaries, talk of mind and consciousness largely ceased in America, and was replaced by descriptions of overt behavior which was always presumed to be determined by environmental conditions. Interest centered on the function or adaptive value of given behaviors, the prediction of future activity, the nature of individual skills and differences, the testing of intelligence, the collection of data and development of statistical methods, and the comparative study of animals—all matters being simultaneously pursued in the British Isles.

In Continental Europe, however, behaviorism was less than favorably received. More convinced of the determining power of heredity, still committed to the centrality of consciousness and subjective experience and to the value of introspection, given to suspicion or disdain of technology, and at best ambivalent about experimentation, European psychologists rejected most of the American behaviorist program. Instead, in keeping with their more philosophical and speculative bent, they searched for the general properties of the human mind, its affective and its cognitive components. It may be said, without undue simplification, that the field of psychology around the turn of the century was essentially divided between these two opposing orientations. Certainly there were psychologists both on the Continent and in the Anglo-Saxon countries who took intermediate positions; but, for the most part, they assented to the view that the future of psychology lay somewhere between these competing images of man.

Two schools which emerged in the opening decades of the twentieth century, however, served notice that neither of these approaches had offered the last word in psychological insight. The Gestalt psychologists—notably Wolfgang Köhler and Max Wertheimer—employed the controlled experimental procedures championed in America in the name of a radically divergent set of psychological principles. They sought to demonstrate that the mind actively constructs the world it perceives, that it naturally and inevitably confers meaning upon stimuli, shapes them and gives them coherent form ("Gestalt" meaning "form" or "configuration"); far from simply reflecting what is "there" in the "real world," the mind seeks out examples of good form, imposing it upon aspects of the environment which are wanting. Where Wundt stressed the atomistic nature of elementary sense data and their combination into mosaic-like wholes, the Gestaltists emphasized the phenomenological perception of intact objects, dynamic forces, meaning and value. If for Wundt the primary elements perceived in a fire were geometrical forms of varying shapes, brightnesses, and hues, the primary elements for the Gestaltists were excited tongues dancing and darting about. Köhler, Wertheimer, and their associates insisted on the priority of the whole (the "Gestalt") over its parts, and stressed the relations among elements rather than the elements themselves: a melody or geometric figure inheres in a relation among tones or lines, not in the individual notes or marks. Where the behaviorists searched for Laws of Learning in order to document changes due to additional experience or training, the Gestaltists sought Laws of the Mind's Organization in order to elucidate the mental faculties and structures governing perception and intellectual processes. As a result of these emphases (motivated in part by the desire to annihilate iniquitous behaviorism), the Gestaltists paid little attention to changes in behavior and perception over time, the influence of parts upon the whole, or, in general, intellectual processes which do not involve the mind's organization of sense data.

At about the same time the Gestaltists were creating a stir in academic circles, Sigmund Freud and his fellow psychoanalysts were launching a revolution in man's conception of his motivation, behavior, and mental health. Freud demonstrated that an individual's behavior was not simply what it appeared to be to his conscious mind or to the naïve observer; relentless unconscious processes were at work in man's dream and waking life, reflecting deep-seated strivings, motives, fears, and anxieties. The founder of psychoanalysis attempted to lay bare the structure of the unconscious, to tease out its principles of functioning, to spell out processes whereby ideas were formed, transformed, repressed, sublimated, and made accessible for conscious consideration. Freud's work initially engendered strident opposition among his colleagues, with some criticizing the absence of empirical studies and statistical support, others deploring his dark and pessimistic view of human nature, still others questioning his models of thought, neurosis, defense mechanisms, and child development. Even those sympathetic to the psychoanalytic perspective often felt that Freud concentrated excessively on the affective aspects of mental processes, paid too little attention to psychologically normal or fully psychotic individuals, and was insensitive to the characteristics of children, members of primitive cultures, and others who differed from the turn-of-the-century Viennese burgher. Nonetheless, the fundamental reorientation of psychological studies that Freud engineered has come to be acknowledged by all but the most carping critics.

The Gestaltists and the psychoanalysts charted vast domains which had been by-passed by the preceding generation of psychologists. The Gestaltists stressed the constructive properties of the mind, the validity of the data of consciousness, and the centrality of perceived relations; the psychoanalysts highlighted the role of the unconscious in thought processes, the crucial part played by motivational factors, and the existence of similar basic personality constellations in "normal" and "sick" individuals. Both schools, despite their many differences and deficiencies, represented visible progress over the earlier stage of psychological thought. There was recognition of the need for empirical observations and theory-building, and a closer tie between data and theory; there were methods which could be applied by any competent investigator and which led to interesting questions. Yet neither the Gestaltists nor the psychoanalysts developed a coherent and comprehensive position on the relationship between child and adult, perception and cognition, thought and affect, part and whole; nor did they devise formal, testable models of the processes which they described. From a structural-developmental point of view, Gestalt psychology and psychoanalysis may be viewed as transitional stages in the evolution of psychological thought. They stand midway between the behaviorism, sporadic empiricism, and introspectionism of the preceding generation and the structural approach adopted by the most productive psychological school of the present time.

3. EARLY INVESTIGATIONS IN ANTHROPOLOGY

As measurements of pain perception and auditory threshold were being recorded in Leipzig, small coteries of dedicated scholars were ensconced in the libraries of London, Oxford, Cambridge, and Edinburgh, poring over the records made by missionaries, travelers, and adventurers of their encounters with primitive people all over the "uncivilized" world and the British empire. These men, more often than not convinced of the essential oneness of mankind, were attempting to account for the apparently striking differences in customs, behavior, and outlook between the natives of the African wilds, on the one hand, and the cultivated gentleman of the Victorian drawing room, on the other. One way of proceeding was that endorsed by such thinkers as Herbert Spencer and Auguste Comte: to postulate a series of stages through which all men would ultimately pass—from savagery to barbarism to civilization—to note the diffusion of knowledge across cultures, and to plot the place occupied by each new tribe or group on this march toward Progress; evolution was synonymous with the perfectibility of man. The more far-sighted of these "armchair anthropologists," however, came to understand the essential futility of such an approach. One could never conclusively prove the validity or falsity of such evolutionary, historical, or diffusionist schemes; devoting one's energies to them simply postponed the vital task of describing in their own terms the life styles of these groups and locating affinities between the life of the primitive and the world of civilized man. Later generations of anthropologists have paid greater tribute to men like Edward Tylor and Lewis H. Morgan, who concentrated upon the customs of particular groups and the common elements among diverse groups, than to investigators like Sir James Frazer, who combed the literature in support of *a priori* notions about what was progressive, scientific, or civilized and what was not. Heightened understanding lay in comparison of kinship systems in order to discern the underlying principles of organization rather than in thinly veiled disparagements of "outrageous" rain dances.

By the early years of the present century, anthropology had emerged as a separate discipline in both Europe and the United States; it became possible, and eventually essential, for those trained in the discipline to conduct their own field work. The anthropologists' invasion of exotic societies had an expected effect: firsthand acquaintance with various tribes and peoples heightened interest in the particular characteristics of individual groups and called into question the facile generalized schemes of the previous generation. An empirically-minded anthropologist, Franz Boas, widely revered for his rigorous intellectual standards, encyclopedic knowledge, and unfailing integrity, virtually decreed that anthropologists should not waste their time on evolutionary, historical, or diffusionist speculation but should occupy themselves collecting data about existing groups and attempting to make inductive sense of it. Following the example of the physical sciences, Boas inspired a whole generation of American anthropologists to make careful ethnographical investigations "in the field" and to eschew *a priori* generalizations about matters which could not be verified empirically.

A figure of comparable importance in England was Bronislaw Malinowski, who spent four years in the Trobriand Islands during the First World War, setting such enviable standards for painstaking field work and empathic immersion in the life and consciousness of a society, that he is still hailed as a paragon for the inspiration of young anthropologists. Malinowski favored a functionalist approach, in which the anthropologist directed his attention to the ongoing life of the culture and attempted to understand how its various aspects fulfilled the biological and psychological needs of its members. "The ethnographer's goal," he said, is "to grasp the native's point of view, his relation to life, to realize his vision of the world. . . . there may emerge [in the investigator] a feeling of solidarity with the endeavors and ambitions of these natives." Rejecting the possibility of "collective ideas" in a society, Malinowski strongly favored psychological explanations of cultural phenomena; as an example, he spent some years in the field initially attempting to verify, and finally modifying, Freud's concept of the Oedipus complex within the context of a matriarchal society.

While Boas's inductive approach and Malinowski's functionalism held sway in the Anglo-American cultural sphere, the sociological approach pioneered by Durkheim remained influential in Gallic anthropological circles. Although Durkheim himself stressed the importance of data collection and empirical analysis, the overall thrust of his approach (particularly in the hands of less-disciplined followers) was toward a rejection of psychological causes, toward armchair theorizing and speculation, and acceptance of such supra-individual entities as a "group mind." As in the psychology of the time, then, the young discipline of anthropology was divided into two camps: west of the Channel were, by and large, the empiricists and functionalists, who favored intensive immersion and energetic data collection in a single culture, who viewed societies as a sum of individuals fulfilling their biological and social needs; to the east were more sedentary anthropologists who rarely visited the field, who searched for patterns underlying diverse cultures, and who viewed society as a "super-organic," or supra-human, entity. On the one hand, dogmatic empiricism and a search for psychological causes; on the other, overarching generalizations and a belief in sociological explanation.

Two transitional figures facilitated the shift from the first generation of anthropological analysis to the more sophisticated approach characteristic of structuralist investigators. In France there was Durkheim's prize student, Marcel Mauss, who collaborated with the master on a study of the methods of classification used in primitive societies, and became leader of the Durkheimian school upon his mentor's death in 1917. Mauss was interested primarily in anthropological investigations and, though never himself involved in field work, saw to it that his students were placed in appropriate cultures. In 1925 he founded and became director of the Institute of Anthropology in Paris; from this position he directed field work, encouraged critical and imaginative investigations of perplexing phenomena, and attempted to preserve what was most worthwhile in the Durkheimian tradition, while de-emphasizing its less viable aspects, such as the belief in crowd psychology and the doctrine of group mystique.

Not one to wield his pen lightly, Mauss exerted his influence primarily through his teaching and his personal example. His genius lay in an ability to perceive profound significance in what at first glance seemed trivial. In his most famous study, *The Gift*, Mauss adduced evidence from such diverse societies as Polynesia, Melanesia, and Northwest America, as well as from Roman, Greek, and Hindu literature, in support of the notion that gift-giving practices among social classes, groups, and individuals lay bare the essence of a social system. Modes of giving, receiving, and repaying are seen as basic means of expressing or reaffirming social bonds and the relative social standing of givers and recipients; an individual is embodied in his gift, or "prestation," which expresses in a fundamental way his concept of himself and his relationship to others. By thus focusing on this seemingly mundane aspect of life as it appears in different groups, "we have been able," said Mauss, "to see their essence, their operation, and their living aspects, and to catch the fleeting moment when the society and its members take emotional stock of themselves and their situation as regards others." Here, Mauss took a fundamental idea of Durkheim's and, by searching judiciously for relevant data and examining phenomena at the appropriate level of generality, carried through the kind of analysis palatable to the broad spectrum of anthropological investigators. His failure to complete the transition to structuralism accomplished by his successors seems a reflection of the paucity of his output, his hesitancy in pursuing an analogy between language and culture, and his reluctance to postulate formal and mathematical models.

Similarly seeking to fuse the strengths of the Anglo-Saxon and Gallic traditions was Alfred Reginald Radcliffe-Brown, a distinguished British anthropologist who sponsored and conducted field work while also promoting Durkheimian views of society and social phenomena. Almost alone in his generation, Radcliffe-Brown did not hesitate to view society as a biological organism and to deal with such relatively abstract notions as social structure and social relations. He construed society as a system of interdependent parts, searched for analogous structures among diverse groups, and attempted to make those general comparisons which would illuminate the nature of social institutions. Unwilling (or unable), however, to divorce himself entirely from the British empiricist tradition, Radcliffe-Brown looked for revelations of social structure and relations in the overt daily interactions among individuals. He thought of society as the mere sum of individual social relations at a given moment, structure as "this network of actually existing relations." This view was sharply criticized by the Durkheimians, who, anticipating a fundamental tenet of structuralism, preferred to posit a model remote from surface phenomena, one which captured the underlying reality, of which the naïve observer or participant might be unaware. Radcliffe-Brown was also vigorously opposed by the followers of Malinowski, who disparaged his efforts to generalize across the boundaries of cultures and societies, his positing of invisible "structures," his manipulation of algebraic equations which purported to deal with kinship and social organization, and his supposed lack of empathy. Radcliffe-Brown was sufficiently occupied defending his formulations from these strong attacks to keep him from ever demonstrating satisfactorily the possibilities of his blend of structural-functionalism. He remains at worst a footnote in anthropological history, at best a transitional figure like Mauss, who anticipated the future evolution of the discipline but was unable to preside over it himself.

The simple developmental analysis we have undertaken above points up significant parallels in the respective histories of psychology and anthropology. Both disciplines were launched in the latter half of the nineteenth century and spread rapidly across Europe and into the United States. In each, before long, two broad camps of workers could be discerned: those of an empirical or behaviorist bent, who favored data collection over theorizing and sought explanations in terms of individual psychological and environmental factors; and those with an introspective and philosophical approach, who spun elaborate theories about human nature, trusted their own intuitions, and attributed greater influence to hereditary and traditional factors. A higher-level synthesis of these opposing views seemed indicated, but this did not come immediately. Instead, a series of transitional figures pointed up the deficiencies of the earlier orientations, and made some progress toward a more satisfactory mode of analysis. It remained for the structuralists to complete the shift to a fully sophisticated approach in the social sciences; and it is the achievements of structuralism's two most eminent practitioners that will concern us for the remainder of the book.

Before focusing upon these men, however, I would like to summarize the results of our inquiry thus far, sketch out briefly some characteristics of the second developmental stage of the social sciences, and describe two schools of thought which could have influenced a young social scientist during the early decades of this century.

4. THE FOUNDATION OF STRUCTURALISM

Even as the determining role of the environment has been a leitmotif of American thought, so—our structural analysis confirmed—has the quest for mind been a perennial concern of the French intellectual tradition. Accompanying this concern has been a belief in the uniqueness of man's cognitive processes, the importance of language, and the appropriateness of a holistic approach to the understanding of behavior and society. Other aspects of the French tradition have proved susceptible to variation: the alternating emphases on the individual or the society, on a single civilized society or the range of cultures, on the logical-mathematical aspects of thought or its affective and intuitive facets. The increasing acceptance of empirical methods, on the other hand, appears to be an irreversible trend in French thought. A projection from this analysis indicated that future workers would be empirical investigators of the mind, who might explore either rational or intuitive thought, and examine either a range of societies and age groups or a single group or stratum.

Our developmental analysis has revealed an initial stage in the evolution of social-scientific thought during which investigators displayed either total commitment to the accumulation of facts or, conversely, a devotion to introspective or philosophical considerations. These polarities were perhaps a necessary feature of pioneering work; but after a time, certain facets of this first stage became irritants. Younger investigators began to question the overarching speculations, introspective evidence, and circular reasoning of the European school, even as they became impatient with the atomism, functionalism, and *ad hoc* explanations of the empiricists. Soon a cluster of new movements emerged, which sought to mediate between the Anglo-Saxon and Continental traditions. Supporters of Wertheimer, Freud, Mauss, and Radcliffe-Brown searched for a middle level of explanation in which facts of significance were isolated and plausible hypotheses advanced. Both the mindless accumulation of facts and the unsupported spinning of hypotheses were gradually supplanted by a search for the fundamental, determining organization which underlay disparate phenomena. The transitional figures generally postulated the existence of unconscious processes of which the individual, the society, and the naïve observer were ignorant; regarded certain enigmatic phenomena (like the nature of gift-giving or the characteristics of early childhood) as especially rich in theoretical yield; favored interplay between perplexing data and broad but precisely formulated theoretical frameworks; and welcomed the judicious application of biology, mathematics, and other disciplines to social-scientific problems.

It was left to the next generation to realize more completely this shift in focus and procedure. The structuralists reasserted the special status of human beings, in opposition to the excessively mechanistic or animalistic approaches to *Homo sapiens* which characterized their predecessors; the priority of mathematical and logical thought; the inadequacy of explanations rooted in affective factors; the belief that various levels of individual and group functioning could be accounted for within a single framework; the interest in the epistemic subject as both a phenomenon to be probed and a valuable partner in the analysis. The structuralists seized upon the *formal properties of thought* as the analytic tool which would allow them to escape from the Scylla of thoughtless empiricism and the Charybdis of factless philosophizing; through an independent description of structures which the analyst could discern and which were also valid constituents of a subject's mind, the structuralist could provide an explanation at the appropriate level: between the nervous system and conscious behavior, between the technical-economic infrastructure and the ideological superstructure of the culture. In short the structuralists sought underlying arrangements of elements which determined overt forms of behavior and thought, could be expressed in logical formal language, and reflected the biological attributes of human beings. The particular solution they wrought will become clearer in subsequent chapters; for the present, the accompanying table may help to clarify the general progression of social science during the early years of this century.

The most salient feature of structuralism, only dimly foreshadowed during the transitional stages, is the belief that diverse sets of phenomena can be related to one another, once relevant factors and their relationships have been ferreted out. The investigator can devise a formal or informal model of the underlying structures which will not only account for the present data in an economical and comprehensive fashion but which will also be applica-

A DEVELOPMENTAL ANALYSIS OF TWENTIETH-CENTURY
SOCIAL SCIENCE

	Anthropology	Psychology
Stage 1 (1900–1920)	Empirical approach: Malinowski, Boas	Empirical approach: Watson (behaviorist)
	Philosophical approach: Durkheim	Philosophical approach: Wundt (introspectionist)
Transitional Phase (1920–1935)	Mauss and Radcliffe-Brown	Wertheimer, Köhler, and Freud
	Linguistics as Catalyst Phenomenology as Negative Example	
Stage 2 (1935–present)	Structural approach: Lévi-Strauss	Structural approach: Piaget

ble to data that have yet to be collected, and to data
expressed in unanticipated form. The formal model must
be divorced from concrete reality to the extent that it can
be stated without reference to the particular phenomena
being investigated; and yet it must be a reflection of observations made by empirically oriented observers, not a
whole-cloth invention of the armchair philosopher.

In our structural analysis of the French intellectual
tradition, we first reviewed the major historical currents,
then attempted to tease out those features which appeared
representative of the underlying "structure" of thought.
Next we composed a model which incorporated synchronic and diachronic aspects of the domain, and which
also had a certain predictive power. This model may be
said to have an independent existence—that is to say, it
can be expressed in purely formal language, equally applicable to the structure of Russian intellectual thought or
the metabolic cycle of a vertebrate. If we term the synchronic factor k, the diachronic reversible factors a and b,
and the diachronic irreversible factor x, $x+1$, $x+2$, etc.,
we end up with the following abstract (or formal) model,

upon which it is possible to perform a set of operations and hypothetical experiments:

	Time 1	Time 2	Time 3	Time 4
Synchronic factor	k	k	k	k
Diachronic reversible factor	a	b	a	b
Diachronic irreversible factor	x	$x+1$	$x+2$	$x+3$

We may presume that Piaget and Lévi-Strauss were sensitive not only to the synchronic and diachronic aspects of the French intellectual tradition but also to the dominant trends in the social science of their time. Possessed of wide-ranging and synthetic intellects, they not only assimilated the work of their predecessors (with whom they had agreements as well as disagreements) but were also attuned to the more general intellectual and social developments of the period. We shall conclude this introductory discussion by describing two of the most prominent of these developments, to which Piaget and Lévi-Strauss reacted in instructive ways.

During the early part of the present century the so-called phenomenological school of philosophy gained prominence in Europe, owing primarily to the innovative writings of Edmund Husserl. The phenomenologists rejected (or, to use Husserl's term, "bracketed") much of the history of philosophy and nearly all of current psychology, arguing vigorously that one must begin any analysis with one's own "phenomenal" experience, one's own living reaction to events, persons, objects, the immediate givens of life. Unlike the introspectionists, who had minimized the value of raw, unanalyzed consciousness and stressed the need for trained self-observation, the phenomenologists honored spontaneous and uncritical human responses. The phenomenological perspective included a radical critique of science, which was viewed as introducing unnecessary and artificial bifurcations and divisions into human experience, creating barriers between subjects and objects, becoming embroiled in futile terminological disputes, deductive entanglements, and "facts," instead of confirming the essential nature and unity of experience. As all perception, even that of the logician or physicist, must begin with momentary experiences, scientists were suppressing the crucial dimension of experience—the intuition of essences—in their preoccupation with concepts, models, and ideal states. For the phenomenologists, one's perception of the self and the body was central; interest inhered in the content of objects, in essential qualities, in the appearance of things: intention, organization, directedness, attractiveness were accepted as valid phenomena which required no demonstration except, perhaps, to satisfy stubborn scientists.

As they did with Bergson, Piaget and Lévi-Strauss seem to have taken phenomenology seriously and to have read its major proponents carefully, but finally to have rejected it with some decisiveness as preventing a serious, objective, and controlled study of any occurrence. Piaget asked how one could determine, except through experimental scientific means, that individuals actually had the same experiences and, if they did, how these came about. Lévi-Strauss questioned the egocentrism of those who placed their own experiences at the center of their philosophy. More generally, both men, after having been enamored of philosophy in their adolescence, became deeply suspicious of the whole philosophical enterprise. As Lévi-Strauss commented, in a characteristically harsh judgment on the possibilities of philosophical analysis:

It is necessary that the philosophers who have long enjoyed a sort of privileged position because one recognizes their right to speak on all topics begin to resign themselves to the fact that many matters of research escape the realm of philosophy. . . . we are witnesses to a sort of dismemberment of the field of philosophy. Maintaining the requirements of all or none has led to a sclerosis of social science.

Indeed, phenomenology served to some extent as a negative example, whose seductive beckonings must be resisted by the serious social scientist. While it would be ill-advised (and perhaps impossible) to ignore one's personal impressions of a phenomenon, no scientist could afford to rest his case on this sort of evidence.

While forming increasingly severe opinions regarding the practice of philosophy in the absence of confirming or disconfirming facts, Piaget and Lévi-Strauss looked with much greater interest and favor upon developments in the field of linguistics. Linguistic study had been an active enterprise at the time of Descartes, and had made considerable progress since then; but by the latter part of the nineteenth century the principal schools were bogged down in the mindless and uncritical collection of details about different linguistic stocks, as well as unproductive studies of comparative grammar, the etymology of words, the origin of human language, the slight changes in language across geographical boundaries. So preoccupied with minutiae and bereft of convincing documentation were many of these inquiries that the Cercle linguistique de Paris actually forbade papers on the origin of language in the closing years of the century.

As a result of the pioneering work of a Genevan linguist, Ferdinand de Saussure, a revolution occurred in the study of language. Just around the time the more farsighted anthropologists were discovering the uselessness of historical and diffusionist inquiries which could never be confirmed or refuted, Saussure was rejecting most of the evolutionary and comparative pursuits of his colleagues. He called, instead, for a study of language as a separate, distinct system with its own rules and properties which could be discovered by careful examination of language *per se,* without reference to historical, geographical, economic, or other "extra-linguistic" factors. Even as chess can be understood through a mastery of the rules, and the relative strength of given players by a study of a

particular game, so language can be analyzed exclusively
in terms of its systematic regularities.

Saussure made many enduring contributions to the
study of language. He argued that the purpose of linguistics was to discover principles operative in all languages;
these in turn could be drawn on to explain the differences among language stocks and historical eras. He
demonstrated that language was an orderly, coherent,
"collective" phenomenon. Above all, Saussure stressed that
linguistic analysis involved determination of the relationships among basic elements; units were devoid of structure when isolated and could only be defined by their
relations with one another; whatever distinguished a unit
or sign from others in the set of units defined it. "In languages," asserted Saussure, "there are only differences."
Just as, in a chess game, a piece has meaning only in
relation to all the other pieces, and any slab of wood so
designated can represent that piece, so, in language, a
part of speech is defined only in relation to other parts
or signs and a concept may be represented by any available sound.

A generation of linguistic scholars took inspiration from
Saussure's reorientation of the field. Foremost among
them was Roman Jakobson, a brilliant, prolific Russian
scholar who, like Marcel Mauss of the Durkheimian
school, attempted to preserve what was most valuable in
his master's tradition while sifting out those aspects which
did not prove viable. Jakobson and his associates searched
for the basic building blocks of a language, the qualities
of the emitted sound which they termed "distinctive features." Once the distinctive features in a domain were
isolated and defined, more complex linguistic entities
could be described simply as a combination of a certain
set of distinctive features. After years of painstaking inquiry, the followers of Saussure postulated a small set of
a dozen or so distinctive features required to produce a
sound; these features could, when combined in various

ways, account exhaustively for all sounds used in the languages of the world. Such a remarkable simplification of what had appeared an unmanageable babble was recognized as a significant achievement by workers in many fields, and served as a model for other linguists who aspired to simplify the realm of syntax and semantics in a comparable way.

The resurgence of interest in language and in linguistics had reverberations throughout the social sciences. Investigators began to examine the differences among various kinds of natural and formal language, the operation of linguistic and nonlinguistic symbols, the relationship between language and thought. Interest in these "semiotic" questions attracted such diverse workers as Freud, Cassirer, Boas, Malinowski, Durkheim, and Wundt; indeed, Mauss held that the key to cultural analysis lay in a comprehension of the laws of language. Not surprisingly, incisive practitioners of the social sciences like Piaget and Lévi-Strauss became interested in the problems of language; and while their enthusiasm for phenomenology had been short-lived, they were sufficiently impressed by the work of the linguists to base their early work on linguistic questions and models.

What was it about the study of language that so attracted French social scientists during the early years of this century? Language was clearly a phenomenon which was central to the human mind, and one which had intrigued their predecessors, from Descartes to Bergson. Saussure and his followers had now shown that language could be studied in isolation from other cultural products, that it was analyzable into systemic elements which could be defined independently, that one could examine the way in which these basic elements were combined in order to produce complex sounds and utterances and meanings. The domain of language was clearly part of the human realm; and yet, more so than the other social or human sciences, linguistics had moved toward the model of the physical sciences: it was possible to devise abstract formal models of underlying linguistic structures, to relate disparate phenomena in this way, and to apply such theoretical models to empirical data collected from diverse sources. By treating language as a set of signs, the analyst obtained objectively determinable units and operations upon which he could base his conclusions; and the prospect then arose that actions, perceptions, and thought itself could be systematically studied along the same lines. It was the promise of studying behavioral and cultural phenomena in a rigorous manner, of developing testable models of pivotal processes, that was most appealing to the young Piaget and Lévi-Strauss; the strides made by the linguists inspired them in their efforts to found a structuralist social science.

II The Architects of Structuralism

3 Piaget

Things and states are only views, taken by our mind, of becoming. There are no things, there are only actions.

—BERGSON

In a word, in the beginning there was action, as Goethe said; then came operation.

—PIAGET

In 1916 a brilliant and sensitive young biologist spent a year in the Swiss Alps, recovering from a condition of nervous exhaustion (what today might be termed an identity crisis). To pass the time and to collect his thoughts, he composed a novel *Recherche* ("Search") which was published two years later, when he was twenty-two years old. In it, he recorded the conflicts felt by a young Catholic concerning the relationship between religion and science, and, with Comtean hauteur, proposed a general synthesis of knowledge. The major part of the novel consisted of a lengthy and wide-ranging tract reviewing, questioning, and criticizing the principal philosophical and scientific views of the time on the nature of life and experience. The work dwelt in particular on the nature of the relationship between part and whole in organic life, the concept of type-of-species, and the meaning of organismic equilibrium:

51

Now there can be no awareness of these qualities, hence these qualities cannot exist, if there are no relationships among them, if they are not, consequently, blended into a total quality which contains them, while keeping them distinct. For example, I would not be aware either of the whiteness of this paper or of the blackness of this ink if the two qualities were not combined in my consciousness into a certain unit and if, in spite of this writing, they did not remain respectively one white and the other black; in this originates the equilibrium between the qualities.

Neither the style nor the message of the novel was of a sort destined to win a wide public, and with the exception of one or two philosophers who expressed indignation at the author's stance, *Recherche* was ignored and forgotten, even by its author. Looking back at it several decades later, however, Jean Piaget could comment that nearly all the ideas which were to guide his subsequent research had been raised in some form in this idle exercise of his spiritual *Wanderjahre*.

What had led to the composition of this adolescent work? Jean Piaget was born in Neuchâtel, Switzerland, in 1896, son of a student of medieval literature who was the historian of Neuchâtel, and of an intelligent and kind, though rather neurotic, mother. With a father of a systematic and critical bent, and a mother who was frequently ill, the son became a serious and industrious child who displayed scholarly promise at a remarkably early age. He enjoyed collecting various kinds of natural objects, such as fossils and sea shells, and was avidly involved in mechanics and bird-watching. At age ten he saw a partly albino sparrow in a park and sent a description of it to a natural history journal in Neuchâtel. The article was published—and, in Piaget's words, "I was launched."

On the basis of this find, the still-preadolescent Piaget became an assistant to the curator of Neuchâtel's natural history museum. There he mastered the biological system of species classification and the methods for handling exhibits. During his "spare time" he collected molluscs, and within a few years became an expert in "malocology," publishing widely in this area during his early teens. (Piaget reminisces that foreign colleagues wanted to meet him, and job offers were tendered, but that he always had to decline these overtures, lest the other party discover his extreme youth.) The articles written at this time were rather primitive, but Piaget was subsequently grateful that this early scientific experience had shored him up against the seductive lures of philosophy.

The years 1911–1916 were a time of deep inner crisis for Piaget. He found himself unable to reconcile the dogmatic religious teachings he had absorbed with his more recently acquired scientific credo. At the age of fifteen, he went to visit his godfather, a Romansh man of letters, who taught him some philosophy and, in particular, exposed him to Bergson.

Piaget alludes to his first encounter with Bergson's work with awe: "It was an emotional shock; I recall an evening of profound revelation." Well prepared for the encounter, he found that Bergson's writings addressed his own need to fit questions about life, religion, and the natural sciences into an overall, integrated world-view. For the first time, he could see that God was identified with life and that biology might be drawn on to resolve philosophical dilemmas. Biology furnished an explanation of all things, including the mind itself.

For a time, Piaget subscribed to the Bergsonian view of knowledge. But he soon came to see epistemological problems in Bergson's approach; in particular, he discerned a need for a rigorous experimental science as a bridge between Bergson's casual Darwinism and his analysis of knowledge and intelligence, between biological investigations and the study of mind.

Piaget feverishly resumed his reading, as well as writing, in philosophy and science, while simultaneously pursuing a varied course of study at the university. He ardently perused the works of, among others, Spencer, Comte,

Darwin, and William James. Eventually, this regimen proved too much for him, and he was compelled to take off a year in 1916 to go live in the mountains. He had already acquired his lifelong habit of thinking issues out by writing, and so kept numerous notebooks of his intellectual development. Several such notebooks, as well as the novel *Recherche* and some still-unpublished tracts were products of this period.

From his year of reflection, Piaget seems to have emerged with his physical and spiritual equilibrium restored. Returning to school, he completed his degree in biology and philosophy under the direction of a mathematical philosopher, Arnold Reymond, the teacher he most frequently mentions as a formative influence in his thought. Through his work with Reymond, Piaget reached a crucial insight: the activity of an organism can be described or treated logically, and logic itself stems from a sort of spontaneous organization of activity. At this time he also formulated the notion that all organisms consist of structures—i.e., of parts related within a whole—and that all knowledge is an assimilation of a given external into the structures of the subject. He concluded that the sense of balance or resolution evident at various intellectual levels corresponds to the biological necessity for equilibration or autoregulation of structures in every domain of life. All of these ideas were to recur in Piaget's writings over the next half-century.

Thus, by the age of twenty or so, Piaget had already set up the program he would pursue in the future. He was interested in the relation between biology and logic and regarded human psychology as the essential link, humans being indubitably part of the biological world and yet also the practitioners and source of logical thought. Piaget thought that he would spend a few years studying psychology and then return to his first loves, biology and logic. Although he was to fulfill much of this program eventually, his scheduling estimates were somewhat off.

As Piaget felt deeply that his nascent system of knowledge was worthless unless it could be put to an experimental test, he elected to go to Paris, where he could acquire the necessary experimental and clinical methodology. He took courses in clinical psychology at the Sorbonne, learned to interview mental patients, and also audited courses on aspects of sensory psychology, perception, and the epistemological foundations of psychology. He was then recommended to Théodore Simon, who had worked with Alfred Binet, creator of the first intelligence tests. Simon hired Piaget to standardize some psychological tests and, perhaps sensing the latter's potential, placed an entire school at his disposal.

Binet had posed many kinds of questions to young children and had set up preliminary performance norms. For example, he determined that an average three-year-old could repeat three digits, identify a picture of a cow, and string beads. An average six-year-old could recognize objects represented in an incomplete picture, trace a simple maze, and define an orange; a nine-year-old could resolve verbal absurdities, field simple arithmetical questions, and give rhyming words; a thirteen-year-old could repeat five words correctly, assemble sentences with the words out of order, and correctly answer questions of this sort: Edith is taller than Susan; Susan is taller than Lilly; who is taller, Edith or Lilly? Piaget's task was to ask children such questions and to determine more precisely at what age most children were able to handle the question. Piaget modified the standard methods used in intelligence testing by applying the clinical method of interviewing he had learned in working with mental patients. Instead of merely recording a response, he encouraged the child to reason about the problem.

While engaged in this project, Piaget happened upon the insight for which he is most renowned. He found that children at certain ages not only gave wrong answers to questions but also exhibited qualitatively different ways of reasoning. The young child was neither "dumber" nor just a few steps behind the older one; rather, he thought about things in a wholly different way, possessing a distinctive conception of the world that was manifested in every application of his reasoning power, whatever its object, and that could be elicited through judicious questioning. This deceptively unimposing conclusion (so simple, said Einstein upon learning of it, that only a genius could think of it) was to be explored by Piaget in literally thousands of investigations over the course of the next half-century.

Piaget studied children's conceptions of number and of cause and effect at Simon's laboratory and wrote up his results in three lengthy articles. The third of these he sent to Eduard Claparède, a leading Swiss psychologist, who was so impressed by it that he offered the twenty-five-year-old scholar a position as director of studies at the Jean-Jacques Rousseau Institute in Geneva, the principal Swiss center of research in the field of genetic psychology. Piaget accepted the offer and initiated many further studies of young children during his first years at the Institute. Within a short time after his arrival there, he had published five major works. He was destined to have a world-wide reputation by the age of thirty and an honorary doctorate from Harvard just before his fortieth birthday.

Surprisingly, Piaget's reputation did not continue its rapid ascent after this first spate of publications. Instead, the early monographs remained the chief basis of his reputation for the next quarter-century, long after he had ventured into other areas of knowledge and indeed had repudiated certain aspects of his early work. Only in the 1960's, after Piaget had been by-passed for many years by the principal psychological schools, was there a resurgence of interest in his pioneering research.

Because Piaget's published works are so numerous and so widely dispersed—he has written or coauthored some fifty volumes, and many hundreds of articles—any effort to give a comprehensive summary of his lifework would be futile. It is likely that, except for his closest associates, there is no one who has read all of this vast output, and, unless someone should deliberately set himself the task of compiling it, it is unlikely that anyone else ever will. However understandable, this is quite unfortunate, for to understand him fully, it is necessary to follow him in all his twists and turns, his repetitions, his slight and not-so-slight revisions of his earlier work.

Piaget is a superbly disciplined individual who spends several hours each day taking long walks, during which he organizes his thoughts, which are then written down on the same or the following day, in his neat, somewhat cramped script. He is especially given to writing in airports, where one is unlikely to be disturbed, and will often arrive at an airport several hours before departure so that he can have an uninterrupted bloc of time in which to work. During the summer months he retreats to a hideaway somewhere in the Alps where he takes long walks, collects shells, and writes page after page, usually producing at least one book or monograph during this estivation.

For Piaget, writing is a form—or better, an extension—of thinking. As a psychologist he believes that thought builds upon itself, that attempts to work and rework a problem hold promise of yielding greater insight, that each fresh formulation of a position may integrate more of the relevant data into an increasingly comprehensive framework. Piaget is faithful to this view in his writings, which are filled with fresh returns to points raised earlier, each revision expanding the given formulation to accommodate a new finding or setting the formulation in relation to a competing or complementary point of view. Attempts to skim what appears to be a rehash of an old Piagetian argument are frequently brought up short as Piaget introduces a new observation which directs the argument along unanticipated and rewarding lines. Piaget views action as the source of knowledge, and for him thinking, reading, and writing are all and equally forms of action. During the act of writing, Piaget's own thoughts become clear to him; by additional thinking and writing, these thoughts and ideas become ever further clarified and integrated.

This distinctive approach to intellectual creativity imposes itself upon all who would hope to grasp Piaget's work. There is, alas, no royal road to mastery of Piaget. His viewpoint is a radically novel one, and, consistent with his theory of how knowledge builds and changes, it is not possible to learn this new way of looking through a three-point program or a simple negation of previous views. When a child first learns that the earth revolves around the sun, he is confronted with an idea counter to his common sense but an idea which, once accepted, can readily be incorporated into his world-view. Piaget's revolution, however, does not allow itself to be expressed or understood simply; and citing his views with approval while simultaneously embracing a contradictory position is a common phenomenon. Certainly the best, and possibly the only, way to appreciate the full subtlety of Piaget's ideas is to read and reread, again and again, his principal writings. In doing this, one is essentially recapitulating the procedure used by Piaget in thinking and in writing; putting forth the major ideas, at first vaguely, then exploring their ramifications, pondering them in the perspective of other views, attempting to square them with one's own views about cognition.

Having issued such caveats, one can perhaps now be overly bold and attempt to list Piaget's cardinal ideas in a few pages. As we later proceed to examine some of his specific contributions in greater detail, the latent implications of these rapidly outlined views may gradually emerge.

Piaget began his life's work as a biologist, and he remains deeply committed to the study of organic life. Like others of his time, he was deeply influenced by Darwinian evolutionary theory, and in fact came to believe that processes and states should be understood in terms of their developmental course. An early experiment convinced Piaget, however, that Darwin's account of natural selection was too simple. Piaget placed some aquatic molluscs which had the normal elongated shape into the great lakes of Switzerland—bodies of water far more turbulent than their customary homes in the marshes of Europe and Asia. Through motoric adjustments during the period of growth to the rough movement of the water, a new breed of mollusc developed which was globular in shape and more resistant to the currents of the water. When this mollusc was placed into a calmer body of water, however, it retained the new, globular shape. Piaget interpreted this result as indicating that, rather than merely being subject to chance mutations, the structure of an organism has the potential to develop in diverse ways, depending on the eliciting circumstances of the environment. Adaptation to new conditions involves an *active* restructuring and accommodation to the environment on the part of the organism which may result in a lasting alteration of form. Organisms have the capacity to respond to stress, and the results of the exercise of this capacity will be manifest in succeeding generations.

By analogy, Piaget reasoned that an organism's intelligence was embodied in a series of structures with latent tendencies for development, which could be brought out by appropriate interaction with the environment. But, again, the organism was not a passive reflector but rather possessed active potentialities which could unfold to a greater or lesser extent, depending upon the nature of the interaction with the environment.

Piaget, seeking the essential property or capacity of organisms, concluded that it was *action*. A paramecium swims, respires, excretes, assimilates food; an infant sucks, cries, exhibits reflexes, incorporates food. Although casual talk treats feeling, thinking, seeing, or understanding as discrete processes, the scientist must appreciate that they are all and equally forms of action. Whatever development occurs in an organism must involve the mastery of the current repertoire of actions, and the combining of actions into new, more complex actions. The order and pace with which this process unfolds are functions both of the extent of the organism's interaction with the environment and of the organism's own "equilibrating processes." That is, the emergence of a new form of action —for example, walking—results from the organism's being placed repeatedly in situations where walking would be adaptive, the maturing of certain muscles and nerve fibers, and the self-regulating nature of the organism, which at certain determinable points produces spurts of growth and emergence of new activity while giving rise at other times to periods of consolidation or stasis.

Piaget's view of action differed markedly from the customary view of motion or random activity. He saw action as potentially intelligent; thus, an organism that used a stick to reach an object it could not grasp by hand would be exhibiting intelligent action. In addition, Piaget saw action as susceptible to logical treatment. That is, he maintained that one could observe a series of actions undertaken by an organism and then extrapolate the reasoning process involved in its actions, ferret out the intellectual structure implicitly reflected in the action, even set up a logical model of what had happened. If a child consistently followed a certain route to and from a park, but returned home one day by a different route, which could be inferred from previous activities, Piaget would attempt to map the logical structure necessary for this novel and intelligent action to have taken place.

The contention that action may be intelligent should be plausible to any parent or pet-owner; but the claim that all thought or intellectual functioning is itself action seems counter to common sense. After all, in reading a book,

watching a movie, or solving a problem, one is clearly
engaging in thinking, and yet it is difficult to discern
actions, other than the trivial moving of eyes or lifting of
pencil. Piaget intends no such self-evident point. He
argues, rather, that all mental states involve a form of
implicit activity upon the world, and that the capacity
to "think" questions through in one's head would not
exist in the absence of a developmental history in which
one has performed physical actions upon the environment.

Although support for this position will have to await
further elucidation, now is an appropriate time to introduce a crucial term in the Piagetian armamentum: *mental
operation*. All thinking involves, for Piaget, a series of
mental operations, and these operations are simply inter-
nalized actions and sequences of actions. The child who
appreciates that one ball has the same amount of clay as
another that has been altered in shape is demonstrating
the capacity to perform an operation of reversibility. Piaget
maintains that such a problem could not be correctly
solved unless the child is able, in his own mind, to roll the
distorted clay back into its original shape, and to confirm
that the two balls thus procured are the same size. Since
the clay cannot simultaneously assume two different
shapes, the child must reason in his mind. Thus, reasoning
involves implicit action—hence the term "mental operation." Of course, for the mature adult such an operation
may not reveal itself to casual introspection, since the idea
of equivalence over transformation is so firmly established
that a rote formula suffices for an answer. Not so for the
young child, whose evolution from a stage where he does
not recognize the equivalence of the two balls to one
where he insists upon it is directly dependent upon his
capacity to carry out an operation of reversibility, i.e.,
implicitly or mentally returning the transformed ball to
its original shape.

From his observations and experiments with children,
Piaget has deduced three principal stages through which

normal individuals in Western culture pass in their march to intellectual maturity. The *sensorimotor stage,* which runs its course in infancy, involves the child's increasing mastery of his actions in a world of objects. By the end of the period he exhibits a "practical intelligence": he is able to demonstrate, through the manner of his inter-actions with things and persons, that he has a sense of space, time, causality, and objects which will enable him to negotiate his way successfully around his environment.

During the years following infancy, called variously the preoperational, intuitive, semiotic, or representational stage, the child evolves toward the possession of *concrete operations.* The capacities evolved during the sensorimotor stage in direct contact with objects are now achieved on an implicit plane—that is, he no longer needs to "go through the motions" in order to test a possible action. By the conclusion of this period, during the elementary-school years, he will no longer have to assume another person's seat in order to see how the world looks to that person. Rather, he will be able to switch perspectives mentally, to form a representation of the view from the other chair. The term "concrete" here indicates that the child is continuing to work in his mind with concrete materials, with objects, physical states, persons and so on; the "operational" aspect involves his implicit actions upon those objects which he is manipulating mentally.

The final broad phase of mental evolution is termed by Piaget the stage of *formal operations.* This is generally attained sometime between the ages of twelve and fifteen, and involves the capacity to carry out experiments in a laboratory and, more broadly, to reason like a practicing scientist, employing deductive thought. Thus the fifteen year-old, in contrast to the nine-year-old, can conduct experiments in which he varies factors one at a time, and then can issue a reasoned judgment about the relevant causal relations. Clearly, this kind of reasoning is opera-tional, for it involves implicit (and sometimes explicit) actions upon the environment, in particular such activities as joining, reversing, and coordinating. The operations are called formal because, increasingly, the child is operating not upon the world of objects but rather upon verbal or symbolic characterizations of this world—upon linguistic, logical, or "formal" propositions. The child's starting point is not the object itself, or even an implicit action upon an object, but rather a statement or possible statements about the object which the child weighs against one another, and performs operations upon. Thus, the child trying to judge which of three girls is tallest evaluates the propositions with respect to one another and draws the appropriate conclusion. Piaget believes that he can specify the logical operations which the child at the level of formal operations is capable of performing; validation of this claim, which is still awaited, would serve as a powerful confirmation of his theory.

Three broad trends characterize the child's mental development in childhood. The first is the decline of egocentrism. The young child is, in Piaget's terms, totally egocentric—meaning not that he thinks selfishly only about himself, but to the contrary, that he is incapable of thinking about himself. The egocentric child is unable to differentiate himself from the rest of the world; he has not separated himself out from others or from objects. Thus he feels that others share his pain or his pleasure, that his mumblings will inevitably be understood, that his perspective is shared by all persons, that even animals and plants partake of his consciousness. In playing hide-and-seek he will "hide" in broad view of other persons, because his egocentrism prevents him from recognizing that others are aware of his location. The whole course of human development can be viewed as a continuing decline in egocentrism, until death or senility occurs.

A second trend in the child's mental growth is the tendency toward internalization or interiorization of thought. The infant either solves problems by his activity upon the world or he does not solve them at all. The older child, on the other hand, can achieve many intellectual breakthroughs without overt physical actions. He is able to realize these actions implicitly, through concrete and formal operations.

Finally, a growing child increasingly relies upon various kinds of symbols—words, pictures, mathematical or artistic concepts. The child of two is able to use words and other symbols as accompaniments to his physical actions, and before long he becomes able to replace overt actions with symbolic representations of them. Such use of symbols is an extremely powerful aid to thought, and its emergence has been designated the dynamic characteristic of the preoperational, or intuitive, stage. Thus, the young child trying to understand the principle governing a pendulum's trajectory is restricted to a series of uncoordinated actions on the object which he is unable to order or assess, while the teenager confronted with the same problem is able to evaluate the possibilities in some sort of linguistic or symbolic code, without making hand or pendulum move. Furthermore, when he finally does begin to manipulate the pendulum, his actions will be guided by the logical analysis he has performed and will be perpetually adjusted in accordance with that program.

Although Piaget's views on intellectual development were, as we have suggested, at least latent in his earliest papers and treatises, his mature formulations rest upon an enormous amount of experimental data accumulated over many years with the help of many colleagues, foremost among them Bärbel Inhelder. We shall now take a look at each of the three major periods of Piaget's work. Throughout we shall, for illustrative purposes, indicate the ages of the children being examined. It must be emphasized, however, that any ages given for a developmental phase are very approximate, at best. What is important for Piaget is not whether a child reaches the stage of concrete operations at age five or age eight, but

only that the concrete-operational stage must always suc-
ceed the preoperational stage, even as it must always pre-
cede the formal-operational stage. It is entirely possible
for a five-year-old to be at a more advanced stage than a
six-year-old; what is not possible is for the child to skip
a stage, or to vary the normal order of progression through
the successive stages.

1. CLINICAL INVESTIGATIONS OF THE CHILD'S WORLD-VIEW

Piaget's earliest series of studies, for which he was catapulted to fame, dealt with the world-view of children aged
four to twelve. This age range was a fertile one to study,
because the four-year-old, a fluent speaker, could convey
to the experimenter his notions about many realms of
activity, yet these notions were markedly divergent from
those of somewhat older children, and so the egocentrism
of the young could be readily seen.

In the research that formed the basis of his very first
book, Piaget sought to uncover the young child's intellectual level by focusing on his use and understanding of
language. He told a simple fairy tale to children and
asked them to repeat the tale to others. From these repetitions, Piaget was able to measure the child's own understanding of the story—could he recapitulate the major
points? did he comprehend the underlying message?—and
the child's capacity to appreciate the amount of information another child would need to "get" the story. Here
is a sample story:

Once upon a time there was a lady who was called Niobe
and who had 12 sons and 12 daughters. She met a fairy who
had only one son and no daughter. Then the lady laughed at
the fairy because the fairy had only one boy. Then the fairy
was very angry and fastened the lady to a rock. The lady cried
for ten years. In the end she turned into a rock, and her tears
made a stream which still runs today.

Consider now how Gio, aged eight, related the story of Niobe:

> Once upon a time there was a lady who had twelve boys and girls and then a fairy, a boy, and a girl. And then Niobe wanted to have some more sons. Then she was angry. She fastened her to a stone. He turned into a rock and then his tears made a stream which is still running today.

Gio's protocol would seem to suggest that he understood little, if anything, of the story: individuals are never distinguished from one another; sex is mixed up; Niobe is never properly introduced. Yet a series of questions asked following his telling indicated that in fact he had understood the story almost perfectly. For example, he knew that the fairy was angry "because she [Niobe] wanted to have more children than the fairy." Piaget indicates that Gio's problem lay in his "style of talking," which made it impossible for someone ignorant of the story to discern which details were crucial. Gio evidently lacked the ability to assume the listener's perspective, i.e., his "egocentric coefficient" was high. It was through such finely honed investigative techniques that the limitations of children's speech were revealed—the fact that a child's language is often too imprecise to permit adequate communication and that his level of understanding is not always reflected in his spontaneous speech.

In addition to revealing that a child's understanding often exceeds his skills in communication, Piaget's study suggested that children aged four to eight have only an incomplete grasp of logical causality and frequently gave implausible verbal accounts of causal relations. Piaget examined this question directly in a companion book, *Judgment and Reasoning in the Child.* He first reviewed the spontaneous use of the word "because" in children's discourse, and found that the word was quite frequently used in what appeared to be an appropriate sense. For this reason many parents of a six- or seven-year-old might declare that of course their child knows the meaning of "because." When, however, Piaget gave children of this age incomplete sentences and asked them to supply the endings, he found an inexpert and often erroneous handling of causal terms. Indeed, the use of "because" varied from its correct meaning to one akin to "in such a manner that" to another suggesting the connective "and." Thus, Sci (aged 7:2) : "A man fell down in the road because he broke his leg." Berne (aged 6:6) : "I teased that dog because he bit me." Don (6:0) : "I've lost my pen because I'm not writing"; "I went for a message yesterday, because I went on my bike"; and "They are playing music [in the next room] because you can hear it."

Piaget interprets these logical solecisms as a demonstration that the child does not have a developed sense of causality: the child dimly perceives that some sort of causal relation obtains, but is likely to blurt out the first idea that comes into his head, and that is more likely than not to be the consequence of the act, rather than its cause. He does not ask whether the connection is causal, consecutive, or logical, but simply expresses the relation by an available conjunction. He tends to juxtapose rather than examine logical implications and to impose a *syncretistic* vision, in which the domain as a whole is vaguely perceived, but its unique details and their interrelations are largely overlooked.

Thus far the Piagetian enterprise seemed to emphasize the child's linguistic errors, logical immaturities, and egocentric tendencies, rather than the more positive features of his mental functioning. In the next phase of his enterprise, however, Piaget focused on the specific contours of the young child's world-view. He did so by applying in his interviews with children the clinical methods he had used in working with mental patients. For example, he would ask a child where the sun had come from. Rather than merely recording the youngster's answer and moving on to the next question, he would use the initial response as a point of departure for further discussion and probing. Taking care not to influence or predetermine responses, he would encourage further discussion through non-directive questions or remarks, such as: *What did you mean by that? ... A little boy told me the other day that he thought ... Suppose the sun were to disappear one day ... Do you suppose the sun has always been there?* There was no set procedure for questioning, for this would limit the child's freedom of expression; but there was a plan of attack for experimenters to follow, and a set of hypotheses which Piaget hoped his subjects would confirm or disprove. This clinical method has continued to be used prominently throughout Piaget's later studies, and an apprenticeship in its use (which may take a number of years) is now required of Piaget's research associates and students.

Characteristically for a scholar reared in the Cartesian tradition, Piaget began his investigations of the child's mental universe by probing his notion of thought. Piaget hypothesized that a being with no clear notion of the distinction between mind and body, with a less developed sense of self, would have a different conception of thought from that held by most adults. He then asked children to tell him their thoughts about thinking.

During the first stage, many children claim that they think with the mouth. For example, Mont (7:0) was asked if he knew what it means to think. When he said he did, he was asked, "What do you think with?" *The mouth.* "Can you think with the mouth shut?" *No.* "With the eyes shut?" *Yes.* "With the ears stopped up?" *Yes.*

Though the child spontaneously introduces the idea that thought comes from the mouth, he does not hesitate to suggest an external source to thought as well. Thus, Ratt (8:10) was asked, "Have words got strength?" *Yes.* "Tell me a word which has strength." *The wind.* "Why has the word 'wind' got strength?" *Because it goes quickly.* "Is it the word or the wind which goes quickly?" *The wind.* Only later does the child adopt a more internal notion of thought; and even then it tends to be rather animistic. Asked if one can touch the mind, Peret (11:7) replies, *No. You can't because you can't see it.* "Why not?" *It's air.* "Why do you think it is air?" *Because you can't touch it.*

Having probed juvenile conceptions of the thought process and the mind, Piaget investigated several other kinds of conceptions, including the child's view of dreams. For the youngest child, the dream is an image or voice coming from outside and manifesting itself in front of your eyes. Banf (4:6) sees dreams as made of "lights" in the room. The lights are "little lamps, like bicycles . . . [which come] from the moon. The lights come in the night." The search for the causes of dreams comes sometime later. Bag's (7:0) dreams come from God "to pay me back because I wasn't good." Other children see dreams as being sent by various external objects like birds, pigeons, or the air. Gradually a movement inward commences as the child, though he still sees the dream as the product of external sources, comes to regard it as existing closer to him, in his room or directly in front of his eyes. It is first in the years immediately prior to adolescence that the dream is understood to be internal and of internal origin. Bouch (11:10) explains, "I'm dressed like other people, then it [the picture] is in my head, but you'd think it was in front of you."

Piaget concludes that the young child's ideas about thoughts, words, and dreams are characterized by three forms of a fallacy he calls "realism"—the attribution of an independent, quasi-physical reality to mental states and constructs. In the first type, the child confuses the mental object and the thing it represents (the sign with the thing signified); to touch the name of the sun would be to touch the sun itself, to curse the sun is to threaten its existence. This realism gives rise to feelings of "participation" in which the name passes to and fro between the object (the sun) and ourselves. The second kind of realism involves confusion between internal and external. The dreams are first found to be in things, then in the room, then in the head, and finally in thought itself; the child often embraces the paradoxical notion that the dream is a voice or air which is both external and internal. The third variety of realism leads to a confusion between thought and matter. Thought or dream is a whisper, or a voice, or smoke; only gradually does the child come to believe that experiences like dreams can have a nonsubstantive basis.

Explorations of children's conceptions in other areas, ranging from the nature of weather to the origin of the sun and the moon, confirmed Piaget's notions about the distinctive quality of the young child's thought. He found a pervasive flavor in the answers given by children of a certain age, irrespective of the topic of the questioning or the particular experience of the individual child. A consideration of the questions and answers demonstrates how unlikely it was that the children were extrapolating their answers from religious training or from what the parents, siblings, and teachers had told them. Rather, it appears that the child had never considered these questions, and that Piaget was uncovering "an original tendency, characteristic of child mentality." Piaget has called this flavor "artificialism" and explored its characteristics at some length.

The artificialist child conceives of all objects, including natural bodies, as artifacts, as each being "made for" a given purpose. The readiest hypotheses are that natural objects are made "for keeping warm," "for boating," etc. —that is, for whatever use they are actually put to—and, furthermore, that these natural objects are made by men. The child behaves as if nature were charged with purpose, as if chance or mechanical necessity did not exist, as if each being tended towards a fixed goal. There is no distinction in the child's mind between physical and moral causes, and therefore the sun appears because it has to give us light or to keep us warm, because men or God so decree it. There is a development to this artificialism; for example, the four- or five-year-old may trace the origin of man to earlier man, whereas a child aged seven to nine is likely to attribute man's existence to animals, plants, or nature itself. But such attributions are merely more sophisticated manifestations of the artificialist mode of thought.

Piaget, with acute discernment, has perceived a relationship among the accounts of the universe woven by children in their early years, the kinds of dream symbolism studied by Freud, and the accounts of cosmology and nature given by primitive peoples. Indeed, he claims that an elementary conception of the world—replete with animism, realism, and artificialism, with objects seen as permeated by spirits and thought as material in substance —will naturally and inevitably color less developed forms of thought, whether in the mind of a child, a dreamer, a madman, or a primitive. Only as the child becomes interested in the mechanisms which govern the functioning of objects—in the construction of a bicycle or the processes of a simple craft—does a trend away from artificialist explanations and toward an understanding of a phenomenon in its own terms emerge.

When the child starts to ask how something works, he can no longer subscribe completely to the notion of human or natural omnipotence, and he has started to test reality with various hypotheses about its processes and structures. At the same time, the child becomes aware of the fallibility of his parents and teachers and stops looking to them as a source or creator of all knowledge. Instead, he tries to explain phenomena in their own terms, and typically seeks to establish dynamic forms of participation between things: the clouds and the rain are attracted to one another; the wind and the clouds act upon one another. Unlike artificialist and animistic hypotheses, these lend themselves to testing and even to refutation—through systematic observation one can see whether the wind actually does depend on the clouds. Once the child has freed himself of spontaneously occurring but deceptive theories about the nature of the world, he has the opportunity to arrive at a more reasonable and less biased version. It is a fascinating phenomenon, one which reminds Piaget of his globular molluscs, that the normal ten- or twelve-year-old in our society is able to reject, with relatively little prompting from his environment, many primitive notions about the world of objects which the greatest philosophers in classical times held to be correct. Although certain characteristics permeate both childhood and primitive thought, the dissemination of modern scientific findings has interacted with factors of development to produce juvenile theories of nature which are increasingly consonant with the findings of science.

2. STUDIES OF INFANCY

While Piaget was discovering the characteristic worldviews of young school children, he was also launching a family of his own. Three children were born in the Piaget household during the late 1920's and early 1930's, and Piaget began what in all likelihood are the most careful observations of infants ever undertaken. These studies were an effort to define and trace the evolution of the most basic aspects of intelligence; they were eventually published in a set of three monographs which constitute the second major phase of Piaget's developmental investigations.

In a little-known article published in 1927 in a British journal, Piaget mentions the great difficulties he had in studying the first year of life of his first child. Any parent who has tried to make sense of the goings-on of infancy can readily sympathize with Piaget. At first, the child seems a totally alien creature, much closer to a primitive animal or automaton, a sum of its waking and sleeping states, sucking rates, plus a reliable but limited repertoire of reflexes. Before one knows it, however, the child becomes able to react to individuals, and many a mother suspects that even her two-month-old recognizes her. Babbling proceeds with seemingly little purpose in the early months, but suddenly a first and then a second word appears. And once words combine into phrases and phrases into sentences, the child has become, to all intents and purposes, a participant in the adult world. In the meantime, he has achieved the ability to walk, run, imitate, use tools, eat, recognize himself, undress himself, and engage in numerous other complex activities with little direct tutelage from his parents.

Children change dramatically within weeks, days, sometimes even hours: a child will pore over a picture puzzle in the morning with no idea of how to solve it, look at it a few minutes in the afternoon and assemble it correctly; he will passively watch a television show for a week, then recite three commercials flawlessly. It is no wonder that parents have expressed marvel, and psychologists bewilderment, about the mechanism of change in the first years of life; it seems easiest to follow the child's example, adopting some sort of artificialist or animistic explanation for this phenomenal progress. And it is not surprising that most parents, when the second or third child comes along, are more struck by the temperamental differences among their children than by the undeniable similarities in behavior, physical growth, or intellectual development. All told, the naturalistic study of children presents strong evidence for the contention that mere observing of a phenomenon will lead to charming anecdotes and a "feeling for the subject" without yielding propositions which can be empirically tested.

Unlike other parents and most child psychologists, however, Piaget drew lessons from the problems he encountered in studying the first year of life of his first child. When there were additions to the Piaget family, he was Pasteur's genius, "the prepared man": he had a theory of how infant development occurred and he was prepared to test it. The theory of infancy was critical for his grand scheme, because if one wanted to understand the development of intelligence, it was necessary to start at the beginning. And if one wanted to pinpoint the role of language in intellectual functioning, it was imperative to begin at the prelinguistic stage.

Piaget's method and materials were deceptively simple. He sat near his child, who was lying in the crib or playing on the floor, watched the infant's spontaneous behavior, and from time to time introduced various kinds of interruptions or "problems," carefully noting the child's reaction to these impositions. The experimental materials were restricted to the most banal objects: pens, berets, pocket watches, boxes. From the years spent in silent observation came what are by common consensus the most brilliant set of observations ever made on children during the prelinguistic stage.

In his first book summarizing his results, Piaget explored the origins of intelligence. He outlined six stages of sensorimotor development, during the course of which the child moves from simple reflexes to a practical mastery of the world of persons and objects around him. We shall now describe each of these stages, with their approximate age ranges. It will, however, be noted that (as indicated earlier) the children vary significantly in the age at which they reach a given stage; moreover, a child who is predominantly at one stage will occasionally evince behaviors associated with an earlier or a subsequent stage.

(1) Use of Reflexes

The newborn infant is seen as a collection of reflexes: sucking, swallowing, crying, making gross bodily motions, and the like. What occurs during the first few weeks of life is that the child becomes quite proficient with regard to these fundamental actions and is able, up to a point, to modify them to make them more appropriate to the given environment. Thus, sucking may proceed in a slightly modified way, depending on the angle at which the child is held, the shape of the nipple, the amount of fluid desired, the degree of pressure needed to get the fluid at a desirable rate. Such modifications are examples of *accommodation*—a basic process of adaptation in which the child alters a behavioral pattern or scheme in accordance with the conditions he finds in the outer world. As a corollary, a wider variety of objects come to be treated as "suckable," and the child not only sucks when hungry at the breast, but also when other objects are put into his vicinity at other times. This complementary aspect of adaptation—in which an increased number of objects or events are subsumed under, and trigger, the exercise of a given behavioral scheme—is called *assimilation*.

The scheme itself may be thought of as the capacity to suck, or the act of sucking; but as the child develops particular components of this ability, more differentiated sucking schemes, involving variations in speed, frequency, or shape of the mouth, will also evolve. More generally, the scheme can be thought of as those aspects of an action or operation which are repeatable or generalizable in a similar action or operation. The scheme of sucking consists not in the particular characteristics of any given suck, but rather in those more general properties which persist through a variety of sucking situations. An infant's (or any person's) behavioral repertoire may be thought of as the sum of his schemes.

(2) Acquired Adaptations and Primary Circular Reactions

When the child no longer sucks reflexively at objects, but undertakes systematic coordinations between behavioral patterns, such as bringing his hand up to his mouth during sucking, he has entered Piaget's second stage: he is

now able to adapt his schemes to the particular dimensions of situations. Characteristic of this phase is the
primary circular reaction, the constant repetition of a
behavioral component so that the pattern is smoothed out
and mastered. Consider the following examples of the
behavior of Laurent during his third month of life:

> From 0:2 (3) [i.e., third day of the second month] Laurent
> evidences a circular reaction which will become more definite
> and will constitute the beginning of systematic grasping: he
> scratches and tries to grasp, lets go, scratches and grasps again
> etc. On 0:2 (3) and 0:2 (6) this can only be observed during the
> feeding. . . .
> But beginning 0:2 (7) the behavior becomes marked in the
> cradle itself. Laurent scratches the sheet which is folded over
> the blankets, then grasps it and holds it a moment, then lets it
> go, scratches it again and recommences without interruption.
> At 0:2 (11) this play lasts a quarter of an hour at a time, sev-
> eral times during the day. At 0:2 (12) he scratches and grasps
> my fist, which I placed against the back of his right hand. . . .
> At 0:2 (14) . . . I note how definitely the spontaneous grasping
> of the sheet reveals the characteristics of a circular reaction—
> groping at first, then regular rhythmical activity (scratching,
> grasping, holding, and letting go) and finally progressive loss
> of interest.

One can see in these jottings that the two-month-old child
at first achieves some mastery of the behavior in a particular situation and then exhibits the behavior in newer contexts, in which he both assimilates objects into his scheme
of grasping and accommodates the scheme to the different
shapes and positions of objects.

(3) Procedures to Make Interesting Sights Last

These trends are accelerated in the third stage of development, during the middle of the first year of life, when
the child becomes capable of performing *secondary circular reactions.* Such a reaction still encompasses the
repetition and mastery of simple behaviors (hence circular) , but these behaviors are now put to various uses—

in particular, to the preservation of interesting sights and experiences. Accompanying this stage is a kind of motor recognition of familiar objects, involving the performance of reduced and simplified (abbreviated) versions of the behavioral scheme appropriate to an object when that object appears. Thus, when a person enters the room, the infant will turn his head slightly, then resume his previous activity. The temptation here is to use mentalistic language, for the child appears to display incipient signs of intention, recognition, and direction.

The child at this third stage is interested in the environmental consequences of his actions. Unlike the younger child, he doesn't merely act or try out; he heeds consequences and attempts to have the more desirable of them repeated. It is at this stage, then, that we find the child fulfilling for the first time a role celebrated in all of Piaget's work: that of an experimenter or investigator who modifies his conceptions of the world as a result of his actions upon it and his observation of their consequences. Particularly instructive are the procedures for making interesting sights last. By his behavior the child reveals that he is interested in phenomena that are sufficiently akin to those engendering his previous actions to be assimilable, but that he has no clues concerning the actual cause of the desired event:

At 0:7 (7) Laurent looks at a tin box placed on a cushion in front of him, too remote to be grasped. I drum on it for a moment in a rhythm which makes him laugh and then present my hand (at a distance of 2 cm. from his in front of him). He looks at it, but only for a moment, then turns toward the box; then he shakes his arm while staring at the box; then he draws himself up, strikes his coverlets, shakes his head, etc. (that is to say, he uses all the "procedures" at his disposition).

(4) Coordination of Secondary Schemes

As he approaches the end of his first year of life, the child exhibits a new level of behavior—stage 4 of Piaget's sequence. He begins to combine his various secondary schemes ("coordination of secondary schemes") and to apply them in new situations. For the first time, the child is able to adapt to new situations through a systematic use and combination of schemes familiar to him. Prominent at this time is the sequence of setting aside an object in order to reach a more desired goal. To do this, the child requires not only a clearly established intention but also the ability to execute a plan so that the appropriate behavioral scheme will occur at the apposite time. To be sure, such a plan will not be made with drawingboard precision; but at the very minimum, the child must have sufficient control of his schemes that it is possible for him to order them appropriately. Such sequences offer, in Piaget's view, an illustration of the spontaneous structuring activity inherent in all intelligent thought; it is difficult to comprehend how such a combination could be derived simply from "past experience" or environmental influences. An example is Laurent's behavior at 0:7 (8) when Piaget presents him with a little bell behind the corner of the cushion. Laurent strikes the cushion, as he had done previously, but then depresses it with one hand while he grasps the new object with the other. Exploration of new objects is characteristic of this stage:

At 0:8 (16) Jacqueline grasps an unfamiliar cigarette case. . . . at first she examines it very attentively, turns it over, then holds it in both hands while making the sound *apff*. After that she rubs it against the wicker of her bassinet, then draws herself up while looking at it, then swings it above her, and finally puts it into her mouth.

The divergence between the child near the end of his first year and the newborn infant is already incredible: the newborn simply exhibits his limited repertoire of reflexes in an unmotivated sequence, whereas the child of one year has control of a large number of differentiated and appropriate behavioral schemes which he draws upon skillfully in exploring objects and attaining goals.

(5) Tertiary Circular Reactions—New Means Through Experimentation

More striking signs of intelligent behavior wait upon the events of the last two sensorimotor stages. In the fifth stage the child evolves tertiary circular reactions and discovers new means for solving problems through active experimentation. In contrast to his earlier, primary and secondary circular reactions, in which he was working with familiar schemes, the child at stage 5 is oriented toward the novel features of an object which are not readily assimilable to the usual schemes. The child makes a new discovery and, rather than falling back upon old schemes, actively pursues the consequences of his discovery by devising novel schemes:

Thus Jacqueline, when fourteen months of age, finds that a certain movement of her fingers leads to a tilting of a box. She then varies the conditions of the movement, keeping track of her discovery, until she arrives at an effective way of tilting the box up.

In addition to this capacity to adapt schemes to new situations, the child is also able to devise new means for solving problems. Hitherto he has relied on familiar schemes or on their combination: at stage 5, however, he lets the problem or difficulty serve as a guide and attempts to devise a solution adequate to the demands of the situation. In a revealing example, Piaget places his watch on a big red cushion. Laurent, at age 0:10 (16), attempts to reach the watch but cannot get it:

But then, instead of letting go of the support at once, as he has hitherto done, in order to grasp the objective, he recommences with obvious interest to move the cushion while looking at the watch. Everything takes place as though he notices for the first time the relationship for its own sake and studies it as such. He thus easily succeeds in grasping the watch.

Not satisfied with this demonstration of use of new means, however, Piaget devises an even more difficult problem. He sets up two colored cushions in front of Laurent. The first one, as before, is placed directly in front of the child, while the second is placed behind the first so that a corner of the second is facing the child. This corner is placed on the first cushion; but the second does not protrude and is not very visible. Finally, Piaget places his watch at the far end of the second cushion. Laurent immediately grasps the first cushion and pulls it toward him. When he observes that the watch does not move, he examines the place where the cushions are superimposed and goes right to the second cushion, thereby retrieving the watch. At stage 5, then, the child has already achieved an effective, supple commerce with the world of objects. Yet, he remains restricted to the world of objects present; when things disappear from view (or when he looks away), he has difficulty incorporating them into his domain of thought.

(6) Invention of New Means Through Mental Combination
The sixth stage, which emerges toward the latter part of the second year, marks a decisive point in the child's development: for the first time, he is able to devise means of solving problems through internal or mental coordinations. If the stage 5 child is placed in a situation in which he cannot readily devise a solution, he will grope around with the means at his disposal, always actively experimenting with overt sensorimotor acts. The child at stage 6, however, will pause and appear to consider the alternatives, to carry out a kind of internal experimentation, an inner exploration of ways and means. An entirely novel sequence of actions can come to pass without trial and error in the world, simply through a mental inventory of possible actions. Two examples will serve to illustrate the unique character of this sixth stage—the invention of new means through mental combinations:

Jacqueline at 1:8 (o) arrives at a closed door, with a blade of grass in each hand. She stretches out her right hand toward the knob but sees that she cannot turn it without letting go of the grass. She puts the grass on the floor, opens the door, picks up the grass again and enters. But when she wants to leave the room things become complicated. She puts the grass on the floor and grasps the doorknob. But then she perceives that in pulling the door toward her she will simultaneously chase away the grass which she placed between the door and the threshold. She therefore picks it up in order to put it outside the door's zone of movement.

In the second example, Piaget hides a chain inside a match-box and leaves only a tiny slit open. Lucienne, at 1:4 (9) , begins by turning the whole thing over, then tries to grasp the chain through the opening. Not succeeding, she simply puts her index finger into the slit and so succeeds in getting out a small fragment of the chain; she then pulls on it until she has completely solved the problem. Next, Piaget replaces the chain in the box and leaves an even tinier opening. Again Lucienne tries her two schemes—turning the box over and sliding her finger into the slot—but this time neither of them works. A pause follows, during which Lucienne manifests a curious reaction:

She looks at the slit with great attention: then several times in succession, she opens and shuts her mouth, at first slightly, then wider and wider. Soon after this phase of thinking, Lucienne unhesitatingly puts her finger in the slit and, instead of trying as before to reach the chain, she pulls so as to enlarge the opening. She succeeds and grasps the chain.

These examples, multiplied by dozens in Piaget's book, suggest that the child's intellectual processes have under-gone a revolution by the end of the sensorimotor period. Rather than starting from overt actions in the world, and letting these actions guide him to the solution of a prob-lem, the child at the age of eighteen months can now apprehend the constraints of a problem on a conceptual level and consider the various possibilities without actually having to run through them. A kind of short-circuiting appears to have taken place whereby an action or behavioral scheme can be contemplated without being unraveled and enacted. We have seen foreshadowings of this trend earlier in the child's development, as, for example, when the stage 3 child faced with a familiar object goes through only a partial enactment of the appropriate scheme. But by stage 6 a much more radical development has occurred: the actions need not be physically carried out at all, for assimilation and accommodation can occur on the "mental" or "representational" plane.

Does Piaget mean to say, then, that the child of age two walks around with pictures in his head? Piaget is appropriately cautious at this point, on which it is virtually impossible to gain evidence. He prefers to suggest that the child, instead of performing an act, is imitating it internally; he is "running through" the act itself "within his body and mind" rather than externally upon the world. This imitation of action can be replete with pictorial images, muscular sensations, or relatively free of physical-sensory accouterments. What is crucial is not its physiological concomitants but the fact that in *some* way the two-year-old is *potentially* able to draw upon an action, evaluating its appropriateness without testing it in the world. Here lies the basis of operational thinking.

Until the sixth sensorimotor stage the child's knowledge of the world is based on the actions he can perform on the world of objects. If a child can bite, suck, throw, drop, and bounce a ball, his knowledge of the ball is as an object which can be bitten, sucked, etc. His knowledge is restricted to the sum of schemes which can be performed on that object. (If there were an action called "zilching" that he could perform, the child's knowledge would include the zilchability of the ball.) But after the sixth stage, two radical reorientations have occurred in the child's epistemology. The first is that he can now view the ball in relation to potential actions as well as to actions actually performed with it: the ball is not only something that he throws, but something that he "could throw" if he wanted to knock down a pan from the wall, or something that he "could suck" if he wanted to alleviate a pain in his mouth. In appropriate situations, the child may run through his possible schemes via mental representation and, without any perceptible prior actions, alight immediately on the correct sequence of movement. The second major consequence is that the world is no longer simply a sum of physical actions related to objects and persons; rather, the two-year-old child has developed an entire theory about the crucial components of experience—about space, time, causality, and objects, and the way they interrelate to constitute experience.

Because the child's changing awareness of objects is a crucial component of his psychological development—and because it is to this subject that Piaget has devoted perhaps the most central chapter in all his work—it merits special mention. First, however, a word on Piaget's methodology may be appropriate. Psychology may be viewed as the science of tasks and tests; it is difficult to assess behavior unless some sort of a standard is defined, and a subject's performance evaluated in relation to this standard. Devising tests for infants is especially demanding, and Piaget was among the first psychologists to have specific tasks in mind when working with children, instead of merely describing what the child does in an unstructured situation.

One risks finding in Piaget's reports merely a series of perceptive descriptions if one fails to appreciate that his interventions into his children's life-space were carefully planned in order to yield information about a range of capacities. Piaget always worked with a hypothesis in mind which could be tested by setting the same task for the child on a number of separate occasions. His highly organized account of his findings may hide the subtlety and brilliance of each of his little tests; these sometimes fade into the background against Piaget's more dominant concern with theoretical concepts and stages of development. Perhaps the magnitude of his achievement can be most clearly realized if one makes the attempt oneself to devise a series of tasks to be used in assessing a child's sense of the world of objects, and then goes on to consider Piaget's efforts in this direction. Only then can his unique capacity to guide the child's behavior without hiding its spontaneous properties be fully appreciated.

For the adult, the world is composed of objects: persons, furniture, astronomical bodies, chemical compounds, cells molecules. Not only are these objects relatively stable, but also the adult has various theoretical notions about objects which are virtually impregnable to challenge. An object endures across time, contains a certain amount of matter which may be transformed but not destroyed, is susceptible to certain transformations but not to others, and exists in a spatio-temporal context with other objects. These sophisticated notions take a long time to solidify, but the most crucial central component—what Piaget calls the sense of object permanence—develops during the first years of life. Let us now take a look at the developmental trajectory Piaget has uncovered.

The core of the object concept is the understanding that objects continue to exist when one can no longer see them. Accordingly, Piaget's tests have focused upon infantile behavior when objects are removed from sight. During the initial two stages (analogous to stages one and two of sensorimotor development) the child shows no special behavior when objects vanish. Though he may smile or behave appropriately when the nipple or parent comes into view, he gives no evidence of perceiving the universe as divided into objects having substance and being external to himself. When an object is removed from sight, it simply ceases to exist for the child, who looks for it no further and becomes preoccupied instead with whatever remains in his perceptual field.

In the third stage, around the middle of the first year of life, the child possesses sufficient expectations that he is moved to action when a desired object disappears from sight. At six months, for instance, Laurent searches in front of him for a paper ball which Piaget has dropped above his blanket. He immediately looks at the blanket but only in front of him—that is, where he has just grasped the ball. When Piaget drops the object outside the bassinet, Laurent does not look for it, except around Piaget's empty hand, which remains in the air. Similarly, Lucienne, at the end of eight months, grabs a small doll and examines it with great interest. When it drops out of her hand, she immediately looks for it in front of her, but doesn't see it right away. When she has found it, Piaget takes it from her, and places a blanket over it, before her eyes. Lucienne evinces no reaction.

During the third stage, then, there is concern about absent objects, but the child apparently lacks a strategy or scheme for finding them. Piaget believes that the child's general recourse when an object vanishes is simply to continue whatever action he has been undertaking and to hope, by invoking magical kinds of procedures, to make the object somehow reappear. In the fourth stage, however, which occurs toward the end of the first year of life, the child for the first time makes an "active search" for the object. At this time, he begins to search for objects outside of the perceptual field; he studies the displacements of objects (where they have been moved) and begins to coordinate his visual sense of where objects are and his actual knowledge of where they are. Indeed, it may seem that the stage 4 child has a sense of object permanence when one learns that Laurent, at nine months, would lift up a pillow to reach a tin box which had been hidden beneath it. But a more decisive test of the child's object concept occurs when Piaget initiates a series of visible displacements:

At 0:10 (18) Jacqueline is seated on a mattress with nothing to disturb or distract her (no blankets, etc.). I take her parrot from her hands and hide it twice in succession under the mattress on her left in A. Both times Jacqueline looks for the object immediately and grabs it. Then I take it from her hands and move it very slowly before her eyes to the corresponding place on her right, in B. Jacqueline watches this movement very attentively, but at the moment when the parrot disappears in B, she turns to her left and looks where it was before, in A.

This attraction to A, the original locus, when the object has been moved in the child's presence to B, is a strikingly dramatic illustration of the undeveloped intelligence of the child near the end of his first year. Numerous other observations of this sort by Piaget confirm that, for the stage 4 child, the object seems to inhere in a particular locus. In his search, the child is not able to take note of the displacements he witnessed, but instead searches for the object in its original place. This indicates that the child does not yet have a sense of an object apart from location, nor an awareness that an object can move to a variety of loci and remain the same object. It is instructive in this regard that cats have also been shown to reach stage 4 and to do so in a much shorter period of time—about three months. Might it be that the longer and more gradual evolution of the child's concept helps to explain why the child advances further than the cat, which never gets beyond stage 4?

Stage 5 is marked by the child's ability to take visible displacements into account. The child no longer searches for the object at A when he sees it moved to B or C, but immediately looks at the correct location. While it might appear that the child's object concept is now fully developed, clever improvisation by Piaget has documented its still fragmentary quality. Trying a series of invisible displacements in front of Lucienne, now one year old, Piaget finds that she succeeds in locating the target only when she has seen it placed. When Piaget hides a watch in his fist, places the fist under a blanket, and then shows

Lucienne his empty fist, she will look at his hand, and all about, but will not look under the blanket, where the watch has been placed outside of her visual field.

The full-blown object concept only emerges in the sixth stage, at about eighteen months, when the child is able to take into account both visible and invisible displacements of the object. The qualitatively different behavior of this stage is well illustrated in the following series with Jacqueline:

At 1:7 (20) Jacqueline watches me when I put a coin in my hand, then put my hand under a blanket. I withdraw my hand closed; Jacqueline opens it, then searches under the coverlet until she finds the object. I take the coin back, put it in my hand and then slip my closed hand under a cushion situated at the other side. . . . Jacqueline immediately searches for the object under the cushion. . . . I complicate the test as follows: I place the coin in my hand, then my hand under the cushion. I bring it forth closed and immediately hide it under the coverlet. Finally I withdraw it and hold it out, closed, to Jacqueline. Jacqueline then pushes my hand aside without opening it (she guesses that there is nothing in it, which is new); she looks under the cushion, then directly under the coverlet, where she finds the object.

In the sixth stage the child is aided by the newly developed ability to represent actions and events mentally— the same capacity that characterizes the sixth stage of general sensorimotor intelligence. This ability to find the object irrespective of what has been witnessed presupposes knowledge of invisible displacements of the object. Piaget explains that this result comes about neither through *a priori* deduction (reasoning from first principles) nor through mere learning by empirical examples (a conclusion based on probability). Were the understanding of the object concept based on *a priori* deduction, there would be no reason for a child to go through a long stage of trial-and-error gropings, where he looked unsystematically for the object or simply waited till it reappeared. On the other hand, if the child were simply learning by association, there would be no way to explain how he was able to locate objects whose displacement he had not seen; nor could a mere accrual of past experiences account for the certainty with which the stage 6 child pursues the object until he finds it. Rather, says Piaget, the evidence suggests that the child actively constructs his knowledge of the object by making certain assumptions about how objects behave, by trying out these "hunches," by rejecting those which are not supported by the facts, and ultimately by devising his own theory, "On the Existence of Objects in a Spatial and Temporal Framework." Needless to say, this construction is not a self-conscious process: it takes place exclusively on the plane of actions. But that fact makes it neither unintelligent nor unconstructive, for actions may have their own compelling logic. Furthermore, the development of the object concept, which itself rests upon the development of sensorimotor intelligence, lays the groundwork for a new plane of reasoning in which problems and situations need not be worked out purely through physical activity but may also be thought out via mental operations. For the reasoning which characterizes the child during the later operational stages of intelligence rests precisely upon the knowledge that the world is composed of substantial, permanently existing objects which can be manipulated and transformed in diverse ways while still maintaining their identity.

At the time he was observing his infants, Piaget was deeply influenced by Jules Henri Poincaré, a leading French philosopher and mathematician around the turn of the century. Poincaré had proposed that the sense of space was innate in human beings, and possessed the properties of the mathematical construct called a *group*; this would mean, roughly speaking, that even a young child was capable of performing specified operations upon a given set of elements—for example, proceeding from one locus to another via one operation, then returning to the original locus by an inversion (or reversal) of that operation. For Piaget, this suggestion that understanding of space could be described in terms of group theory was of great importance, for it confirmed his own conclusion that behavior (or action) could be treated in logical terms. He added, however, that Poincaré, not being a psychologist, mistakenly regarded the group of spatial displacements as *a priori* knowledge instead of recognizing it as the product of thought processes developing within the individual.

Piaget's research on the development of space, time, and the object concept revolutionized the perspectives of Kant and Poincaré, by demonstrating that the infant lacked an innate "adult" sense of these dimensions of experience and therefore had to "construct" them (build them up through his own actions) over the course of years. Nonetheless, Piaget was very much in sympathy with Poincaré's practice of introducing logical models for intellectual conceptions. Not only did such models confer neatness, elegance, and power upon one's formulations, but they also reflected Piaget's own major preoccupation in child development: the child's increasing approximation to logical consistency in his actions, behavior, and knowledge. Accordingly, even in this early work on infant intelligence, Piaget proposed that the child's sense of space, which evolves in the first eighteen months of life, possesses the characteristics of a "practical group." This meant that the child could reveal

DIAGRAM 1. THE SPATIAL GROUP

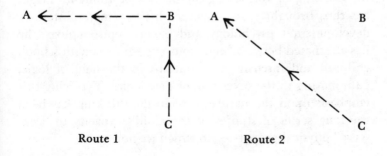

Route 1   Route 2

through his movements within and about a given area, or realm, his understanding of its spatial layout. (See Diagram 1.) If a child was able to come back from point C to starting point A, either by tracing his way through B or by proceeding directly from C to A, and was able without difficulty to employ diverse routes in order to make interconnections within different parts of the realm, Piaget concluded that the child's behavior was analogous to, if not isomorphic with, a mathematical group. This claim is neither obvious nor beyond dispute; yet whether or not it is substantiated, the line of thinking it reflects is crucial for an understanding of Piaget. From this time onward in his work, Piaget would be increasingly eager to provide mathematical models for the behaviors he discerned; these formal analogies constituted for him the underlying structures of behavior.

3. STUDIES OF CONCRETE AND FORMAL OPERATIONS

Having described the child's characteristic world-view during the 1920's, and the origins of intelligence in infancy during the thirties, Piaget subsequently devoted his prodigious energies to investigations of the development of the capacity to think scientifically. His studies have traced the genesis of operational thinking at the concrete and formal levels, and he has simultaneously sought to describe the underlying structure of operations through the positing of formal-logical models of thought. Piaget has thus brought closer together his two major interests, developmental psychology and genetic epistemology; he has alternated between ingenious experiments with schoolchildren and intensive explorations in the field of logic, culminating in the invention of new logics. Typifying this emphasis upon the nature of scientific thinking has been the long series of studies of the child's capacity to "conserve" physical properties, to which we now turn.

Just as an appreciation of objects is necessary for reasoning about, and negotiating one's way within, the environment, so the awareness of various forms of conservation is the precondition for working consistently with specific material. Conservation is a global term which covers a range of phenomena; that a substance may be bent or twisted, that liquid can be poured into diverse containers, that melodies may be sung at different pitch levels, that land masses may have dissimilar shapes and yet remain in crucial ways the same, are all examples of conservation taken for granted in adult society. One of Piaget's most striking findings was that, until the age of seven or eight —the advent of the capacity for concrete operations—the child is aware neither of the conservations nor of numerous other forms of consistency assumed by older children and adults.

DIAGRAM 2. CONSERVATION OF LIQUIDS

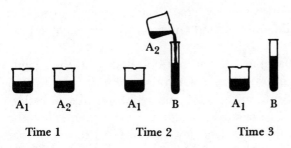

(which has more water, A₁ or B?)

To study conservation of liquids, an experimenter pours water into two identically shaped containers (A_1 and A_2) and gains the child's assent that both containers have the same amount of liquid in them. (Alternatively, the child may pour the water himself.) Then either child or experimenter pours the water from one of the containers (A_2) into another container of a completely different shape— for instance, one that is much longer and thinner (B). The child is then asked whether the first container (A_1)

and this new container (B) each have the same amount of
water or if one has more than the other. (See Diagram 2.)
Almost invariably, the young child of four or five will
declare that one container has more than the other "because it is taller," or because "water goes higher" in it.
Efforts to dissuade the child from this contention are to
no avail, for even if one convinces him of the correct
answer, he will lapse into a misconception of the same
sort on the next task. Various "check" tasks verify that the
child really believes that the quantity of liquid changes
when it enters into a different-sized container with different dimensions. For example, if the child is asked to
pour the same amount of liquid into two containers of
different sizes, he will pour the water to the same level
irrespective of the disproportion in amount which results.
Counterarguments that the child does not understand the
meaning of the term "same" miss the point: it is true
that the child does not understand the term in the adult
way, but this is precisely what Piaget is documenting. For
a young child, amount and sameness are matters of appearance.

Other Piagetian demonstrations flesh out the characteristic *Weltanschauung* of children at this age. In con-
servation-of-substance tasks, the child regards a ball of
clay rolled into a sausage shape as having more clay (because it's longer) or less clay (because it's thinner) than
one which retains its round shape and was originally declared to be of the same size. Or, shown a collection of
diverse objects and asked to place together those which
belong together, the child will come up with a range of
possible groupings but will be unable to make classifications which are internally consistent. For example, he
will put a blue ball and a yellow ball together "because
they are both balls," then a yellow triangle and a yellow
circle because they are "both yellow," and a large ball and
a large square because they are "both large." If the incon-

sistency of this procedure is called to his attention, he will be unconcerned, because as he is unable to bear in mind at the same time all the various dimensions involved, his classifications do not appear to him as inconsistencies. The child associates from part to part, but never succeeds in integrating the parts within a hierarchically arranged whole. Finally, a child shown seven beads, five white and two black, and asked whether there are more *white beads* or more *beads,* will insist there are more white beads, because there are only two black ones. He will resist the necessary comparison of the whole set of beads, including black and white, with one subset of beads, all white, because, according to Piaget, the preoperational child is unable to maintain a simultaneous awareness of a whole and a part.

Understanding what is involved in comparing white beads with all beads is crucial for a grasp of Piaget's theory. The preoperational child can compare white beads with black beads if both are visible, because this task merely involves a perceptual discrimination between lighter and darker spheres and an assessment of which pile is bigger. However, he cannot compare the class of all beads with the class of white beads, because it is impossible to compare a set *physically* with its subset—i.e., it is physically impossible to form two groups, one consisting of all the beads, the other of all the white beads, as the white beads would have to belong to both groups, and hence be in both places at the same time. For such a comparison a *mental operation* is required, of which the preoperational child is incapable. Almost invariably, therefore, he will reinterpret the problem as, Are there more white or more black beads?, a question which can be answered simply by visual inspection. The operational child, on the other hand, mentally compares the class of all beads (seven in number) with the class of white beads (five in number) and answers Piaget's puzzle correctly. It is this capacity to perform actions mentally—to form the two groups in the mind and to compare them in size—which is crucial for all of the higher cognitive functions studied by Piaget.

Piaget's largest body of research, embodied in about two dozen monographs, has been concerned with the period of concrete operations. He has sketched out the characteristic cognitive map of the preoperational child, the child en route to concrete operations, and the child who has finally reached that higher stage. Remarkable though it may seem, a child of six or so who misses all the questions described above and seems quite unaware of his inconsistency will, six months or a year later, step again into the experimental laboratory and not only answer the questions to perfection but also ridicule the idea that anyone, least of all himself, could ever entertain another interpretation of these phenomena. Piaget claims that what has happened in the interim is that the child has become able to think operationally. Let us try to understand the meaning of this claim.

In Piaget's view, the child's intellectual development reflects the nature of his actions upon the world, and the degree of coordination among these actions. The infant possesses the capacity for a diverse set of actions at birth, but only gradually becomes able to coordinate them; for example, he combines his vision and his grasping at five months or thereabouts, and within the next year becomes able to integrate a set of actions in order to achieve a goal. He synthesizes all of his potential actions toward an object at about a year and a half, and constructs a theory of the object at that time. While the events of the first year of life are restricted to the sensorimotor plane, the advent of representational thought—i.e., the ability to imagine actions—enables him to contemplate a series of schemes without actually carrying them out "in the world." At the same time, of course, more advanced and complex actions are also becoming possible, as the child matures physically and acquires various skills. What has happened in the preoperational period, according to Piaget, is that the child now has at his disposal a variety of actions, both actual and potential, which he can direct toward objects, but which he has not yet been able to coordinate into an integrated and holistic structure.

The child on the verge of grasping the principle of conservation of liquids will consider two alternative schemes of actions: (1) pouring liquid into thin containers makes the liquid go higher; (2) pouring liquid into thin containers makes the liquid have narrower width. An incorrect answer will focus on either the height or the narrowness of the container (whichever happens to be more salient), thereby revealing that the child has not succeeded in coordinating the actions with one another; he has focused on a perceived state rather than on the transforming act. When, however, the child realizes that these two actions complement and can be coordinated with each other, that the action which increases height is the same as the action which decreases width, and that the two cancel each other out, he has developed an operation called *compensation*. In more technical language, he may be said to understand that in transferring liquid from the standard beaker A to the new beaker B, one changes aspect x of A to x', which is greater than x, but one has simultaneously changed aspect y of A to y', which is less than y, so that the two changes compensate for one another (though, needless to say, the child does not put the matter this way himself). At about the same time he comes to realize that the act of pouring water from beaker A into beaker B is equivalent to the act of pouring water from B back into A, and thus has developed the operation Piaget calls *reversibility*.

Piaget argues that the child has fully achieved a grasp of the principle of conservation of liquids when he succeeds in combining into a "structured whole" these two operations and a third—that of *identity*, the quantitative notion that nothing has been added and nothing taken away from the object despite its change in appearance. Indeed, this total system of operations, this structured whole, underlies all conservations, and is fundamental to the attainment of concrete operations.

The cognitive capacities of the concrete-operational child may be described mathematically, according to Piaget, in terms of nine interrelated "groupings" (a variety of group devised by Piaget himself). These mathematical structures and their behavioral counterparts account for the whole range of behaviors which the eight-to-eleven-year-old (but not his younger brother) is able to perform. For example, the grouping of "composition" expressed as $A + A' = B$, $B + B' = C$, etc., where $A \times A' = 0$ and $B \times B' = 0$, is said to underlie a variety of operational tasks having to do with addition of sets, position of groups in a hierarchy, composition and decomposition of classes, and class inclusion. That is, this one formal expression designates the structure underlying a variety of cognitive capacities of the eight-year-old. A child who can solve this range of tasks is presumed to have a behavioral structure isomorphic with that grouping.

It is not as yet possible to verify Piaget's claim about these groupings, although Piaget believes that analogues of these mathematical structures will eventually be found in actual behavior and, ultimately, in the nervous system as well. It *is* possible, however, to verify or disprove the particular hypotheses and findings reported by Piaget; and hundreds of researchers all over the world have consistently been able to replicate his findings. More controversial is his discussion of operations, inasmuch as these hypothetical mathematical formulations cannot be readily translated into workable experiments. Piaget's disputes with American psychologists—for example, Jerome Bruner—have often centered on the usefulness of these elusive constructs.

What strikes one in reading Piaget, however, is that operations are intensely real and vital for him. In watching

a subject explore, examine, weigh factors, and reach conclusions, Piaget vividly discerns actions and operations,
just as a behaviorally oriented psychologist spontaneously
spots stimuli and responses in the workaday activities of
college sophomores or Norwegian rats, a psychoanalyst
finds repression or Oedipal fixation in his patients. For
Piaget, thinking is a process which seizes and transforms
the reality of a given moment into that of another moment
—it is the organizing principle of the Bergsonian flux, the
motor of the mental mechanism which makes sense of rich
sensations and feelings and tensions. To think of something in one's head is as active a matter as to push it or
eat it or "zilch" it and, as a result, operations seem no
more hypothetical to Piaget than the balancing motions
of a juggler or the compensatory adjustments of a cyclist.
He goes on to say that one's own knowledge of states of
reality comes about through transforming them; thus, the
very actions which constitute thought lead ultimately to
knowledge of thought. To understand a state, you must
understand the transformation from which it results; to
understand a structure, you must focus on its genesis and
its development. These positions are developed in an
increasingly technical epistemological exposition, and it
requires considerable immersion in Piagetiana before they
become comprehensible, let alone convincing. Yet one cannot hope to understand Piaget fully and in depth unless
this is done.

The stage of intellectual development which follows
concrete operations is called formal operations. Piaget has
devoted less study to this area than to the other levels of
intelligence; yet here, too, his conclusions have become a
point of departure for other psychologists. Formal operations develop at the time of early adolescence and may
conceivably depend upon certain of the neurological or
hormonal changes of that period. But biological or environmental factors can never be sufficient for the appear-

ance of new structures. Rather, the structures of formal operations are dependent upon thought working on itself and reaching what Piaget regards as a new and permanent form of equilibrium.

When Piaget first worked in Simon's laboratory, his task involved, among other things, standardization of verbal reasoning problems, such as those of the "Edith is taller than Susan" ilk. At that time he noted that reasoning exclusively in words was extremely difficult for preadolescents, who were much more competent at manipulating objects or contemplating potential actions upon objects. Only in the formal-operational stage does the child become able to act not only upon real or imagined objects but also upon propositions expressed in words or mathematical symbols. The clearest examples of these problems are ones posed and answered exclusively in words, such as the brain-twister about liars and truth-tellers familiar to puzzle buffs. But Piaget's examples tend to be drawn from the physics laboratory: the child is given a task which cannot be conclusively solved simply by physical manipulations on the objects. Instead, any correct solution should reflect the hypothetico-deductive thought processes characteristic of a scientist.

A child enters Piaget's laboratory and is shown a kind of billiard game in which a plunger is pulled and a ball shot against a wall, in order to hit one of several targets spread at various points across the table. The angle of the plunger in relation to the table can be varied, and the size of the angle will determine where the ball will ricochet and which of the targets is hit. Presumably the child does not know this principle: he is expected to tinker with the game and to find out the governing law.

Six- or seven-year-olds are concerned with their practical success or failure; they do not consider the variety of *means* of achieving success and generally pay no attention to the rebounds. Indeed, they appear to believe that the ball's trajectory is a sort of curve, rather than a set of rectilinear segments. Piaget talks to the subjects and tries to determine their reasoning about what happens but subjects at this age are usually restricted to general statements like "It goes there and turns the other way." Piaget concludes that the child of this age never internalizes his actions as operations, not even as concrete operations.

The eight- or nine-year-old child is aware of the rectilinear nature of the trajectory segments and the course of rebounds. He comes up with general formulations of the sort "To aim to the left, you have to turn the plunger to the left" or "The more the plunger moves this way, the more the ball will go like that, and the more I push it in the other direction, the more the ball will go like that." Such subjects can work out the concrete correspondence between the relevant rank orderings (the greater the angle, the greater the rebound). However, they are constrained to remain at the concrete level because they do not look for the reasons behind the correspondences. They cannot explain the behavior of the apparatus in terms of formal reasoning involving implications.

Adolescent subjects of age fourteen or so search for a general hypothesis which can account for the concrete correspondences between angles. Unsatisfied with the empirical correlation between angle and rebound, they seek a necessary reason for this relationship. They begin to search for the precise angle, and achieve a convincing demonstration of the relevant principle when they pull the plunger directly perpendicular to the wall and with some excitement see the ball return directly to the point of departure. They begin to talk of necessity: "You need two angles: the inclination . . . equals the angle that the trajectory of the ball makes . . . therefore the two must be equal." For these subjects, the idea of a correspondence between the incline of the plunger and the path of the ball seems to lead inexorably to the idea of a necessary reciprocity.

In sum, only at this stage is the child able to view

the experiment in terms of the total number of possibilities and the necessary relations. This capacity is achieved only at the formal-operational level, where the child formulates verbal propositions about what he sees (let $x=$ the angle of incidence) and then relates these propositions to one another in a logical way. Whereas the younger subject starts from the phenomenon and tries unsystematically to tease out a general principle—commencing with the concrete event and searching for the underlying structure— the older subject starts out with the belief that there *will* be a system and performs various experiments in order to ferret it out—proceeding from an assumption of structure to an account adequate to the specific event.

With reference to any single Piagetian experiment, it is always possible to offer counterexplanations. For example, one might claim that the younger subjects do understand the law as well, but that, ignorant of geometry, they cannot speak in terms of angles and equivalences. Although this objection carries some weight, it does not explain why the younger subjects do not even try to find a necessary rule—a failure that does not seem attributable to a lack of geometrical training. However, the Piagetian demonstration becomes more fully convincing when one considers another problem which elicits the same principal stages as those described above.

The child is given a series of bottles of chemical substances: four similar flasks containing colorless, odorless liquids and a bottle, with a dropper, that contains an indicator. Since oxygenated water (bottle 3) oxidizes potassium iodide (the indicator) in an acid medium (dilute sulfuric acid in bottle 1), a mixture of bottle 1, bottle 3, and the indicator will produce a yellow color. The experimenter shows the subject that it is possible to produce a yellow color but does not tell him which bottles must be used. The subject is simply given some empty flasks and asked to produce the yellow elixir.

At the preoperational level, subjects are limited to mixing randomly two elements at a time, noting the result, and giving some sort of a prelogical explanation. For instance, Mam, aged five years nine months, first mixes the indicator with a burette containing caustic soda and says, "It's like wine," then mixes the indicator with sulfuric acid and says, "It's like water." Asked if there is any color, he replies, "It went down to the bottom, it went away like that" (he gestures), and then mixes the indicator with more caustic soda. After repeating the mixing of the indicator with the sulfuric acid, he comments, "The red runs away in the glass—the color disappeared at the bottom, you don't see it any more. It melted."

At this age, neither a systematic approach nor a search for principles is evident. Subjects in the second stage, that of concrete operations, spontaneously and systematically associate the indicator with all the other liquids; they fail, however, to make any other combinations. Even when the subject is encouraged to combine several factors simultaneously, he makes only a few tentative multiple combinations, and, even if he does happen to produce the correct color, is unable to demonstrate that there is but one way to achieve it. Somewhat later on in this stage he does develop the idea of making $n \times n$ combinations. But he still lacks a system—he only makes trial-and-error combinations without ever organizing them in a comprehensive manner. The source of the color is sought in individual elements and not in the combination of them.

Whereas concrete-operational subjects start from an individual event and go in search of an underlying structure, formal-operational subjects often have a systematic plan from the first. Subjects at this higher level say, "You have to try all the bottles." They also label the purposes of the bottles: "This is the substance that keeps it from coloring"; "this must be water"—because, say, it didn't influence any combinations. The subjects ask for a pencil and talk to themselves in an attempt to insure that they haven't missed any possible combinations. And once a subject has found the correct combination, he does not cease working, but attempts to determine whether alternative solutions are possible. His interest, in other words, is not merely in achieving practical success by a particular combination but also in understanding the role which a given combination plays among all possible combinations. The subject seeks to determine if specific substances play equivalent roles; if certain ones are necessary for any chemical reaction; whether he can present a theoretical basis for his findings.

More than a dozen experiments by Piaget and Inhelder and their associates have amply buttressed the contention that the adolescent subject is behaving in the experimental laboratory in a qualitatively different way from his concrete-operational forerunner. The subject at the stage of formal operations confronts the implications of each of his acts, has an overall view of the possible combinations, and has arrived at the insight, essential to experimentation, that one can only make distinct causal determinations if one holds constant all the variables in an experiment save one. Younger subjects, by contrast, will often proceed in an orderly way, only to vitiate the prospect of success by changing two variables at a time, or by missing a whole set of combinations.

As has happened at all previous stages, a new set of structures coalesces during this last period. Concrete operations become the subject matter of formal operations, which are operations to the second degree, involving linguistic descriptions of actions rather than actions themselves. The resultant structures are not the incomplete mathematical groupings of the concrete stage but the sixteen binary propositions of formal logic. That is, in his procedures and in his interpretation of the laboratory experiments, the adolescent is reasoning the way a formal logician does. This should not be taken as a claim that the bell-bottomed teenager is ready to make original contributions to symbolic logic, nor that he is even likely to be

aware of the canons of modern logic; it does mean, however, that he has the necessary cognitive structures for
performing the full range of operations involved in ratiocination: the capacity to express relations in terms of
linguistic propositions and to consider systematically the
relations of the propositions to one another, to make deductions and implications, and to draw conclusions from a
set of statements about a phenomenon. He is capable of
reasoning from the general to the particular and back
again.

With the appearance in adolescence of this last and
highest stage, Piaget ends his account of human intellectual development. No one as yet has seriously challenged
this account; to do so, it would be necessary to demonstrate
that post-adolescent individuals are capable of a qualitatively different level of reasoning, rather than merely a
more expert application of formal operations to more
recondite or complex areas of concern. What seems more
likely from other studies, however, is that formal operations reflect a level of reasoning which is reached, with
effort, by most adolescents in Western society but which is
not a vital part of the lives of most, and which achieves
facility and full use only in those who go into the sciences.
One retains always the capacity to reason logically in areas
that interest one, but the kinds of suspension of reality
and of belief in hypothetical possibilities characteristic of
logicians ("If tomorrow is Saturday, every Irishman is a
native") are of interest chiefly to those professionally or
avocationally concerned with such matters.

Although no one is a formal operator in all his pursuits,
the advent of formal operations has considerable impact,
in Piaget's judgment, with manifestations far beyond the
realm of academic study. For the first time, the teenager is
comfortable dealing with hypothetical possibilities and reasoning about the contrary-to-fact. He becomes a dreamer,
interminably considering the possibilities of his life; he
begins to understand various philosophical theories and

speculations. Piaget attributes the idealism and revolutionary tendencies of many adolescents to their initial encounters with the exciting world of pure thought. (His autobiography documents the enormously stimulating role which the reading of Bergson played in his own adolescence.) This emergent ability to reason deductively and hypothetically confers tremendous power on the adolescent, but may also be somewhat disconcerting for him as, for the first time, he confronts the manifold possibilities open to him. Identity crises or uncritical involvement in mass ideological movements may result for those who experience difficulty in adapting or accommodating their fascination with absolutistic theories to the relevant aspects of their social world.

The newly developed structures of these adolescents must go on to attain a state of *equilibrium*. The notions of equilibrium and of the process of equilibration which underlies it are very important ones for Piaget, who believes that intellectual development has its own pace and rhythm and involves the same kind of organismic regulation as do physiological and motivational processes. He conceives of equilibrium as a mechanism of change and continuity, a state of balance between competing actions; a system is in equilibrium when a perturbation which modifies the state of the system has its counterpart in a spontaneous action which compensates for its effect. Consequently, equilibrium is a function of the actor's behavior.

Although Piaget has worked extensively on his theory of equilibrium, it still, in the view of many observers, requires further elaboration. Nonetheless, it serves as a reminder that, while the delineation of childhood intellectual development would constitute a lifework for many of the most knowledgeable and talented psychologists, it represents only one of Piaget's manifold interests and contributions. We can do little more than mention some of the other areas of study to which Piaget has devoted attention in the last half-century.

4. OTHER CONTRIBUTIONS

With his associates, Piaget has developed a theory of perception which, not surprisingly, emphasizes the amount of active construction involved in judging visual arrays and illusions. Piaget has studied the history of the various scientific disciplines, examined in detail the interrelationships among the sciences, and founded a whole new field, genetic epistemology, which traces the development of scientific thought in the various disciplines and in the life of the individual, and notes the relationship between these two developmental trajectories. Piaget has done original studies in sociology and pedagogy, wherein he displays loyalty to Durkheim's ideas, to the latter's conviction that morality arises from the need for interpersonal cooperation, and to his belief that there is an optimal rate at which structures should unfold. This last conclusion has placed him in some disfavor with meliorists like Jerome Bruner, who contend that intellectual development is susceptible to rate changes and that complicated concepts can be presented "at [a child's or young person's] own level." Lastly, but of great importance, Piaget has returned to his earliest passion—biology—not only pursuing his studies of molluscs, but also penning a major work of synthesis, *Biology and Knowledge,* in which his manifold findings on intellectual development are related to pervasive principles of biological functioning. His overall conclusion is that cognitive activities promote organic regulation—that is, they help maintain physiological and bodily equilibrium—and constitute, in effect, an organ that regulates exchanges with the environment, analogous to the more purely physiological organs, which also achieve a form of equilibrium. Whether in the realm of bodily function or of scientific thought, development consists in the unfolding of structures according to innate principles of functioning, in the active construction of new structures out of earlier ones, in the steady alteration of a subject's relationship to the external world, and in the increasing comprehensiveness and integration of that relationship.

It is as a genetic epistemologist that Piaget primarily views himself, deeming psychology a tool by which he can get to the roots of knowledge in biology and in the history of scientific thought. It may well be that his longest-lasting contributions will come in this area, for he may have succeeded in redirecting the entire thrust of scientific and philosophical thought. At present, however, he is perhaps more readily identified as a psychologist who has chosen a vast and formidable area to investigate. He has investigated it with vigor and the most penetrating insight, and has demonstrated, quite conclusively, that children at different developmental levels have characteristic ways of thinking about the world. He has undermined "common sense" notions of the child as either a passive reactor to the environment, a mere imitator, or one in whom "innate ideas" will automatically unfold, replacing them with a more comprehensive and intricate concept of the child as an active constructor, one who acts upon the world and, in so doing, comes to increase his knowledge of the world as well as of his own thought and person. Piaget has made an impressive attempt to replace the behaviorist emphasis on the primacy of the environment and the Gestaltist emphasis upon the primacy of developed structures with a less elementary and more enriched picture of intelligence, as a product of the interaction between constantly evolving structures in the child's mind and ever-varying aspects of reality which the child becomes able to assimilate or accommodate. The world is not just "out there," waiting to impress itself on a blank slate; it is a product of our actions upon it, of the relation between these actions, of the symbolic embodiments of those actions.

Piaget has, furthermore, provided evidence that a whole variety of mental actions and underlying schemes reflect structures which come to be integrated at certain points in development and can be expressed in terms of mathematical groups, groupings, and logical propositions. This mathematical approach is of enormous promise, for it suggests the possibility of a common language in which biology, psychology, and logic can be related to each other, without loss of their individual integrity. Piaget is hopeful that evidence for the structures he posits can be found in the nervous system, and he places a premium in this regard on Warren McCulloch and Walter Pitts's contention that the nervous system has the character of the mathematical function called a lattice.

A final contribution rests in Piaget's claim to have demonstrated the distinct limitations of traditional philosophical conceptions of the nature of knowledge. He has shown that many long-standing questions in philosophy—for example, the nature of space, time, and number—can be illuminated by considering their genesis in the young child; this approach suggests that the contradictions found among traditional solutions to these questions were only apparent rather than real, in that some of these solutions related to the development of such concepts, while others were concerned exclusively with the end state, or point of ultimate development, toward which all thought tends.

Piaget makes a key distinction between *wisdom*—which is the end result of an interaction between objective knowledge and personal values, and constitutes the particular domain of philosophy—and *knowledge,* which requires built-in controls and fixed criteria for truth and thus belongs to the realm of science. He claims that reliable evidence is now available which will elucidate the origin, terminus, and fundamental nature of a variety of realms once thought the exclusive province of the philosopher, and that this evidence can be elicited through the kinds of epistemological studies of the foundation of knowledge which he has undertaken. While old-school philosophers have not lain down and surrendered, as Piaget sometimes implies he would like them to, it seems a certainty that his trenchant reflections on philosophical wisdom and knowledge will have increasing impact in the years to come.

Many philosophers have simply ignored Piaget's work; others have dismissed as naïve his attempts to "define" number or causality genetically. Numerous psychologists have found his work of little importance, and still others have questioned both the methods he uses and the conclusions he draws. The founding of a theory of infant intelligence on the study of a mere three children—and one's own, at that—has disturbed many empirically oriented workers, who expect large samples to be taken, experimenters to be completely free of bias, and systematic hypotheses to be tested. Talk of operations, equilibration, schemes, groupings, and other invisible, nontangible concepts has rankled even more sympathetic workers, who wonder if evidence for or against the system will ever be accrued. Even Piaget's most basic assumptions have been challenged: perhaps, it has been suggested, thought derives from modes of perception which are built into the sensory system rather than from groups of actions gradually evolving in the motor system; perhaps the ability to conserve various properties is a trivial one, of little importance in other societies; perhaps Piaget's view of knowledge is parochial, his emphasis on logical thought unwarranted, his picture of scientific thought too rational and orderly; perhaps, indeed, the whole impetus to study change over time, and to postulate its basic mechanisms, is misguided, as being a form of reductive thought which inevitably distorts the full-blown phenomenon. Numerous other misgivings about Piaget's enterprise have been voiced, some serious and worth responding to, others not; Piaget has paid more attention to his critics than most other social scientists would, but has wisely not allowed his desire to convert skeptics to distract him from pursuing the researches in which he believes.

And his work and output continue unabated as I write.

Ensconced in his Center for Genetic Epistemology in Geneva, Piaget—now in his seventy-seventh year—continues his arduous schedule of teaching, lecturing, traveling, walking, and writing hundreds of lines a day. New research monographs come out with numbing regularity, as do unexpected pronouncements in one or another of the few fields on which he has heretofore failed to comment. Piaget has the benefit of help not only of many research assistants from the university, but also of his collaborator of thirty-five years, Bärbel Inhelder, and of many visiting scholars who brief him on recent findings and join him in his quest for a science of genetic epistemology. The questions he is addressing, no less than those that he has raised in asides, will continue to occupy him and his co-workers for many years to come.

In 1967, Piaget made one of his intermittent trips to the United States to give an address. Over the years he has made thousands of speeches, and has received a score of honorary degrees. Yet, as David Elkind reports, Piaget was particularly nervous on this occasion, for he was speaking at Clark University, scene in 1909 of Freud's only visit to the United States and of his famous lectures on the origin and development of psychoanalysis. The significance of the invitation to Worcester had not been lost on Piaget, and it was clear during his two evenings of lectures that he was extremely moved to be visiting this historic site. And, unable to speak English and uncertain of the loyalties of his audience, he was understandably anxious when the series began.

In the chairman's introductory remarks, he alluded to a time when Piaget, an addict of pipe-smoking for many years, had been restricted for health reasons to only three pipefuls a day. Although crestfallen, the master of conservation was equal to the doctor's challenge: he availed himself of his pipe six times a day, but only placed half a pipeful of tobacco in each time, thus giving himself the genuine feeling, and the intellectual illusion, that he was in fact having six pipes a day. As this story was told, Piaget, who understands more English than he lets on, smiled and gave his pipe a tiny clutch. This action was not lost on the audience, whose affection he won at that moment.

The contrasts between Freud's Clark lectures and Piaget's addresses on "Memory and Identity" were notable. Piaget, speaking through an interpreter, felt no need to introduce or defend his system, but proceeded at once to treat two highly technical aspects of his theoretical framework. He was harsh on American critics of his work, assumed knowledge of technical logic on the part of his audience, and made few jokes or direct comments to the audience. And yet, as with Freud, his rapport with the audience was so powerful that his remarks received rapt attention, even as his voice and his emphatic facial and bodily gestures conveyed his sincerity and humanity. Piaget's talk had that directness, self-confidence, command of the material, seriousness, incisiveness, sensitivity to nuance, and methodical thoroughness which belong only to the most far-seeing and productive of minds. Through both the content and the manner of his presentation, Piaget affirmed again his central position among the psychologists of today and his claim to the mantle of Freud.

It is related that when Freud came to America, the ailing William James made a day-long pilgrimage to hear the Viennese doctor and that, at the conclusion of the talk, he told Freud, "The future of psychology belongs to your work." Could James's words perhaps be extended in application to include the more recent visitor to Worcester, Massachusetts, on that wintry night fifty-eight years later?

4 Lévi-Strauss

*Common readers, pardon my paradoxes, they must
be made whenever one thinks seriously. And whatever you may say, I would rather be a man of
paradoxes than a man of prejudices.*

—ROUSSEAU

*The tendency of modern inquiry is more and more
toward the conclusion that if law is anywhere, it
is everywhere.*

—EDWARD TYLOR

In a semidelirious state at the conclusion of his enervating
trip through central Brazil, having reached the point
where an anthropologist questions the meaning of what
he is doing, Claude Lévi-Strauss conceived a play, which
he entitled *The Apotheosis of Augustus.* Essentially a new
version of Corneille's *Cinna,* the play dealt with two men
who had been friends in childhood and encountered each
other at moments of crisis in their highly divergent
careers. Augustus had been singled out at birth for participation in the world and its honors, only to find that
all his efforts were undermining this world and its mock-
ing plaudits; Cinna (or Lévi-Strauss) had rejected the
world of material comforts and satisfactions in order to
proceed away from civilization, only to find that he was
heading back to it by a complicated route and, in so doing,
had destroyed the value of the alternative which he had
supposedly embraced.

111

As Augustus undergoes the process of deification, he comes to realize that his hold over his people is lessening, that his flatterers are scheming behind his back, that he is being sanctified only because people want to remove him from the scene. Cinna, meanwhile, having been away from civilization for ten years, living an adventurous life among the savages, is being lionized by the hostesses of Rome, intent on learning of his exploits. Only he is aware that the celebrity he has acquired at such cost is based on a lie. His adventures and his journey have been a deception and a myth; for even as he thought to demonstrate his humanity by caressing every flower, tasting every food, exploring every emotion, he became increasingly inhuman and lost everything of value to him. Yet, as he attempts to convey the emptiness and futility of his experience, it unavoidably becomes transformed into a "traveler's tale" which delights and mesmerizes all.

Both Augustus and Cinna have seen their goals revealed as fraudulent, their aspirations as impossible to realize; the balance of forces in their lives has been overthrown. The two men work out an elaborate scheme: Cinna will murder Augustus, who will thereby win official immortality; Cinna will have the dark immortality of the regicide, which will allow him to rejoin society even as he continues to reject it.

Lévi-Strauss describes this drama in his masterly autobiography, *Tristes Tropiques,* a work whose impact upon the French intellectual world matched that of Cinna's voyages upon the salons of Rome—it catapulted its author into a position of notoriety. Lévi-Strauss has, nonetheless, the most serious of intentions in introducing this fiction: it is his attempt to delineate "the disordered state of mind" produced by the abnormal conditions of a traveler's existence.

A traveler, of course, is a mere—and admitted—spectator. But an anthropologist must confront a deeper riddle: why does he reject his own society while reserving for

societies distant and different from his own the patience
and diligence he has deliberately withheld from his own
people? For Lévi-Strauss, the irony extends deeper still,
for while he rejected the French way of life, he concluded
after his travels in the Brazilian wilds that the characteristics of man are everywhere identical, the apparent differences between Western European and primitive peoples
a delusion. Further, upon returning to France with these
findings, this somewhat retiring man, who has a strong
distaste for fads and fashions, was treated as a culture
hero. However disconcerting these paradoxes for the observer, they are part of Lévi-Strauss's life and character;
for his major argument about the nature of thought and
of society centers on the role of contradiction, opposition,
and paradox in the experience of man.

Claude Lévi-Strauss was born in Belgium in 1908, son
of an artist and member of an intellectual French Jewish
family. During the First World War he lived with his
parents near Versailles, where his grandfather was a rabbi.
Although Lévi-Strauss says little in his published works
about his early childhood, one gathers that he was a serious
and somewhat romantic youngster who loved to take long
walks, to pause over the flora and fauna, to muse upon
philosophical questions. This interest was poetic and
humanistic in tone; Lévi-Strauss did considerable reading
among literary masterpieces and was deeply immersed in
classical and contemporary serious music. Yet there was
also a scientific bent to his pursuits, reflected largely in a
deep interest in geology.

Indeed, Lévi-Strauss acknowledges geological excavation
and theory as one of the three major intellectual influences
in his life, the others being psychoanalytic theory and
Marxism. Geology taught him to seek for origins of manifest features in the past history of an object. He learned
to explore various rock strata, looking for the subtle differences in jumbled arid rocks which would indicate
where an ocean once flowed. Or he would note two plants

of different species on opposite sides of a hidden crevice and simultaneously observe that one of the fossils embedded in the rock had less complex involutions than the other. "We glimpse, that is to say, a difference of many thousands of years; time and space suddenly commingle: the living diversity of that moment juxtaposes one age and the other and perpetuates them." Such explorations not only heightened one's perceptual and aesthetic sensibilities, but also pointed in Proustian fashion to the untold wealth of history and lost experience latent in a tiny manifestation.

A first reading of Freud reinforced the lessons of Lévi-Strauss's geological excavations. In both cases, the investigation starts with apparently impenetrable phenomena (dreams, slips of the tongue in psychoanalysis), and in both cases a delicately refined perceptiveness is needed to disentangle the elements of the situation and note crucial differences. Yet the resulting order is anything but arbitrary; rather, it all fits into a coherent scheme and thereby reveals fundamental properties of the physical or psychical universe.

A Belgian socialist introduced Lévi-Strauss to Marxism when he was only seventeen, setting off in him that feverish excitement which occurs perhaps only once in each young intellectual's development. Not only did Marxism provide an entranceway to the whole school of German philosophical thought of which he had previously been ignorant; it also demonstrated to him, conclusively, that social science is "no more based upon events than physics is based upon sense perceptions." What the scientist did was to construct a model, examine its properties with reference to laboratory tests, and then apply these observations to the study and explication of empirical events.

From his trio of "mistresses," Lévi-Strauss learned to look at sensory phenomena and to expect that if he took great care, they could reveal to him the underlying nature and order of events. These intellectual influences suggested that understanding consists in the reduction of one type of reality to another, that true reality is never the most obvious of realities, and that its nature is already apparent in the care which it takes to evade detection. All three of these realms posed for the young Frenchman the question of the relation between reason and sense perception, a question which was to play an increasingly dominant role in his thinking and writing over the next forty years.

Lévi-Strauss entered the Sorbonne, where, as a member of a brilliant group which included Simone de Beauvoir, Maurice Merleau-Ponty, and Paul Nizan, he studied philosophy and law. Law was never really an interest—rather, a concession to family—and philosophy increasingly antagonized him, although he was as expert as his peers in the statement of thesis, antithesis, and synthesis, in the exercise of hypothetico-deductive reasoning and conceptual clarification. For he soon came to a sense of the uselessness of these mental gymnastics, the stagnation of the different philosophical schools and their mutual exclusiveness, and the impossibility of ever reconciling conflicting cosmologies. After taking his degree, he set his foot on the first rung of the French academic ladder, becoming a teacher in a *lycée*. But he felt vaguely dissatisfied, and was constantly "on the lookout" for some more attractive occupation.

Two events around this time were pivotal in determining Lévi-Strauss's future course. The first was his reading of Robert Lowie's *Primitive Society,* a deeply moving firsthand account of the meaning of anthropological experience. Lévi-Strauss has described the book's effect on him in glowing terms:

My mind escaped from the closed circuit which was what the practice of academic philosophy amounted to; made free of the open air, it breathed deeply and took on new strength; like a townsman let loose in the mountains, I made myself drunk with the open spaces and my astonished eye could hardly take in the wealth and variety of the scene.

Enamored of the life described in Lowie's book, Lévi-Strauss did not take long to exploit the opportunity afforded by the second event. When an acquaintance, Célestin Bouglé, phoned him in the autumn of 1934 and asked whether he might be interested in the post of professor of sociology at São Paulo University, he accepted within three hours. This decision made possible four years of occasional travels among the Indian tribes of central Brazil. The story of these memorable journeys is related in *Tristes Tropiques,* and the empirical data and intellectual capital of those years have been a major source of ideas for all of Lévi-Strauss's subsequent work.

Anthropology gave the youthful scholar the opportunity to achieve the goal of all philosophy—illumination of the dimensions of human experience—by allowing him to come into contact with the lives of men of different cultures, rather than just Western man. Antagonized by Gallic culture, Lévi-Strauss seems to have begun his studies and journeys with the usual tendency to view primitives as "wild, different, romantic"; but, as he relates with compelling detail in his autobiography, he was gradually disabused of this stereotype. At first, he went in search of what Rousseau called "the barely perceptible advances of the earliest times," seeking the pristine state which had so fascinated that renowned philosopher. And he thought he had found it in the long-isolated Nambikwara of the Amazon jungle, whose society he saw as one of extreme simplicity. As his stay with them went on, however, his views changed; he was impressed by their sense of humor, their petty rivalries, the political acumen of their chief. Ultimately he came to the epiphanous realization that the similarities between the Nambikwara and himself far outweighed the differences, that they, like himself, were "nothing but human beings." Looking for infinite variety, for a natural society "reduced to its simplest expression," for bloodthirsty cannibals or noble savages, Lévi-Strauss had instead discovered the common humanity of savages and savants—and with it the central theme of his lifework.

In spelling out over many years the conclusions derived from his field work, Lévi-Strauss has surveyed the range of cultural institutions and artifacts, from social organization to myth and art, in an effort to document the underlying continuities between the disparate forms found in diverse cultures. His way of approaching a problem—his way of thinking, if you will—is to make a logical analysis of the arrangements possible in a given type of institution and then, through both careful observation and leaps of intuition, to relate theoretically possible forms to the ones actually realized in a society. Variations among societies are treated as experiments in nature; unusual or unexpected artifacts in one culture are regarded as questions which await an answer in the form of a "structurally related" artifact to be discovered, hopefully, in another culture. Lévi-Strauss's thinking is characterized by a dialectical interplay between two dominant tendencies: a penchant toward logical analysis and systematic comparisons on the one hand; a flair for the suggestive metaphor, the unanticipated link, the synthesis of two apparently contradictory notions, on the other. And this curious amalgam of the precise and the poetic is reflected, naturally enough, in his writing, which consists in methodical, dry presentations, sporadically and dramatically interrupted by enthusiastic pronouncements, unlikely similes, sweeping generalizations.

Similar polarities enter into the very substance of Lévi-Strauss's work. Thus, he considers primitive thought to be essentially logical in nature—the perception of opposites and contrasts being the underlying common ground of all human thought—while at the same time savage thought exhibits a heightened sensitivity for the raw sensory data of the world, colors, smells, sounds, together with the intuitive capacity to perceive links based upon sensual parallels. His proposal of such an unlikely combination of intellective proclivities is perhaps a principal reason why

Lévi-Strauss engenders both extravagant praise and hostile criticism: those who share his dual vision applaud his perspicacity, those who find his descriptions strangely alien are repelled by both the substance and the style of his work. We shall repeatedly encounter this curious mixture of art and logic, sensuality and rationality, myth and philosophy, as we review the major products of Lévi-Strauss's pen.

In stressing the logical properties of primitive thought, Lévi-Strauss diverged markedly from his famous predecessor Lucien Lévy-Bruhl, the leading theme of whose work was the differences between primitive and advanced societies. And in contrast to the functionalist school of Malinowski, which focused upon the "uses" of institutions and the needs of people, Lévi-Strauss emphasized the essential autonomy of cultural institutions and the extent to which they reflect the untrammeled operation of the human mind. He embraced strongly the conclusion that the full gamut of human possibilities and human experience is rooted in, and limited by, the intrinsic structure of the mind, and that it can therefore be specified:

The ensemble of a people's customs has always its particular style; they form into systems. I am convinced that the number of these systems is not unlimited and that human societies, like individual human beings (at play, in their dreams, or in moments of delirium), never create absolutely; all they can do is to choose certain combinations from a repertoire of ideas which it should be possible to reconstitute. For this, one must make an inventory of all the customs which have been observed by oneself or others. With all this, one could eventually establish a sort of periodical chart of chemical elements, analogous to that devised by Mendeleev. In this, all customs, whether real or merely possible, would be grouped by families and all that would remain for us to do would be to recognize those which societies had, in point of fact, adopted.

Making this bold and exciting claim was one thing, substantiating it another. Lévi-Strauss's first anthropological contributions were in the traditional vein: ethnographies of peoples he had visited, with particular emphasis upon their family life. Owing to the vicissitudes of the Second World War, however, he ended up in New York where, while teaching at that bastion of European refugees, The New School for Social Research, he met the noted linguist Roman Jakobson. Jakobson had been instrumental in introducing a scientific approach into the study of language, and Lévi-Strauss soon became convinced that the revolution wrought in linguistic study was of critical importance for anthropologists. Just as Jakobson had been able to show that, underlying the tremendous diversity of language groups and phonological components, there was a small set of distinctions which could generate diversity of systems, so, too, Lévi-Strauss felt that, if one could determine the underlying units of culture, one could give an economical and accurate account of the range of cultural systems—kinship, social organization, and myth.

In a programmatic manifesto, Lévi-Strauss announced that anthropologists must follow the lead of their linguistic brethren. He outlined the steps which must be taken in order to make a structural analysis of cultural phenomena analogous to the analysis of linguistic phenomena undertaken by the Prague school: one must study the unconscious infrastructure of cultural phenomena rather than their surface manifestations; one must treat not the terms or units of the realm, but rather the relationships between those units, as independent entities; one must regard the entire domain as a system, and search for general laws, using the methods both of induction and of deduction. One can see here not only the affinity between Lévi-Straussian analysis and linguistic procedures, but also strong influences from Lévi-Strauss's original masters—geology, psychoanalysis, and Marxism.

Linguistic systems dealt with symbols or signs, arbitrary units which "stood for" objects or concepts in the world and acquired meaning only when so associated. In a linguistic analysis, then, it was heuristic to examine the relationships among these signs and to consider the effect of various logical operations upon a system of signs. As regarded the realm of culture, however, the procedure was less clear. There were no necessary or conventional symbols in the domains of family relationships, social organization, or political processes, but instead distinct behavioral acts involving or performed by individuals. The application of structural linguistic methods to anthropological investigations thus remained problematic until Lévi-Strauss proposed that all cultural phenomena were of an order comparable to linguistic phenomena and that *cultural phenomena should therefore also be considered in terms of signs.* This crucial insight—based on an assumption that cultural phenomena could for analytic purposes be treated as arbitrary—enabled Lévi-Strauss to undertake a structural analysis of various cultural realms; he could search for signs (or symbols) which reflected the principal factors in these domains and then operate upon such signs, with some confidence that the relevant operations would reflect genuine relationships among the phenomena themselves. In other words, he could, following Marx, erect a model of the relationships in a given cultural realm, perform operations upon this model, and then determine from ethnographies and observers' reports whether these operations produced the predicted empirical correlates. Let us now look at the four principal phases of Lévi-Strauss's scholarly work and see how he implemented his ambitious research program.

1. KINSHIP STUDIES

Dating back to the time of Lewis H. Morgan, the great American scholar who made detailed studies of the Iroquois' system of kinship, ethnographers have searched for laws or regularities among such systems; indeed, kinship relations have traditionally been the area of greatest interest to anthropologists. Accordingly, it was in this realm that Lévi-Strauss made his first efforts to apply the methods of structural linguistics to anthropological data. He published his findings in a series of important articles which appeared in the 1940's.

After rejecting more traditional approaches to the subject because of their lack of generality, Lévi-Strauss makes a preliminary suggestion: he proposes that kinship terms be equated with linguistic phonemes, the smallest perceptible units in speech. Just as one might analyze the distinctive features of a phoneme—e.g., is the sound p relatively low-pitched or high-pitched? is it produced through the nasal cavity or not?—so, analogously, one would ask of the term "father" whether, with reference to Ego (the subject), it is positively or negatively scored on such dimensions as sex, age, and generation. After a brief flirtation with this approach, however, Lévi-Strauss discards it as well, as being neither accurate nor simplifying nor explanatory, and so as incompatible with the goals of any scientific analysis. He then introduces an alternative suggestion. In addition to a system of terminology (a vocabulary system), a kinship network also involves a system of attitudes held by kin toward one another. The system of attitudes, of affective relations among individuals, is more directly analogous to the principal dimensions of linguistic analysis, and accordingly affords the proper basis for the structural analysis of kinship.

A long-standing concern in kinship theory has been the relationship involving the maternal uncle. A boy and his mother's brother often have a special bond; either they are on familiar terms—a "joking" relationship—or there is a rigid and distant relationship between them, with the boy fearing and submissively obeying his uncle. Lévi-Strauss suggests that a formal transposition of the method of structural linguistics can help to penetrate the mysteries of this phenomenon. He reviews with sympathy Radcliffe-Brown's pioneering attempt to account for the variations in this relationship, but concludes that the British analyst failed to recognize the full extent of the avunculate. For it includes not only the boy and his uncle, but a number of other family members as well; the avunculate, in fact, is a global system, containing four kinds of organically linked relationships or attitudes. Of these, the crucial one is that among, and embodied in, four persons, and can be expressed as a formula: the relation between the maternal uncle and the nephew is to the relation between brother and sister as the relation between father and son is to that between husband and wife. If one knows that among the Tonga, a Polynesian people, the husband has a harmonious relationship with his wife and the nephew enjoys a similar relationship with the uncle, it follows that the relationship between father and son is distant, and that a taboo exists between brother and sister. Similarly, among the Siuai of Bougainville, if one knows of the affection between brother and sister, and between father and son, one may then infer a distant and submissive relationship of a nephew to his uncle, as well as a lack of harmony between husband and wife. And so on.

It would be misleading to claim that Lévi-Strauss's assertion is confirmed by all the relevant data, or even that there is complete consensus about the meaning of his claim. (Which pair of relationships precisely is he referring to? How does one resolve ambivalent feelings into positive or negative? What would constitute counterexamples to the claim?) Indeed, most commentators are skeptical about this analysis, no matter how it is interpreted. Still, there is no denying that this kind of approach to kinship structures has had enormous influence in anthropological circles and that use of the linguistic model has created a revolution in the field. Even if the avunculate is not in some sense the basic unit of kinship, the mere challenge it offers to the primacy of the nuclear family is itself a significant contribution. The possibility that one may find basic units or structures in cultural realms, translate them into signs, determine the relationships among these signs, and then make predictions about factors heretofore unknown, has been seen by many anthropologists as a promise that their field may soon take on the substance as well as the trappings of a true science.

Having provided a solution for the puzzle of the avunculate, Lévi-Strauss proceeded in his first major work to propose a key to the understanding of all kinship structures in all primitive societies. This enormous book, in "the grand tradition," as a sympathetic critic put it, began by considering the universal taboo on incest—a rule found in all societies and therefore *the* rule of Society, the one which sets it off from Nature. Lévi-Strauss went on to provide abstract models for the major kinds of kinship systems, pausing along the way for incisive discussions of gift-giving, the relationship between Nature and Culture, the place of women and words in a society, the mental capacities of children, the absence of incest among the anthropoid apes, and wine-tasting in France. Although the detailed discussion of kinship algebra which occupies a major part of the text has little meaning except for professionals, the book's principal themes *are* accessible to the lay reader and have become a crucial part of Lévi-Strauss's enduring legacy to the field of anthropology.

Standing behind and inspiring *The Elementary Structures of Kinship* was the pioneering work of Marcel Mauss on the centrality of the gift. Mauss had shown that exchange and the giving of gifts formed the solder which held individuals and groups together, and had presented extensive documentation concerning the various kinds of exchange found in diverse societies. He had argued that gifts were social facts over which the individual had no control, that there were no truly free or pointless gifts. Lévi-Strauss recalls his experience in reading *The Gift* as "like Malebranche hearing Descartes lecture, the heart throbbing, the head seething and the mind invaded by a certainty still indefensible but domineering, at having attended an event decisive in the evolution of science." In Lévi-Strauss's view, Mauss was the first anthropologist to comprehend fully that universal phenomena must be studied in their unconscious as well as their conscious form, that empirical reality must be transcended in order to penetrate to more profound structural realities, and that careful research may enable one to uncover the innate structure of the human mind. The principle of reciprocity represented one such basic form of human thought and behavior.

And yet, though Mauss's contributions were of the highest order, he had not carried his work through to its ultimate conclusion; he had led anthropology to the Promised Land, but had not entered there himself. For, as Lévi-Strauss was to show, the centrality of giving extends not merely to material goods, but also to the exchange of words and to the transfer of women. Indeed, Lévi-Strauss was to find in the exchange of women among social groups the basis for the incest taboo and for the very origin of society itself.

Lévi-Strauss begins his discussion in *The Elementary Structures* by questioning why the incest taboo is found in all societies. He rejects previous interpretations (e.g., the development of physical repulsion between siblings, familiarity breeding indifference) and suggests that the phenomenon can only be explained by considering the nature and function of kinship systems. In these terms, the fatal flaw of incest is that it prevents the formation of larger units: if one marries one's sister, the possibility of exchanging women and so of establishing alliances is precluded. Inasmuch as society and survival are thought to depend upon the building up of such alliances, incest cannot be tolerated, and strong sanctions are devised against it.

The prohibition is seen as a manifestation of giving or self-sacrifice, as the group's way of saying that, in sexual matters, a person cannot do as he pleases. Among primitive peoples, incest is regarded as socially absurd rather than as morally repugnant, reflecting a sort of Cartesian principle that one cannot marry oneself, or a part of oneself. Lévi-Strauss cites a vignette which points up the primitive person's understanding of the reason for the incest taboo:

> [In answer to a question put by an anthropologist] What, you would like to marry your sister? Don't you want a brother-in-law? Don't you realize that if you marry another man's sister and another man marries your sister, you will have at least two brothers-in-law; while if you marry your own sister, you will have none? With whom will you hunt? With whom will you garden, . . . whom will you go to visit?

Lévi-Strauss regards his explanation of the origin of the incest taboo as the solution to a profound mystery: the transition from the state of Nature to the state of Culture. Whereas animals have no incest taboo, and more generally no rules, the capacity to state a rule binding upon all men is the decisive factor in the formation of culture; from this epochal step, marriage, social alliances, and reciprocity of all sorts follow. For Lévi-Strauss, as for his Rousseauian forebears, the transition made by man from being a part of Nature, along with plants and animals, to a creature of Culture, with language, customs, and traditions, was an issue of overriding philosophical and humanistic importance; the claim to have clarified this mystery was a critical one, of interest to many outside the anthropological field. However, as already indicated, the major portion of *The Elementary Structures* consisted of a detailed consideration of the various kinds of kinship structures possible, and, in this area, he gave his anthropological contemporaries much aliment for thought.

Surveying the hundreds of different kinship systems reported in the literature, Lévi-Strauss claimed to be able to reduce them to a few basic types. In a restricted form of exchange, the obligation of reciprocity was fulfilled by a direct exchange of females between two groups (A and B). This direct exchange had the advantage that one saw and knew what one was getting, and got it immediately, but the more damaging consequence that possibilities for building up strong and complex networks of interrelated alliances were effectively precluded. Thus, a more advanced form—generalized exchange—developed in which A gave a woman to B, B to C, C to D, and so forth, and each group took the calculated risk that this chain-letter kind of exchange would eventually result in a fuller and more varied mesh of social structure. Lévi-Strauss, placing a high value on the increasing integration of social networks, argued strongly and cogently for the superiority of this form of exchange.

The elegance of his work on kinship is discernible in a number of contributions. He was able to take diagrams of basic kinship forms and show how a simple change of one factor in the diagram would give rise to another kinship structure; he could explain why certain of these structures were frequent among primitive groups, whereas others seldom or never occurred. Here was a literal representation of a kinship structure and the application of a logical mathematical operation upon it—remarkable demonstrations in a field which had often been pervaded by confusion. Yet, Lévi-Strauss went beyond such algebraic computations in his insistence that while, from the formal point of view, men and women were interchangeable and equal, they were not so from societal points of view: men exchange women, and not vice versa. Theoretically, women *could* exchange men—"it would only be necessary to reverse all the signs in the diagram and the total structure would remain unchanged"; practically, this never happened. Thus certain transformations which might have been anticipated on mathematical grounds simply never occurred. In addition, Lévi-Strauss made the in-

triguing discovery that two forms of cross-cousin marriage
—a male marrying the daughter of his mother's brother
or of his father's sister—which were equivalent formally
were not equivalent in distribution in the world. This
was because, given the nature of exchange, it was productive to marry a mother's brother's daughter, but not the
father's sister's daughter. The former course would lead
to a widening of kinship ranks, the latter to a cutting off
of possibilities. Thus, marriage with the father's sister's
daughter could only yield a multitude of small systems:
kinship relations which were equal from biological and
formal viewpoint were shown to be dissimilar from the
viewpoint of social utility.

Lévi-Strauss believed he had reduced all the multitudi-
nous systems and elaborate rules to three structures and
two forms of exchange, and that these structures and
forms depended in turn upon a single differential in a
regime—its *harmonic* or *disharmonic* character. All principles of kinship came down to the question of the relationship between rules of residence and rules of descent,
with a disharmonic regime leading to restricted exchange,
a harmonic regime to generalized exchange. He had demonstrated, further, that exogamy (marrying outside one's
group) was the archetype of all practices based upon
reciprocity, and that marriage alliances were the essential
basis of the social structure. He claimed to have shown
the existence of basic mental structures: the universality
of rules, the principle of reciprocity, the socially solidifying
nature of the gift. He had shown kin relationships to be
analogous to linguistic systems, with members of society
standing in binary relation to one another, the members
as lexicons or repertoires of terms, the exchange rules as
the grammar. Finally, he disclosed his personal value system with his declaration in favor of generalized exchange
as leading to greater degrees of solidarity, and in his conclusion that language tended to "impoverish perception,"

stripping it of its affective, aesthetic, and magical implications. Lévi-Strauss was to adopt this elegiac tone increasingly in his later writings.

What are we to make of Lévi-Strauss's specific thesis
regarding such systems as the avunculate, and his general
one about the transition from Nature to Culture? It is
only fair to point out that he has excited and delighted
readers more than he has convinced them, and that his
reputation, even during the early years of his career when
he was writing on traditional subjects, has always been
more exalted among the general intellectual community
than among his anthropologist colleagues. The reasons for
his mixed critical reception are manifold, and do not
always redound to the credit of the critic. Yet, nearly all
but his most devoted followers would concede that the
empirical observations cited by Lévi-Strauss can often be
differently interpreted, and that his theories about the
nature of Nature and the elementary forms of thought
would be as difficult to prove as to disprove. This said, it
can be added that the stimulation provided by his pathbreaking work may be unequaled in the modern history
of anthropology.

2. STRUCTURAL STUDIES OF CULTURE

The publication of *The Elementary Structures of Kinship*
made Lévi-Strauss's reputation in the anthropological
world, though it was probably a book more talked about,
in praise or condemnation, than actually read; his publication of *Tristes Tropiques* several years later made him
a well-known figure in humanistic circles everywhere. In
the meantime, however, he published a considerable number of influential articles on other aspects of culture, in an
effort to test out his general notions about structuralism
and to unify diverse kinds of ethnographical data. Some of
these articles, selected by Lévi-Strauss himself, appeared in

book form in *Structural Anthropology* in 1958—a collection that is indispensable reading for those who want to
apply structural methods to various realms.

As the work represents the master's selection from over
one hundred essays written in this period, nearly every
piece is seminal from one or another point of view.
Worthy of special mention, however, are the papers on
social structure among the Bororo, artistic representation,
shamanism, and the analysis of myth. In these writings,
Lévi-Strauss demonstrated that the perspective he was
developing could uncover important facets in the most
unlikely kinds of realms. In his treatment of the Bororo,
for instance, he detailed first the people's own claim about
dual organization in their culture: that there are two
halves of the village which exchange women and gifts and
bury each other's dead. This duality is reflected in the
physical layout of the village, which is divided into sym-
metrical parts and then for other purposes, subdivided
symmetrically again. Next, however, Lévi-Strauss presents
evidence that each clan is also subdivided into three
groups—upper, middle, and lower—and that, in practice,
one regulation takes precedence: uppers from one clan
marry only uppers of the other, middles only middles,
lowers only lowers. Despite appearances, then, the Bororo
are really made up of three endogamous groups. Lévi-
Strauss suggests that the various "aboveground" institutions among the Bororo represent merely a rationalization,
covering up a true structure which the natives feel compelled to hide. The crucial differences between the native's
conscious model of his society, his unconscious model of
the society, and the observer's or anthropologist's model
of the society are then discussed. Pervading this discussion
is the belief that thinking in oppositions—one moiety vs.
another; endogamy vs. exogamy—is a fundamental property of the human mind.

Lévi-Strauss's comparative discussion of the shaman and
the psychoanalyst provides an astounding example of the

way in which apparently diverse personages may be
viewed as participants in closely related structures. The
urbane and literate psychoanalyst, meeting alone with his
patient daily for years on end while the patient relates his
life and attempts through rational interpreting to determine its meaning, is shown to function in a manner strikingly akin to that of the primitive shaman, who chants
before a large group about the events in his clan and the
particular crisis they are confronting and can elicit an
"abreaction," or sudden release of affect, by invoking
supernatural forces.

In both cases, Lévi-Strauss proposes, physical or organic
changes in the patient or group are brought about through
a structural reorganization, as the "patient" comes to live
out a myth—either one received, or one created, by him.
The structure of the myth is, on the unconscious level,
analogous to the structure which underlies the disturb-
ance on the organic level. That is, the abreaction evoked
by shaman or therapist brings about changes in the patient's interpretations of meaningful symbols which reflect
changes in bodily chemistry. Both healers work with
symbols which can be understood by the individual and
which, when properly understood, bring about a powerful affective reorganization tied to the use of words. In
other particulars, such as the source of their material
and the activeness of their participation, the shaman and
the psychoanalyst are diametrical opposites, so that here
their roles have structures related by a single transformation, that of negation. Freud's findings are thus assimilated
into a more comprehensive framework even as the specific
details of the psychoanalytic encounter are placed in a new
perspective.

In his study of split representation in the art of Asia
and America, Lévi-Strauss examines the unusual artistic
practices found among American Indians of the Northwest
Coast. Among the features of this art are intensive styliza-
tion, schematization, and split representation; the animal

is cut in two, there is a deep depression between the eyes, and the head appears not as a front view but as two profiles adjoining at the mouth. Sometimes the animals are depicted as split in two with profiles joined in the middle;

SPLIT REPRESENTATION

Painting from a house-front representing a bear.

FROM Franz Boas, *Primitive Art,* Dover Publications, New York. Reproduced by permission.

alternatively, a front view of the head is shown bordered by a pair of adjoining profiles of the body. The existence of a similar art form among the Chinese could, of course, stem from reasons of history or diffusion, one group transmitting it to others; but once this possibility has been eliminated, as impossible or highly improbable, the traditional approach is reduced to speculation about chance conditions or about the mysterious unity of mankind. Lévi-Strauss instead makes a sociological analysis of the two societies and concludes that, in each, split representation expresses a deeper and more fundamental splitting, namely, between the individual as a biological entity and the individual as a social role which he must embody. The cultures emphasizing this split representation are in fact "mask" or "tattoo" cultures in which the face receives its position in a social structure, its social dignity and mystical significance, only through decoration of some sort. Such civilizations are characterized by prestige struggles, rivalries between hierarchies, competition between social and economic privileges, and split personalities; both the masks and the decorative split representation are embodiments in graphic art of the underlying structure of such cultures.

Finally, in a major essay first published in 1955, Lévi-Strauss introduces a method for investigating the nature and significance of myths. Contrasting his interest with those of his predecessors, who were likely to regard myths either as meaningless conglomerations or as "charters for social action," Lévi-Strauss proposes instead a breakdown of the myth into its component parts or units, and a grouping together of those units which refer to the same point or theme. When these groups of points are considered in relationship to one another, the major themes as well as the structure and the message of the myth can be deciphered. Proceeding through an elaborate analysis, Lévi-Strauss illustrates how the Oedipus myth in all of its versions has to do with either the over- or the under-valuation of the importance of kinship structures and with the question of men's origin on the earth through either autochthony (emergence from the earth) or childbirth. The myth does not resolve these issues—myths by their very nature deal with insoluble problems, the great enigmas of human experience—but it does provide a point of equilibrium between competing notions derived from social experience and from cosmology. (The procedure of myth analysis devised by Lévi-Strauss will be illustrated further when we come to consider in some detail Edmund Leach's examination of the Genesis myth, "Lévi-Strauss in the Garden of Eden.")

The essay on myth analysis appears to have marked a turning point in Lévi-Strauss's development as a thinker. Up to that point he had been intent on demonstrating the relevance of his structural approach to classic anthropological problems: social organization, kinship, primitive artifacts. In each of these domains he attempted to determine what the elementary structures were, in both nuances of that phrase: *structures,* in that he discerned integrated complexes which could be transformed through systematic operations into other related and integrated complexes; *elementary,* in that the dimensions of kinship structures, social organizations, and art forms were supposed to be basic expressions of "the human spirit," basic to human culture—the building blocks out of which the more complex or hierarchical forms characteristic of advanced civilizations were to be constructed.

3. THE SAVAGE MIND

At a conference of linguists and anthropologists held in the early 1950's, Lévi-Strauss remarked that all the discussants had been pointedly avoiding the "uninvited guest": the human mind. Although he had referred only infrequently to "mind" in his earlier writings, it is evident in retrospect that he attributed the existence of a compact set of universal structures to the construction of the human mind (and beyond that, to the constitution of the brain and the nervous system). Restricted and generalized exchange, split representation, dual organization were widespread, and possessed a certain priority because of the way in which the human mind worked. But, as the linguist Saussure had pointed out many years before, the development of elements of culture such as kinship structures was constrained by certain "reality factors": the length of the lifespan, the location of other tribes, the supply of women, the needs of reproduction and alliance. As a consequence, the mind operated in these areas only under severe limitations. If one wanted to see the mind working spontaneously, Lévi-Strauss reasoned, it would be vital to examine realms in which there were fewer givens and restraints, and the mind could accordingly have "free rein." For this reason his later work has fixed upon domains such as myth classification, in which the mind can more directly reveal its organization and its rules of functioning. And it is the study of mind that he has come increasingly to regard as properly the primary concern of anthropology.

In an interim period before embarking on his *magnum opus,* a four-volume study of the myths of Indians in North and South America, Lévi-Strauss composed two of his most pivotal works: *Totemism* and *The Savage Mind.* His purpose in these was twofold: to illustrate the basic principles by which the human mind works, and to demonstrate that the mind of a so-called "primitive" is no different qualitatively from that of a member of an advanced Western culture.

Anthropologists of the nineteenth century were captivated by a widespread practice called totemism, which involved the conferring of animal or plant names upon individuals or clans. Various theories of totemism were advanced, but none seemed to account for the majority of cases, and so the theories, and the problem as well, disappeared from sight. Lévi-Strauss begins his treatment with an interesting account of past failures. Totemism, he argues, is like hysteria, in that once one assumes that the hysteric (or totem society) is qualitatively different from the normal person (or non-totem society), it becomes impossible to explain the puzzling phenomenon. It was Freud's great insight that there is no sharp dividing line between illness and health, that what is salient in the hysteric can be discerned in more muted form in the normal person. By a parallel line of argument, Lévi-Strauss demonstrates that the totemistic way of thought is simply a phase of all human thought and that, with this realization, the mystery of totemism dissolves.

Reviewing earlier explanations with characteristic incisiveness (and perhaps a shade of condescension), Lévi-Strauss is able to dismiss all except those that posit some sort of resemblance between totem groups and the names they choose. Such a resemblance, he stresses, is analogical, not literal. It is not that members of, say, the Beaver Clan look, or live, like beavers, while those of the Eagle Clan look, or live, like eagles. Rather, as animals differ from one another—eagles and beavers live at different heights and differ in speed and grace—so clans differ from one another in analogous ways, wearing different masks, residing at different ground levels, featuring distinctive life styles; and totemism is that system which seeks out and captures these analogous differences between groups of men and groups of animals or plants. Thus, one clan lives on the mountainside, and has high social prestige, while the other lives in the valley, and has lower prestige, and this difference is captured in their names, with the higher group having the same relationship to the lower one as eagles are seen to have to beavers. In Lévi-Strauss's succinct formula, "it is not the resemblances but the differences which resemble each other."

This aphorism embodies much of Lévi-Strauss's view of the mind. The mind builds upon its perceptions of the world, and its tendency is to perceive oppositions, contrasts, differences. It does not perceive just height alone, or depth alone; to see one dimension is to see, and comprehend, the other. Nor does it see height or depth merely in one sphere; rather, the mind is driven to look for analogies in various realms and, upon finding them, to encompass such analogies in its systems of names and classification. Consciously, of course, people are aware of concrete manifestations rather than of relations *per se*; but the tendency to perceive relations is fundamental, though unconscious. Lévi-Strauss wittily proposes that the primitive does not name his clans after eagles and beavers because of their functional use—they are not good to eat—but because they are "good to think": they are appropriate vehicles for capturing the perceptual distinctions which have impressed themselves upon the individual or group. In the theory of totemism, one must pass not only from subjective utility to objective analogy, but also from external analogy to internal homology.

Although the mind—primitive or advanced—is aware first of contrasts and oppositions, it also is impelled to mediate between them. For this reason, the animals, plants, or other objects that the mind finds "good to think" are those which have within them the opposing qualities by which it had originally been impressed. Thus, twins and birds are popular characters in myths and totemistic systems, not primarily because of their utility or their occurrences, but because in the primitive mind both occupy an intermediary position between the Supreme Spirit and human beings: twins are Children of God; birds fly between earthbound humans and the Heavenly Spirit. Tricksters and jokesters—who have a touch of the supernatural while also appearing estranged from society and somewhat ludicrous—and crows and ravens, animals which eat carrion, are similarly seized upon by the mind as intermediaries. All such "middle terms" aid in resolving contradictions or, at the very least, in holding them in suspension so that they can be pondered.

Lévi-Strauss makes the provocative observation that modern structuralism confers a certain validity upon traditional associational psychology, which emphasized the way in which the mind builds complex ideas out of simple associations. The true insight of the associationists was that the mind does work by a kind of elementary logic of conjunctions between percepts; their flaw was the belief that this elementary logic simply reflects the structure of the environment. Instead, Lévi-Strauss proposes, the perceiving of associations is *the way* the mind and brain are structured: the logic of oppositions and correlations, exclusions and inclusions, compatibilities and incompatibilities explains the laws of association, and not the reverse. Linguists have demonstrated the mind's capacity to make $+/-$ distinctions. Similarly, the human brain uses nonverbal elements of culture to form a sign language; the selectional system used—the "algebra"—is an attribute of human brains everywhere. With some satisfaction, he concludes that an analysis of totemism has guided him beyond simple ethnographic generalization to the laws of language and even thought.

Specifying these laws of mind in ever-greater detail has become Lévi-Strauss's mission in his most recent writings. In *The Savage Mind*, he seeks to inter for all time the (then) widely accepted notion that primitives think in a childish way—with regard to totemism, for example, that they literally believe they are animals or plants—that they are incapable of conceptual thought or abstraction, that they are creatures of magic rather than science. He advances his argument in two ways: by citing impressive instances of conceptual or scientific reasoning on the part of primitive persons, and by showing that the thought processes of contemporary civilized man display many modes of perception or reasoning which are unhesitatingly labeled as primitive when they are encountered in other societies.

As an instance of advanced thought among primitives, he cites this ethnographical account of the Hanunóo of the Philippines:

Almost all the Hanunóo's activities require an intimate familiarity with local plants and a precise knowledge of plant classification. Contrary to the assumption that subsistence-level groups never use but a small segment of the local flora, ninety-three percent of the total number of native plant types are recognized by the Hanunóo as culturally significant. . . . the Hanunóo classify all forms of the local avifauna into seventy-five categories. . . . they distinguish about a dozen kinds of snakes . . . sixty-odd types of fish. . . . the thousands of insect forms present are grouped by the Hanunóo into a hundred and eight name categories, including thirteen for ants and termites.

And, to provide an instance of a so-called primitive custom which is an integral part of our own lives, Lévi-

Strauss has resort to the primitive belief in the churinga, a stone or wooden object which is supposed to be the physical body of a definite ancestor and is formally conferred on the living person as his ancestor's reincarnation; he forestalls our laughter at this improbable notion by reminding us (or at least his fellow Frenchmen) of the

documentary archives which we secrete in strongboxes or entrust to the safekeeping of solicitors and which we inspect from time to time with the care due to sacred things, to repair them if necessary or to commit them to smarter dossiers. On these occasions we too are prone to recite great myths recalled to us by the contemplation of the torn and yellowed pages: the deeds and achievements of our ancestors, the history of our homes from the time they were built or first acquired.

He alludes to the horror many individuals would feel if a document important to history—say, the original of the Declaration of Independence—were destroyed; he underscores the irrationality of our attitude to such relics of the past in noting that, when we make our pilgrimages to see Van Gogh's house or Lincoln's bed, it is in the last analysis not crucial whether what we see is genuine or not. As in the case of the churinga, what is important is only that we be shown it, told it is *the* house or *the* bed, and undergo the appropriate emotion.

Although Lévi-Strauss is intent upon revealing identities between primitive and advanced thought, he is not so rash as to claim that the primitive is operating exactly like the Western scientist. Rather, he proposes two kinds or levels of science, and claims that the primitive practices the *science of the concrete*. Both primitives and scientists may be said to operate scientifically in that both engage in the classification of objects and phenomena, which philosophers have identified as central to all scientific activity. The primitive, however, bases his classifications upon the sensory properties of materials: he groups together wild cherries, cinnamon, vanilla, and sherry because they smell alike, whales and sharks because they look alike. Such arrangements certainly have their own validity, and the Western scientist might well make the same grouping of foods, for all contain aldehyde. But the scientist would also separate the whale and the shark on anatomical and evolutionary grounds, and this kind of classification is likely to be missed by the primitive, who does not, in his science of the concrete, give weight to the results of dissection or to the twigs on evolutionary trees.

Lévi-Strauss suggests that the science of the concrete and the science of the Westerner are two parallel modes of acquiring knowledge, both capable of giving rise to organized, self-consistent systems. They require the same kinds of mental operations—the identification of properties, and grouping consistently in terms of these properties —but often differ in the types of phenomena to which they are applied and in the bases upon which the salient or relevant properties are determined.

In a revealing, if somewhat overdrawn analogy, Lévi-Strauss suggests that the thought of the primitive is akin to the technique of the *bricoleur*. A *bricoleur* is, in France, a kind of professional handyman who helps with odd jobs, and who uses means which a skilled craftsman might consider clumsy or devious. Faced with the task, say, of repairing a faulty machine, he looks over the materials at hand and improvises a solution. If the materials available do not suffice, he may try to modify them in some way; but he is unlikely to seek new tools or to redefine the problem.

In contrast, the scientist or engineer will not even bother to determine what tools are available until a much later stage. Instead, he will refresh his knowledge of how the machine is supposed to work, drawing a diagram or even consulting a manual. Then, still proceeding on the plane of thought, he will specify the points at which something could have gone wrong and the set of possible repairs. Only at this point will he inventory the tools that are at hand; and if the appropriate ones are missing, he

will secure them, or, if necessary, even invent them. As
Lévi-Strauss puts it, the *bricoleur* begins with the event—
the broken machine and the tools available—and attempts
to build a structure—a set of operations with the tools
which will repair the damage. The scientist begins with
the structure—his knowledge of the intact apparatus, his
deductions about possible flaws—and then gradually con-
verges upon the event—the specific tools and actions
needed to repair the damage.

The thought of the primitive, and preeminently his
myths, form a kind of intellectual *bricolage*. The primitive has "in his mind" a vast set of perceptions, ideas,
events, objects, persons, and so on. Like the *bricoleur,* he
knows these percepts well and can put them to diverse
uses. Yet the possible application of each percept remains
limited by the particular history of each, and by its
original use and the alterations it has undergone for other
purposes. In other words, the ideas and beliefs of the
primitive, like the tools of the *bricoleur,* comprise a large,
but not an indefinite or open set: there are only so many
possible combinations to which they can be put and, as
with the pieces in a kaleidoscope, all possible combinations are preordained by the structure of the machine.

While the engineer or scientist is always trying to break
free of the limitations imposed by his available set of
elements and devise new ones, the *bricoleur* or the mythic
thinker is content to make do with the elements at his
disposal and simply continues rearranging them. Each
choice made will involve some degree of reorganization
of the structure, and so the repaired machine or the content of the finished myth will never be quite the same
as it was before. Like scientific thought, mythic thought
works by analogies and comparisons, but unlike the products of scientific thought, its products are restricted to
rearrangements of old elements. Myths and ideas are
built up out of remains and debris, odds and ends of
thought put to service to help resolve philosophical prob-

lems or issues confronted by the society, such as the origin of man or the discovery of fire. They seem to be cemented in the same nonrandom but not completely foreseeable way as the reveries of young children falling asleep: fragments of phrases, poems, and songs occasioned by casual observations, combined in a novel creation with its distinctive rhythm, tempo, and phrasing.

Having proposed a model for the way in which primitive mythic thought is structured, Lévi-Strauss goes on in *The Savage Mind* to discuss practices of naming, classifying, categorizing, universalizing, and particularizing which are exemplified most clearly in primitive societies but are reflected as well in our own customary thinking. He seeks to demonstrate that there is a rationale for the labeling and grouping done by primitives, that this rationale is based not on utilitarian or functional considerations, but on the way in which the mind sorts, clusters, opposes, and mediates percepts and qualities. In this discussion, Lévi-Strauss remains fairly close to the level of sensory perception, and so it has been argued, with some justice, that he is presenting a *logic* of sensory, qualitative, or even aesthetic perception. Given his perennial attraction to this problem, we may presume that he would not be displeased by such a judgment.

Any honest evaluation of *The Savage Mind* must acknowledge that it is an enormously erudite and recondite work which moves uncontrollably out of focus even after numerous readings. Lévi-Strauss is a master stylist who seldom misses the opportunity for a *double entendre* or a paradoxical opposition, and is not beyond stretching a point in order to turn a neat phrase. One example may illustrate Lévi-Strauss's cultivation of paradox, the difficulty of reading *The Savage Mind,* and the charge that things are seldom as clear as he contends.

Having discussed certain animal-naming practices found in modern Western society, Lévi-Strauss summarizes as follows:

If, therefore, birds are metaphorical human beings and dogs metonymical human beings, cattle may be thought of as metonymical inhuman beings and race horses as metaphorical inhuman beings. Cattle are contiguous only for want of similarity, race horses similar only for want of contiguity. Each of these two categories offers the converse image of one of the two other categories, which themselves stand in the relation of inverted symmetry.

It would take many pages to define and place in appropriate context all the terms and implications of these sentences. We can, however, bring into focus the general point Lévi-Strauss is trying to make, as well as the evidence for it.

Lévi-Strauss observes that we tend to give names to animals with which we have regular contact. This practice is in itself of interest, since we could number them, use their Latinate names, choose not to name them at all, or fail to notice their distinctive appearances. But naming is the way in which we declare our relationship to them, and their relationship among themselves, and this is an important aspect of mental functioning. Given that we name animals, then, do we draw their names from the same set? Do we name dogs as we do race horses, cattle as we do birds? Lévi-Strauss thinks not, and offers an explanation for the particular naming practices in each case.

In France, birds tend to have names like Pierrot or Margot or Jacquot (we may analogize these to Fritz, Peter, Florence) which are drawn from the lexicon of human names; dogs, on the other hand, have names like Sultan, Fido, or Medor (Fala, Spot, Butch), which are somewhat similar to human names but not really of the same type— they are closer to stage names. Both birds and dogs are kept around the house and thus are part of our human society (and thus regarded in some sense as human beings); but birds are thought to have among themselves their own society, with its own relationships. We can afford to give them human names because they have a parallel existence and will not be confused with our society. Domesticated dogs, however, are a part of the family and do not have their own society. Thus, rather than giving them human names, one confers upon them names which are parallel to the kinds of names humans have, but do not come from the same set.

Race horses and cattle are housed in the vicinity of human beings but in no way form a part of our own society—thus, they are inhuman beings. Race horses are intimately involved with a particular human custom or practice (gambling on an animal's performance); their individual identities are important, and they are individually groomed and carefully evaluated. They are given names which are not descriptive of them but which underscore their distinctiveness and reflect upon their owner's cleverness or imagination: Beautiful Night, Native Dancer, Man o' War. Cattle, on the other hand, tend to be treated as objects, because there is no interest in their individual identities, but only in the uses to which they can be put. Their names, if they are given names at all, tend to come from the oral rather than the learned tradition, and are broadly descriptive: Rustaud, Rousset, Blanchette, Douce (Spotty, Bossy, Sweet). Whereas the horses, though isolated, seem to belong to a different and duly constituted society based on competition for prizes—and are therefore parallel to humans—the cattle, like the dogs, are seen more in their relationship to human beings as an extension of our technical and economic system. In contrast to dogs, however, their subjective personal qualities are not appreciated.

Even this abbreviated exposition should suggest that Lévi-Strauss is on to something. It is evident that animals are *not* carelessly or randomly named, and that each category of animal names has distinctive properties. And yet the particular propositions Lévi-Strauss advances should not be accepted without challenge. Domestic animals are sometimes named after individuals whom they resemble in one way or another, race horses not infrequently have descriptive or qualitative names, dogs are sometimes given Christian names, and on their own birth certificates. Furthermore, the division between being a part of human society and not being a part is in practice very difficult to draw, and as Lévi-Strauss himself has shown, primitive people tend to incorporate all animals into their group. Indeed, one could argue that any animal on which one bothers to confer a name is *ipso facto* being seen as part of human society. None of this in any way vitiates Lévi-Strauss's overall point about the importance of naming and the different practices found in various realms; what is being called into question are the specific refined discriminations he makes here.

Similar reservations can be introduced on either the common-sense or the ethnographic level about nearly every argument expounded in *The Savage Mind*; but, revealingly, such disagreements are more and more coming to be presented within Lévi-Strauss's own framework. He himself has remarked that he is like a woodsman who has entered a virgin forest and must make broad swathes before individual bits of pruning can be contemplated. Thus, he would be satisfied if his overall orientation should become the basis for future discussion about the nature of primitive thought and the savage mind. It is toward this goal that the present phase of his research is directed.

4. THE LOGIC OF MYTH

If *The Savage Mind* challenges all but the most sophisticated philosophers and ethnographers, even the latter group has experienced great difficulty with Lévi-Strauss's analyses of myths in his series of monographs collectively called *Mythologiques*. One well-known anthropologist remarked that reviewing the second book in the series was the most arduous task of that sort he could remember having assumed. These books are rich in ethnographic data about dozens of Amerindian societies, and contain, all told, well over eight hundred myths whose details must be kept in mind as Lévi-Strauss guides one through a labyrinthine exposition of their components and meanings. We shall attempt to come to grips with this enterprise through a general overview of it, and through an excerpt from the work of Edmund Leach, Lévi-Strauss's colleague and his principal interpreter to English-speaking readers.

When weaving myth, the mind is freed from the obligation of dealing with objects. Therefore, it should be able to reveal directly its own law of operations and, indeed, "to imitate itself as an object." Myths should reflect the mind's structure, reasoned Lévi-Strauss, as he commenced his study of the huge corpus of American Indian myth. If a visitor to Western society who did not speak the language were to watch a series of card games being played, he should eventually be able to figure out both the rules of the games and the construction of the deck—the content and the form of the domain of cards. Similarly, someone who samples the variety of myths produced across different ethnographic settings should be able to pick out both the bits and morsels which constitute the essence of the myth and the various rules of combination which reflect the structure of the mind that is producing them. This, in brief, was Lévi-Strauss's project.

If the language analogy was helpful in the earlier studies of cultural phenomena, it was obviously relevant to the study of myth. It was necessary to find units—in this case, the shortest meaningful utterances or "basic constituents" —to discover their distinctive features and their rules of combination, to note how they were combined in any given version of a myth and how they were transformed over a range of myths. Lévi-Strauss was convinced that many myths in a culture work with the same set of materials and that myths containing the same material do not have merely an accidental relationship to one another, but that rather there are specific laws of combination or transformation which can enable one to get from one myth to another; indeed, he has even devised an (admittedly obscure) formula for doing so.

And yet, noted Lévi-Strauss, there are aspects of myth not easily assimilated to a linguistic model. Consider, for example, the widespread tendency to repeat parts of myths with great frequency, the numerous variants of a given myth, the way in which the principal elements of myth gradually "sink in" as the listener's intuitive familiarity with them grows. These and other aspects of myth seemed more akin to music, and so it was such correspondences that Lévi-Strauss chose to emphasize in the *Mythologiques*. Music, in turn, has often been observed to have logical qualities: a melody is composed of discrete tones or pitches combined in a certain way, and various kinds of orderly transformation (e.g., diminution, augmentation, retrograde inversions) can be imposed on a musical passage. This transforming aspect was very important to Lévi-Strauss, and in this regard also—instead of embracing the most recent view of language, which stressed its own transformational aspects—he relied on music as an analogy. The *Mythologiques* are filled with musical references, including such section titles as "Recitative Theme and Variations," "A Short Sonata and Well-tempered Anatomy," "Rustic Symphony in Three Movements," and "A Fugue of the Five Senses."

In Lévi-Strauss's treatment of myth, then, there are several competing models: language as spoken in everyday discourse, formal or mathematical language and its logical transformations, and the harmonic structures of music, each of which can in turn be related to the other models, to the ecology of the society, and to the myths themselves, singly or collectively. This complexity, compounded by the richness of hundreds of unfamiliar tales about jaguars, smoke, fire, peccaries, and cross-cousin marriage, makes the landscape of the *Mythologiques* a strange and at times forbidding terrain.

What of Lévi-Strauss's goals in the *Mythologiques*? Quite simply, he seeks to demonstrate beyond a reasonable doubt the method and the logic inherent in myth corpora. He tries to show that simple empirical categories—the perception of light, darkness, smell, noise, silence, etc.—can be treated as conceptual tools for such abstract ideas as the relationship between Nature and Culture, the characteristics of the incest taboo, and the importance of certain kinship and social arrangements; and that these ideas, moreover, can be incorporated into logical propositions. Indeed, he contends that myths must be converted into symbolic logical terms if they are to be understood. The relationships among the myths are seen as quasi-biological in character, analogous to the physical transformations of anatomy and physiology which relate animal species to one another.

In the first volume of the *Mythologiques,* entitled *The Raw and the Cooked,* Lévi-Strauss attempts to present a logic of qualities based upon the difference between the raw or uncooked, which is part of Nature, and the cooked, which is part of Culture, depending upon man's discovery of fire. He proposes that the opposition between raw and cooked on the plane of food is the same as that between Nature and Culture on the plane of society, between profane and sacred on the plane of religion, between silence and noise on the plane of sound. In the next volume, *From Honey to Ashes,* which also features the eating of food as its central image, his aim is to convert content into structure "without impoverishing it." He tries to show that there is a logic of form—contained and uncontained, inside and outside—underlying the logic of qualities: honey is taken directly from Nature and constitutes the meal; tobacco is of Culture and is consumed outside the meal. In a third volume, *The Origin of Table Man-*

ners, Lévi-Strauss argues that a logic of propositions underlies all systems or codes in a culture. And in the finale, *The Naked Man (L'Homme Nu),* he explores the role of costume and commercial trade in man's relationship to the natural world; considers the closed nature of the corpus of myths found among the Indians of North and South America; and reveals how, taking as a point of departure a single tale of a family quarrel, one can elucidate the major oppositions of earth and sky in the physical order, man and woman in the natural order, and kin relationships in the social order.

The *Mythologiques* represent, overall, Lévi-Strauss's comprehensive effort to demonstrate that all patterns of human behavior are codes; that the mind's inherent structuring tendency—operating in terms of a limited set of inborn principles—conditions and determines the form of social phenomena, and of important forms of relations among human beings: differences in status, networks of friendship, feelings of hostility, etc. Such relations are dealt with in myths by means of various codes relating to categories of food, sound or silence, smell and taste, landscapes, seasonal changes, climate, celestial bodies, shelter, animal and plant life. The terms or objects appearing in myths may differ, but the underlying laws of discourse, and the operative ecological and social constraints, are invariable. Myths are designed to deal with problems of human existence which seem insoluble; they embody and express such dilemmas in a coherently structured form, and so serve to render them intelligible. Through their structural similarity to given "real world" situations, myths establish a point of repose or equilibrium at which men can come to grips with the crucial components of the problem, and become aware of the "fix" they are in. Thus, a myth is both intellectually satisfying and socially solidifying.

Lévi-Strauss was here making claims of a boldness rarely paralleled in contemporary social science. He was suggesting, first of all, that the kinds of principles which govern the use of language are also discernible in all other realms of cultural activity, ranging from sex and cooking to hunting and child-rearing. Each of these realms contains "languagelike codes," which the human mind imposes upon the flux of sense and experiential data and which are embodied in the words and the musiclike qualities of myths. If one has a sufficiently thorough understanding of the myth corpus, it should prove possible to predict the form of myths which are as yet undiscovered, just as an astronomer can predict the presence, size, and trajectory of a body which has never been detected by his intruments.

Lévi-Strauss has drawn parallels between language and reality because he believes that, in the last analysis, they both reflect the structure of the universe. Culture, he feels, shares with Nature this underlying structure, since Culture is a product of men's minds and men's minds are themselves a part of Nature. Whereas animals may reflect the mechanisms of life in a disjointed, fragmentary way, the human mind, endowed with reason, provides a relatively faithful reflection of the structured universe. And it is most peculiarly in myth, where the mind is freed of the pressures of daily existence, that it comes to "imitate itself as an object," and thereby to give expression to that reflection. The laws of the world are seen as identical to the laws of thought, and one's thought is seen as susceptible to study like any other object.

In addition to these claims about the essential continuity between thought and its object, Lévi-Strauss attempts the stupefyingly difficult task of analyzing the experience of the senses in a logical way. Whereas the standard scientific inclination has been to ignore qualitative aspects of experience as much as possible and to focus upon measurable correlates (or noncorrelates) of these properties, it is Lévi-Strauss's aim to create a logic which will retain the particular qualities of experience. For the experiencing person, and particularly for primitives, objects are charged with affect and meaning, and the operation of myths and of mind is comprehensible only if these qualitative aspects are somehow retained. Lévi-Strauss seeks to achieve this by allowing percepts and images to function as signs, by treating them as counters in a game which permits their expression in rules, while allowing them to maintain their empirical significance; he aims to transcend the contrast between the tangible and the intelligible by operating at the level of the sign, by reducing experiences to the objectivity of signs while alluding to their qualitative properties through inclusion of the particular sign. Thus, Lévi-Strauss specifies the qualities of raw and cooked, rather than of large and small, of pure and polluted, of x and y; only by maintaining some link to the content of experience can he hope to communicate his basic theses about the laws of mind. The crucial question is whether he has succeeded in bridging the gap between phenomenal experience and the logical analysis of the world, or whether his effort falls between these poles, without capturing the essence of either. Put another way, the *Mythologiques* constitute an experiment designed to determine whether the sciences can elucidate qualitative and aesthetic phenomena.

Any thoroughgoing critique of Lévi-Strauss's program and achievement would still be premature, since the *Mythologiques* have just been completed, and most scholars lack sufficient information and familiarity with the materials to evaluate his enterprise properly. It is not even possible as yet to offer a specific, detailed example of Lévi-Strauss's approach, because the material is so unfamiliar to those unschooled in Brazilian ethnography as to make pages of introduction necessary. Nonetheless, a picture of the sweep and nature of Lévi-Strauss's claims may perhaps be partially conveyed if one considers some examples drawn from a much more familiar source—the Bible. Lévi-Strauss's colleague Edmund Leach has devoted his considerable energy and creativity to making various structural analyses of Biblical material and it is to these that we now turn.

First, let us consider an example of that oft-alluded-to operation, mythic transformation. Leach summarizes Judges 11:30–40 as follows:

(a) Jephthah the Gileadite makes a vow to present a burnt offering to God if he is granted victory.
(b) God grants Jephthah victory.
(c) By implication, Jephthah plans to sacrifice an animal or a slave in fulfillment of his vow.
(d) God, in the form of chance, imposes a substitution whereby Jephthah is made to sacrifice his only child, a virgin daughter.
Outcome: Jephthah has no descendants of any kind.

—and Genesis 22:1–18 in this manner:

(d) God requires Abraham to sacrifice his only son Isaac as evidence of his faith and obedience.
(c) As Abraham prepares to obey, God imposes a substitution whereby Abraham in fact sacrifices an animal in fulfillment of his duty.
(b) Abraham thus demonstrates his faith and obedience.
(a) God makes a vow that Abraham shall have countless descendants.
Outcome: Children of Israel claim descent from Abraham.

Leach maintains that while the superficial resemblance between the passages is slight, a structural analysis reveals these two stories to be mirror images of each other. He suggests the following substitutions: "God" is changed to "father," "father" is changed to "God"; "virgin daughter" is changed to "virgin son"; the sequence represented by the clauses (a) – (d) is simply reversed across the stories and so the outcome itself is reversed. Leach concludes that the two stories have an identical structure, since the second can be obtained from the first by the simplest possible transformational rule: For each element, substitute its binary opposite.

It is certainly an exaggeration to claim that the stories

are mirror opposites of one another—an assertion that
critical consideration of any two clauses will quickly re-
fute. Meaningful passages are not easily converted into
arbitrary signs in this way. Yet Leach is convincing when
he insists on a strong structural parallel between the two
seemingly unrelated and independent passages. The claim
here is reminiscent of the observation that there are only
a few basic plots, which can be varied and converted into
one another by simple modifications. Lévi-Straussian analysis would insist that the myths were formed by a process
of *bricolage*: certain perceptual elements were isolated
because of their salience and opposition; these elements
came to be embodied in persons and characters, thereby
becoming the bits and morsels out of which myths could
be made. The ways in which they could be combined were
conditioned and limited by the structure of the mind (the
kaleidoscope), and the relationship between any two variants could be mapped by transformational laws.

A more elaborate illustration of these points is to be
found in Leach's brilliant, somewhat overwhelming, *tour
de force* on the opening verses of Genesis—appropriately
called "Lévi-Strauss in the Garden of Eden."

Leach views the opening chapters of the Bible as a
series of three episodes which have the same general structure and which reflect the same narrative impulse in the
course of confronting various crucial questions. The first
story has to do with the creation of the world (Chapter 1
of Genesis), the second with the Garden of Eden and the
expulsion of Adam and Eve (Chapters 2–3), the last with
the story of Cain and Abel (Chapter 4). Leach's discussion
is rather dense, and oscillates back and forth between a
text and a complex diagram; I have attempted to simplify
and clarify both, but would counsel readers to refer
directly to the opening chapters of Genesis, reprinted as
an appendix to this book.

In each of the three episodes, one can discern a series
of categorical oppositions, mediated by an intermediary

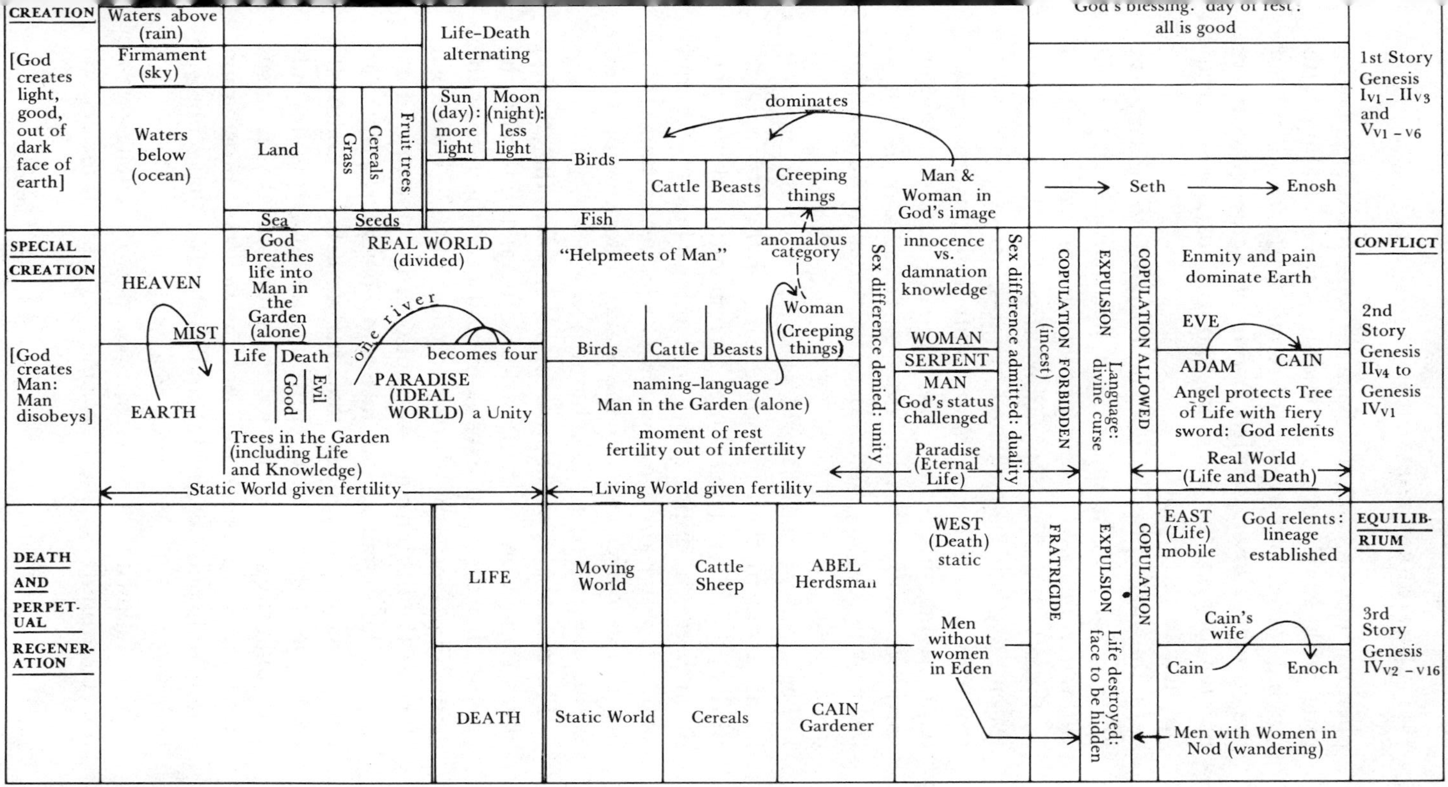

GENESIS ACCORDING TO LEACH

Row labels (left column):

CREATION — [God creates light, good, out of face of earth]

SPECIAL CREATION — [God creates Man; Man disobeys]

DEATH AND PERPETUAL REGENERATION

Top band:

CREATION | Waters above (rain) | Firmament (sky) | Waters below (ocean)

God's blessing, day of rest. all is good

1st Story Genesis I v1 – II v3 and V v1 – v6

CONFLICT — 2nd Story Genesis II v4 to Genesis IV v1

EQUILIBRIUM — 3rd Story Genesis IV v2 – v16

Creation section:

Life–Death alternating

Sun (day): more light | Moon (night): less light

dominates

Birds — Fish

Land | Sea

Fruit trees | Cereals | Grass | Seeds

Seth → Enosh

Creeping things | Cattle | Beasts

Conflict / 2nd Story:

Enmity and pain dominate Earth

EVE
ADAM — CAIN
Angel protects Tree of Life with fiery sword: God relents

Real World (Life and Death)

COPULATION ALLOWED

EXPULSION — Language: divine curse

COPULATION FORBIDDEN (incest)

Sex difference admitted: duality

Man & Woman in God's image

innocence vs. damnation knowledge

WOMAN | SERPENT | MAN

God's status challenged

Paradise (Eternal Life)

Sex difference denied: unity

anomalous category — Woman (Creeping things)

"Helpmeets of Man"

Birds | Cattle | Beasts

naming-language
Man in the Garden (alone)
moment of rest
fertility out of infertility

Living World given fertility

REAL WORLD (divided) — becomes four — PARADISE (IDEAL WORLD) a Unity

one river

Trees in the Garden (including Life and Knowledge)

Life | Death
Evil | Good

God breathes life into Man in the Garden (alone)

HEAVEN — MIST — EARTH

Static World given fertility

Equilibrium / 3rd Story:

EAST (Life) mobile

God relents: lineage established

Cain's wife
Cain — Enoch

Men with Women in Nod (wandering)

COPULATION

EXPULSION — Life destroyed: face to be hidden

FRATRICIDE

WEST (Death) static

Men without women in Eden

ABEL Herdsman | CAIN Gardener

Moving World | Static World

Cattle Sheep | Cereals

LIFE | DEATH

phenomenon or category. Each episode features a beginning with static forces, a middle section dealing with
moving forces, and a point of repose at the conclusion of
the episode. Closer parallels among the three episodes are
pointed out in the diagram, and various themes recur
throughout the narrative.

In the first episode, light is separated from darkness,
heaven from earth, and fresh water above (rain) from
salt water below (sea). These oppositions are mediated
by the sky; the next opposition introduced, that between
sea and dry land, is mediated by grass, herb-yielding seed,
and fruit trees. Here we have a shift from inanimate matter to living things; and the reference to seeds, and in
particular to fruit-bearing trees, serves as a transition to
the moving objects discussed in the latter sections of the
first episode.

The dead or static world is opposed to the moving,
living world in the concluding parts of the first episode.
Birds and fish are living things corresponding to the opposition between things above and things below: sky and
land, salt water and fresh water. Cattle, beasts, and creeping things correspond to the static collection of grass,
cereal, and fruit trees (in column 3).

The conclusion of the first episode involves the creation
of man and woman, expressed in general terms, and the
proviso that they will have dominion over the rest of the
earth. Thus, there are three references to God, who stood
alone at the beginning of the episode: the notion of dom-
inance; the statement that men and women are created in
God's image; the remark that, his work being complete,
God took a day of rest. However, the first episode ends
with unanswered puzzles, for the problems of life versus
death, stasis versus motion, and incest versus procreation
—how will one be fruitful and multiply?—have not yet
been faced.

The following episode—the Garden of Eden story—
does confront these questions, and also expands the general

picture of Creation through more specific creative acts. The episode begins with an opposition between heaven and earth, this time mediated by a fertilizing mist drawn up out of the dry infertile earth. Adam is formed, like the animals, from the dust of the earth. The dry lands of the real world are fertilized by a river coming out of the ground of Eden, and fertile Eve is formed from the rib of infertile Adam. Here, then, in briefer and more specific form, is a recapitulation of the Creation described in the first episode.

Next, oppositions are introduced: the man and the garden, and (by implication) the Tree of Life and the Tree of Death. The Tree of Death is called "the Tree of Knowledge of Good and Evil," which, according to Leach, refers to potentially pernicious knowledge of sexual differences and knowledge of logical categories. The positive aspects of language are introduced as Adam names the animals about him. Then a moment of rest occurs; Adam falls asleep, Eve is created from part of him, and they are of one flesh. The structural parallels between the first and second episodes suggest the following to Leach: Eve is equivalent to the category "creeping things" of the first story; creeping things are anomalous in the categorical opposition "cattle versus beasts," and Eve is anomalous in the categorical opposition "man versus animal"; the serpent, an actual creeping thing, is anomalous in the categorical opposition "man versus woman" (the snake may be hermaphroditic).

The serpent also serves as an antipode to God and raises in concrete and dramatic guise the questions of knowledge, temptation, and disobedience. The incident that follows is the structural center of the three episodes taken as a whole. At the climactic moment, Eve accepts the apple from the serpent, she and Adam partake of it, become aware of sexual differences, acquire knowledge, and face the inevitability of death. At the same time, of course, pregnancy and generational life become possible. God shows wrath toward both humans and the snake and pronounces curses upon them, revealing the less positive aspects of language. Enmity, hostility, and pain are introduced for the first time. At the conclusion of the second episode, Adam and Eve have been barred from Paradise and innocence; the "idyllic world" has been opposed by the real world and by conflict. God does relent to the extent of clothing his children; but he expels them from the Paradise, and the episode ends without our knowing the fate of Adam and Eve and their prospective progeny.

Finally, but more briefly, the third episode recapitulates and epitomizes the same structure. Cain and Abel are introduced as polar givens in the opening section of the work, as static oppositions who foreshadow life and death. Cain tills the soil (the static world) and Abel tends herds (the world of motion), but paradoxically Cain must eliminate Abel and substitute a wife in order that a sterile homosexual world may become a fertile heterosexual world (*And Cain knew his wife and she conceived. . . .*). Again God becomes angry, confronts his child with an accusing question, and places the curse of the earth upon Cain. Like his parents, Cain is estranged from the life of peace and plenty; but it is this separation that makes possible the copulation necessary for survival of the line. God again relents, for he places a special mark upon Cain to spare him from all attempts on his life. The episode ends with the first long recital of lineages, as if to confirm that, for better or worse, the line of man has been unambiguously established. Leach points out several other interepisodal parallels which are included in the diagram, but which I will not dwell on further.

Although any contention that these episodes are completely identical in structure is excessive, I am in agreement with Leach that the parallels are too strong to be unmotivated accidents. As Leach comments:

I do not claim that this kind of "structural analysis" is the one and only legitimate procedure for the interpretation of myth. It seems to me that whether any particular individual finds this kind of thing interesting or stimulating must depend on personal temperament; some may think it is too like a conjuring trick. . . . the pattern is there: I did not invent it. . . . No one will ever again be able to read the early chapters of Genesis without taking this pattern into account.

Skeptics are invited to accept Leach's challenge and to tackle the opening chapters of Genesis without applying the above approach. What is especially fascinating is that, even as the first chapters of Genesis provide an account of how the most mysterious and central questions about man may be resolved, these ancient writings serve as well as a model for all literature and stories: the introduction of contrasting characters, the building-up of a conflict, a central crisis, and a resolution. It is especially neat that each of the episodes embodies in a small way the essential structures of a narrative, while the three episodes together form a carefully worked out and integrated whole.

That Edmund Leach, a noted anthropologist who has not hesitated to criticize many aspects of Lévi-Strauss's work, should produce such an impressive structural analysis is a significant tribute to the Frenchman's pioneering genius. If structuralism is to be more than a skillful display by an imaginative writer, its method must be transferable to other scientists; Leach's success indicates the possibility of such a transfer. Yet two men who can produce convincing structural analyses are hardly enough, either, to prove the method's scientific validity. The real question is whether a *number* of analysts, having studied Lévi-Strauss's exposition (and Leach's examples) could each produce structural analyses of the same text, and whether these analyses would point up the same factors, relations, and underlying structures. Such a demonstration has yet to be done and would probably be extremely difficult to carry out.

Herein lies the principal difficulty with Lévi-Strauss's contribution. His ingenuity, brilliance, and resourcefulness are denied by few; but whether his method has been sufficiently defined as to enable it to be meaningfully used by others has been questioned by many persons, including those fully aware of what he is trying to do. Not a few critics complain that Lévi-Strauss is *overly* clever; that he makes distinctions and syntheses where data are lacking or ambiguous; that he ignores information incompatible with his theories and overemphasizes the limited amount of information in their favor. Furthermore, they resent the frequent inconsistencies and *volte-face*'s in his work; they point to the numerous different ways in which he employs a term like "model" or a discipline like linguistics, and they complain that he is constantly changing direction—as when he first claims that the line between Nature and Culture is absolute, then denies its importance, but continues to refer to it nonetheless; they cite apparent contradictions, as when he first argues that myths are means of considering or solving social problems, only to declare in later writings that myths are untrammeled reflections of the human spirit.

It must be admitted that Lévi-Strauss can be irritating, particularly when one is trying to determine exactly what he is saying, rather than merely taking in the varied and beautiful illustrations, seductive prose, and brilliant intuitions. Nonetheless, too many of his critics, in my view, are overly concerned with proving him wrong on one or another point, rather than in accepting such errors as the unfortunate concomitant of a courageous attempt to take on issues of dizzying difficulty and to make some kind of tentative sense out of them.

Although Lévi-Strauss's output continues at an unabated rate, his lectures treat new topics each year, and further surprises are no doubt in store, it seems fair to say now that his major influence has been of two sorts. On the one hand, his exquisite sensitivity and his ability to write with grace and poignancy about the anthropological calling have made him a hero to a whole generation of young humanists, as well as to many youthful ethnographers or anthropologists *manqués*. On the other hand, he has grappled boldly with many of the most difficult technical problems in the field, and though he has excited perhaps as much opposition as adulation among his colleagues, his vastly stimulating impact overall is denied by virtually no one. Let us, in conclusion, consider each of his contributions.

Lévi-Strauss considers anthropology a way of life. He insists that his students undertake field work and he encourages them to do anthropological research even within their own society. As he attempted to convey through his dramatic alter ego Cinna, the anthropologist is someone who consciously rejects his own society in order to immerse himself in an alien one and must live with the consequences of this decision. One's going into the field is considered a rite whereby one confronts the past tradition of the anthropological discipline and one's own ability to remain estranged from the society in which one has been formed. For a youth soured on Western civilization, yet searching for commitment and self-definition, this perspective is as appealing as Sartre's existentialism, and far less ethnocentric. Rather than viewing contemporary civilized man as the hallowed terminus of all previous evolution, structuralism calls into question the unique status of particular human groups, while also challenging traditional humanistic assumptions about free will and infinite cognitive creativity.

On the subject of the disappearance of primitive societies, Lévi-Strauss is passionate and inspiring. He notes that these groups represent our last connection to the world of the past, and laments the fact that modern techniques of investigation could not have been brought to bear on them when they were still in their pristine state at the time of the first expeditions to the New World. He inveighs against the ravages wrought by conquistadors, mission-

aries, and land-hungry frontiersmen who wreaked havoc
with the mores of these societies and reduced them to dis-
ease, dysfunction, death, and disappearance. Addressing
a distinguished assemblage commemorating (in 1965)
the birth of the founder of the Smithsonian Institution, he
paid tribute to the prescient anthropologists of the last
century and urged scientists and governments to give the
highest priority to the study of primitive life while there
is still time:

> If a planet were nearing the earth only once, we would spare
> no expense. . . . Should not the same be done at a time when
> one-half of mankind, only recently acknowledged as such, is
> still so near to the other half that except for men and money
> its study raises no problems, although it will soon become
> impossible forever . . . for native cultures are disintegrating
> faster than radioactive bodies. . . . That mirror which other
> civilizations still hold up to us will have so receded from our
> eyes that however costly and elaborate the instruments at our
> disposal, we may never again be able to recognize and study
> this image of ourselves which will be lost and gone forever.

This somber, anguished appeal, especially impressive coming from a man devoted to dispassionate analyses of kinship systems and myth components, recalls the classic
concerns of Rousseau, Bergson, and other great figures of
the past, even as it reflects the more advanced perspective
of the present day. Lévi-Strauss has cultivated that tone of
detachment coupled with emotion which is particularly
attractive in a society wedded to intellectual style yet
sensitive to sentiment; and its appeal has extended far
beyond the boundaries of his own culture.

As regards the technical details of his work and his overall contributions to the field of anthropology, Lévi-Strauss
may be viewed as one who has sought to wed the empirical
concerns of the American and English schools with the
interest in pervasive and underlying structures characteristic of the Durkheimian tradition. Although he may,
and should, be faulted for his less than scrupulous ad-

herence to the positivistic aspects of his own program, there is little argument that the course he has proposed for anthropology is an attractive and perhaps a necessary one. Lévi-Strauss persuaded a generation to look at the model of linguistic study, and even where this model turned out to be irrelevant to their own concerns, the kind of analytical rigor characteristic of such studies and the search for underlying structures beneath the surface of a protean and diffuse reality were positive influences. Just as Marx altered the intellectual community's ideas about historical change by applying the methods of political economy, so Lévi-Strauss has drawn upon the methods of structural linguistics in order to elucidate the constancies in social and cultural institutions. His notion of societies as having their own equilibrium, brought about through regulative exchanges of various sorts, was also a needed antidote to the diffusionist and functional approaches prevailing before his time.

Lévi-Strauss's most substantial—and most controversial —contribution to anthropological studies has been his insistence on the importance of the structure of the human mind. This idea is more foreign to the themes of mid-twentieth-century anthropology and is felt by many to be outside its proper scope. It was thus incumbent upon Lévi-Strauss to demonstrate that the elementary structures which he and others had found in the realms of kinship and social organization reflected the basic structures of the mind rather than simply the environmental or evolutionary forces usually cited. To achieve this, he had to map out the rules of the mind, its predilection for contradictions, contrasts, oppositions, mediations, perception of relations, associations, and so on. This pursuit continued to draw upon the insights of the linguists but also brought him closer to psychology and soon carved out a place for logic and music as well. Lévi-Strauss chose to focus on those areas where the mind's own operation would be least obscured by external factors, and so examined classifying and naming practices, myth-making, and the numerous relationships between these manifestations as found in different societies, including his own. He also examined the various codes built up by humans on the basis of their sensory perception and argued vigorously that there was an underlying logic in qualitative perception which studies of myth could bring to the fore.

The chief aspiration of Lévi-Strauss's program is clear. He has hoped, by focusing on the mind, to bring out the nature not only of human psychology but also of cultural and social organization. He wants to bring into a fruitful harmony the diverse traditions of social anthropology, to integrate the central insights of Freud concerning the relationship between affect and cognition, symbols and reality, with those of Marx concerning the relationship between the technical and economic capabilities of the society and its ideology. Learnedly interpolating quotations from Virgil, Euripides, Mallarmé, and *Playboy* in analyses of the disparate myths of the American continents, he has sought to dramatize the affinities between savage thought and the thought of "advanced" civilizations. Indeed, he wants to dissolve the borders between disciplines, to remain close to and illuminate the relatively nonrational realms of intuition, feeling, sensory perception, and dreams, while revealing the scientific basis for such thought and underlining its essential affinity to more logical forms of thought. He wants to illuminate the meaning of myths by focusing upon their structures, and the solidarity and endurance of societies by focusing upon their kinship practices. If his achievement in all these areas has been less than complete, the grandeur of his vision is inspiring.

III An Assessment of Structuralism: Problems and Prospects

5 The Relationship Between Two Varieties of Structuralism

Every psychological explanation comes sooner or later to lean on biology or on logic.

—PIAGET

Suppose you, as the proverbial visitor from a distant planet, were to land in Yankee Stadium. A baseball game is in progress and, curious about the folkways of earthlings, you follow the action with great attention. At first, the activities seem senseless; you do not understand the reasons for uniforms of two patterns and colors, the crowd of people in the stands, the numbers on the scoreboard, the public-address system, the peculiar behaviors of the players. Ignorant of the spoken language, you must rely exclusively on your visual perception of these activities if you are to unravel their meaning. Within a reasonably short period of time, however, you should begin to discern certain regularities. You notice that the men in the dark blue uniforms remain stationary throughout; that the "players" fall into two distinct groups, housed in two separate "dugouts"; members of each team alternatively remain each at one place in the field, then take their turns at bat; after about three hours everyone leaves. It would take longer to discern the subtleties of play: the way in which balls and strikes are determined, the rules governing runs, hits, and errors; the system of innings and complete games. And you would probably have to watch for many months before successfully sorting out the gyrations of the first- and third-base coaches, ground-rule doubles, earned-run averages, pennant races, the unique features of each contest. Eventually, however, given sufficient ingenuity and patience, you should be able to achieve a fairly complete picture of the game, teasing out the merely incidental features (color of uniforms, the seventh-inning stretch, peanut vendors, size of the ball park) from the essential ones (number of men on a team; rules for pinch-hitting; procedure for a double play) .

1. TOWARDS A DEFINITION OF STRUCTURALISM

In its broadest outlines, the task confronting the structural analyst is akin to that of the outer-space visitor to Yankee Stadium. In both cases, the observer stands removed from a human activity, one which he does not understand, but which he assumes to be characterized, like all other forms of behavior, by perceivable regularities. He first watches the activity very carefully, making preliminary guesses about what is going on. He tries out these hypotheses, dropping those which are consistently refuted, embracing those which receive consistent confirmation, waiting for crucial tests of ambiguous ones. He devises preliminary models of what is going on, utilizing those elements he feels are basic to the activity, and reduces to a secondary status those features—often equally salient— which appear to be random or nonfunctional. Ultimately, he may well decide that the actors themselves are only partially aware of the rules governing their behavior; they may be enacting their parts in a structure while innocent of its wider significance. The man from outer space may see the ballplayers as part of a larger social and economic

structure serving interests of which the athletes are ignorant.

Crucial to the analyst's view is the assumption that
despite the numerous apparent differences between one
game, activity, or culture and another, a sufficiently probing analysis will detect deep-seated continuities across
the range of individual occurrences. The analyst not
only points out these underlying regularities, but also
singles out for particular attention those rules or factors which can account for the differences between
two games, activities, or cultures. Basic elements in the
two specimens will be the same; only their arrangement
will be different. Therefore, the rules of transformation
between the possible arrangements of elements become a
pivotal concern for the structural analyst.

Considering, for example, the outcomes of two baseball
games, the analyst may propose that a combination of
three basic elements—pitching, hitting, and fielding—
will account for a team's performance. In the case of game
1, a team triumphed through a combination of good pitching and fielding, despite poor hitting, while in game 2,
success followed upon strong hitting, despite indifferent
pitching and fielding. The simple operation of reversing
the signs of pitching, fielding, and hitting—all positive
elements become negative, all negative ones positive—
establishes the winning combination in the two games.
Although the value of each constituent factor varies from
one contest to the next, the underlying structure of victory
or defeat is shown to be a simple structure or its complement (algebraically: $P + F + H -$ or $P - F - H +$). Another
example: A structuralist interested in the relationship
between football, baseball, and basketball would point to
the existence of two competing teams, a set of different
positions, the alternation of offensive and defensive phases
as common features of all these activities. The relationship
among these sports can be appreciated by contrasting the
stress on physical contact and power in football with the

comparatively high premium on agility and timing in basketball and in baseball; the possibility for scoring many points at one time in football and the large possible payoff from the home run in baseball, with the repetition of many low-scoring plays in basketball; the penalties for fouls in basketball and football with the relative absence of penalties in baseball; the equal opportunities for scoring in baseball, each side having twenty-seven outs, with the stronger possibility for controlling the ball in the other two sports. It should be possible to carry out an exhaustive structural analysis of these and other sports (e.g., hockey) by noting their distribution on such pivotal dimensions; once this has been done, a method for transforming one game into another by changing the signs on these components becomes feasible.

Such an analysis suggests that basketball and hockey are structurally similar games, although hockey employs equipment and places a relatively higher premium on physical power. Football has a structure somewhat apart from the other sports by virtue of its emphasis on a central player, assignment of ball possession to a team for a certain number of plays, greater possibility for rapid change in the teams' respective scores, highlighting of physical contact. Baseball, finally, comes close to being a structural transformation of basketball, as the two sports come out differently on virtually every dimension. Each game is defined by its differences from other games, rather than on its own terms. One might infer from such an analysis that a trend in spectator interest away from baseball would work to the benefit of basketball; one could then relate such a trend, say, to the fact that baseball players and basketball players differ in average educational level. Then, one might attribute the growing popularity of football to the fact that football scores positively on nearly every dimension which, for the contemporary fan, adds excitement to the game, and so is perhaps the "most glamorous and dramatic" of spectator sports.

A STRUCTURALIST LOOKS AT SPECTATOR SPORTS

	use of equipment / no equipment other than the ball	relative emphasis on power and contact / speed and non-contact	possibility of dramatic change in score / total composed of repeated little scores	central player directing team / players roughly equivalent	penalties (influencing play of game) / no penalties
Baseball	+	−	−/+	+	−
Basketball	−	−/+		−	+
Football	+/−	+	−/+	+	+
Hockey	+	+/−	−	−	+

	each team has spatially localized goal / common goal	regularly timed schedule for control of ball / quick shifts, possibility for controlling ball
Baseball	+	−
Basketball	−	+
Football	+/−	+
Hockey	−	+

Key

+ = dimension before the dash
− = dimension following the dash
+/−, −/+ = aspects of both dimensions

The kind of an analysis I have been attempting here, though drawn from an unpretentious domain, is representative of structuralism. Piaget, Lévi-Strauss, and their colleagues focus on separate domains, search for the crucial variables, attempt to map the latter's relationships with one another. The size of the domain, the nature of units, the degree of precision with which rules of transformation are spelled out will vary for different analyses and different analysts; but one can discern an underlying set of principles governing their activities. Here I propose to sketch out the philosophy which I believe motivates those associated with the structuralist movement. Subsequently, I will initiate a direct comparison of Lévi-Strauss's and Piaget's views on various crucial aspects of human culture and development, concluding with my own suggestions about how a resolution of the differences between these two thinkers might come about.

A method or approach rather than a carefully formulated catechism, structuralism is an attempt to discern the arrangements of elements underlying a given domain isolated by an analyst. The structuralist notes variations in these arrangements; he then attempts to relate the variations by specifying rules whereby one can be transformed to another. Structuralism in psychology and anthropology takes its inspiration from mathematics and allied disciplines, such as logic, linguistics, and physics. Typically, one seeks a structural model whose elements and transformations can be couched in formal-mathematical terms. And just as mathematics and linguistics have come to be regarded as autonomous fields, susceptible to exhaustive description in their own terms, so, too, the newer domains explored by structuralists are seen as self-sufficient, having certain necessary properties, subject to lawful transformations. The structuralist is particularly eager to find underlying regularities among seemingly disparate phenomena, since a "determination of basic structures" will result in simplification of a mass of data as well as confirmation of the existence of laws governing that domain. Thus, Lévi-Strauss searches for structures—a myth formula, a kinship unit—which will unify disparate cultural products or the mental structures of primitive and civilized man; while Piaget demonstrates that a wide range of performances and tasks are isomorphic with the nine groupings of concrete operations. The structures discerned—be they in the realm of folklore or of child reasoning—are viewed as self-regulating, closed, and whole, reflections of the organized human mind. Nothing is more likely to please a structuralist than a demonstration that the behavior of crowds at an athletic event and the behavior of microbes in a diseased region of the body or the globe are reflections of the same mathematical function.

One may discern three principal elements in the structural approach. The *strategic aspect*, demonstrated in our discussion of games, refers to the customary way in which structuralists proceed. The strategy is to focus upon the unconscious infrastructure of a realm, rather than upon its superficial aspects; to look at the relationship between elements rather than at the elements *per se*; to search for an organized system governed by general laws. The guiding principle postulates that meaningful accounts of structures can be given; that structures really exist in the behaviors under observation and are not merely the product of the analyst's imagination; that structures in disparate realms will ultimately be related, perhaps by a meta-theory of structures unifying the Babel of disciplines which plague contemporary social science. The level at which one searches for structure is a matter of crucial importance; both Lévi-Strauss and Piaget see it as an intermediary—Piaget, between the nervous system and conscious behavior; Lévi-Strauss, between the economic infrastructure and the ideological superstructure.

The *formal aspect* involves the structuralist use of mathematics and related disciplines. Once the elements of a structure have been isolated, the aim (not always realized) is to formalize all relationships through some sort of logical model or system. Particularly influential is the work of the anonymous school of French mathematicians that signs itself "N. Bourbaki," which has daringly set out the three basic or "mother" structures giving rise to all mathematics. One of these structures—the algebraic group—has particularly inspired structuralists of a formalistic bent, and structuralists in general are ever watchful for new mathematical tools.

At the same time that structuralists look to mathematics, they are also drawn to biological science. The *organismic aspect* reflects a belief that structures are not a pretty invention of man or machine, but rather a reflection of the biological properties of organisms. Even as a biological organism is viewed as a totality whose parts are integrated into a hierarchical whole, so structures are seen as biological wholes, with a dynamic as well as a static aspect to them. Any change in an organism will affect all the parts; no aspect of a structure can be altered without affecting the entire structure; each whole contains parts and is itself part of a larger whole. Following the biological motif, the organismic aspect of structuralism stresses the integration of related facts; the perception of relations rather than absolute properties; the centrality of configurations and Gestalten. Human products are thought to reflect man's biological, rather than mechanical, nature; structural principles reflect the nature of the brain and of human psychological functioning; all biological functions are assumed to have meaning. Even though the organismic aspect is often implicit rather than explicit, appreciation of structuralism is enhanced by the knowledge that Piaget was trained as a biologist, and that Lévi-Strauss was deeply influenced by the work of the naturalist D'Arcy Thompson on growth and form, and by the school of Gestalt psychology.

By speaking thus of "aspects" of structuralism, I have sought to underline that there is no "essence," or unique definition, of structuralism. Nor is there a single method of approach: Piaget and Lévi-Strauss will usually tackle problems in a different way each time, although they do have a few methods that might be termed characteristic; others under the structuralist umbrella will embrace yet other techniques. The justification for speaking of a single movement inheres in the fact of a group of workers having arrived at certain tacit understandings and procedures which yield analyses of a related sort and may constitute a new paradigm in the social sciences. They look for organized totalities which may be said to exist at a level between the biological and the logical; they seek to express in formal terms the relations which govern the behavior of organisms; they focus on questions and domains which seem on an intuitive basis to have coherence and to be central in human experience. It is unnecessary (and would be misleading) to claim that the structuralists have achieved their ambitious goals; even the two men under discussion here frequently change their views, seldom concur completely on an interpretation, and often proceed in divergent ways. Yet structuralism is worthy of study, and potentially of great significance, I feel, 'because its foremost practitioners have sensed which questions need to be asked, have developed methods which significantly elucidate these questions, and can be seen as laying the groundwork for a more completely integrated social science.

Because they most fully reflect the development and the aims of the structuralist movement, I have chosen to focus on the writings and achievements of Lévi-Strauss and Piaget. These thinkers stand out because they have so tenaciously and productively adhered to the three strains in structuralism cited above. Both men embody the structuralist desire to capture the biological properties of the human mind and its processes in formal logical models through careful attention to underlying properties of behavior and institutions.

Thus far I have considered the two men individually. Now, however, I propose to make a comparison of their work and ideas, taking into account both their similarities and their differences. As regards the former, they appear to have embarked on similar investigations and to have achieved considerable agreement and complementarity on major issues in the realm of cognition. The differences between them, while also significant, lie in areas other than is usually supposed, and are themselves illuminating for the study of the human mind.

2. A COMPARISON OF PIAGET AND LÉVI-STRAUSS

What, then, are the similarities between Piaget and Lévi-Strauss? Both men were born in the shadows of 1900, both were precocious students, both rejected the illusions of philosophy while finding themselves increasingly taken with the formal elegance of mathematics and linguistics. Their scholarly careers have parallels as well: each man traveled unexplored paths, working initially in isolation, examining the relations among various biological and mathematical disciplines, inspiring much abuse and misunderstanding, as well as a small group of devotees who understand well. Both men have finally achieved international eminence, though they are somewhat mistrusted by colleagues of the older generation, and they epitomize for many the Continental approach to psychology and anthropology.

Yet all these biographical and circumstantial considerations are (relatively) insignificant compared to the intellectual or philosophical parallels in their lives and careers. For, first, Piaget and Lévi-Strauss are offshoots of the same stem in that they are both deeply steeped in the French intellectual tradition, and have accepted its problems as their problems; and second, they have both created original and powerful new methods for probing the nature of thought, language, and the human condition. Consistent with the trend toward an empirical approach in examining cognition, each has chosen for investigation a group the study of which promises to shed light on humanity as a whole: Piaget has looked to children of various ages, Lévi-Strauss to primitives of diverse cultures. In so doing, they carry on the work of Darwin and Freud, who helped define and delimit the human condition by specifying the relationships between man and animal, sickness and health. They have searched for the significant detail in the commonplace, the revealing link between seemingly disparate data, the apt example or pregnant metaphor which can illuminate a hitherto obscure area. With one eye set on the biological nature of man, the other on the logical nature of all thought, they have forged ahead in detailed observations and investigations of human beings, and then have stepped back, searched for underlying structures, and put forth their best guesses as to the ultimate nature of the mind. In sum, the thrust of their inquiries, the methods they have evolved, and their provisional findings have all been strikingly similar.

Piaget and Lévi-Strauss have sought to prove that the range of human cognition is not unlimited: human knowledge can be studied and known just because it has specific ascertainable structural properties. Piaget has proposed three broad stages of human development and has claimed that a small number of logical-mathematical formulations embraces the nature of each. Given these demonstrations, a plethora of observations and test data can be organized, an underlying structure postulated, the role of actions, coordinations, operations, and structured wholes spelled out. Lévi-Strauss, for his part, has insisted even more explicitly that the forms of human thought are limited and specifiable. Relying heavily on an analogy with structural linguistics, he has uncovered evidence of a basic mental propensity to think in opposites and contrasts, to extract perceptual information from the environment

along certain predetermined lines, and to freeze and combine these percepts in classifying, naming, and mythic
systems. These systems can be related to their variants
through a series of ordered transformations, expressible in
mathematical forms which themselves exemplify human
thought processes.

Our two thinkers, then, share a deep conviction that
mental structures "really" exist, and that some reflection
or manifestation of them—describable in mathematical
and logical terms—will eventually be discovered in the
human brain and nervous system. Both men lay strong
stress in this connection on "group" functions and the
logical system of the propositional calculus, believing that
it is these two types of mathematical constructions that
are most likely to prove descriptive of the workings of
the central nervous system; and they speak approvingly of
biologists and mathematicians who have done work along
these lines. By this profound faith—one perhaps not
entirely justified by current evidence—that mathematical
constructs are a key to the understanding of human cognition, one sees that in Piaget and Lévi-Strauss the spirit
of Descartes lives on.

Were the two men in substantial agreement on all outstanding issues, such a state of affairs would be interesting,
but might render careful study of both superfluous. One
need not master the evolutionary arguments of both Darwin and Wallace, since Darwin stated their shared ideas
with such thoroughness and competence. It happens, however, that there are also strong divergences between Piaget
and Lévi-Strauss. These differences make it worthwhile
to return to their formulations once more, in an attempt
either to discern the stronger position or to reconcile
differences. We shall look at some questions which have
intrigued social scientists, examine the views of each man,
and then assess the amount of disagreement or potential
convergence.

When one is attempting to solve a problem, an assortment of mental processes undoubtedly occur. We tend to use the blanket term "thought" to refer to these processes, but the identity of the components of thinking has been heatedly debated by philosophers and scientists. Perhaps most controversial is the role played by language in thought. Some observers have believed that all thought is simply a reflection of language: the thinker is speaking aloud or to himself and in either case his solution emerges from words, their interrelations, and their referents. Growing out of this position is a belief that language determines the subject matter about which one thinks as well as the way one thinks about it; in this case it follows that individuals who live in cultures with widely different languages will never be able to communicate with one another, since their words and concepts, the members of different species, cannot be mapped onto one another.

The opposite view states that language or speech is, at best, one of many components which enter into the thinking process. Chimpanzees can solve problems involving tool use, maze-running, or complex visual discriminations; since they lack language, but evidently can think, they must be using images, gestures, and assorted kinesthetic cues which should be regarded equally as vehicles of thought. Champions of this view also question the depth of differences between languages. All speakers, they feel, are dealing with the same world of sounds, colors, and sights; although languages may well slice up the verbal world in somewhat different ways, such differences are superficial compared to the wealth of common sensory and motor experience.

At first glance, Piaget and Lévi-Strauss seem to take opposite positions on the relationship between language and thought. In his early writings, Piaget stressed the contributions which language made to thinking. He asked questions in words and carefully noted children's verbal retorts; a decline in the "coefficient of egocentrism" was seen as an index of intellectual advance. His observations of his own infants convinced him, however, that the key to thought and intelligence lay not in language and speech but rather in action. An individual's intellectual level was determined by the range of actions he could perform on the world, the extent of coordination among actions, the degree to which these actions could be performed implicitly or mentally as "operations." More recently, Piaget has underscored the centrality of action by arguing that the child's operational level determines his use of language rather than the reverse. He enthusiastically cites studies which demonstrate that the congenitally deaf, who presumably have no access to language as we know it, are capable of operational thought because they have acquired knowledge through action. And with even greater exuberance he dwells on the research of his colleague, Hermine Sinclair-de-Zwart, who has studied the language used by children solving conservation problems.

Sinclair found that preoperational children spoke of objects in terms of absolute qualities: "the big one," "the little one," etc. Even when attempts were made to alter such usage, to get preoperational subjects to use the comparative forms spontaneously embraced by operational children (e.g., "longer than but thinner than"), only a slight trend toward conservation responses was noted. Once, however, the child's operational level had changed —presumably because the crucial actions of reversing, negating, and compensating had coalesced into a structured whole—his language became permeated with relational terms. Piaget interprets these findings as a strong demonstration that language makes at best only a small contribution to thought, that for the most part the reverse is the case, i.e., operational level determines the use and level of language. Indeed, Piaget speaks of the "prelogic" inherent in language usage: a child may appear to be thinking logically because he uses certain expressions like "because," "if . . . then," etc.; but careful investigation may reveal that such terms are actually being employed in a prelogical way.

Piaget, then, has come to minimize the role of language in thought. The thrust of Lévi-Strauss's work, however, has been in the opposite direction. Lévi-Strauss not only takes his lead from the structural linguists but attributes to language a determining role in thought. One probes the minds and cognitive structures of primitive peoples by noting their naming and classifying systems; one discerns the basis of kinship, customs, art, and social organization through a determination of the *codes* governing these realms. Mechanisms which presumably underlie language use—alertness to opposites, sensitivity to distinctive features, capacity to relate units to one another, or transform utterances—are also posited as the basic components of thought. Indeed, Lévi-Strauss has remarked, with characteristic sweep, that "Language, an unreflecting totalization, is human reason which has its reasons . . . of which man knows nothing."

Here, then, appears to be a clear dispute regarding the constituents of thought, with Piaget starting from action and denigrating language, Lévi-Strauss proceeding from language and minimizing the significance of specific behavioral acts. Final resolution of this conflict must wait upon an overview of both systems; but it is worth pointing out that at least part of the disagreement may be terminological rather than substantive.

Whereas Piaget inveighs against language, and Lévi-Strauss finds it the source of all reason, neither man, when confronted with a given specimen of language, is particularly concerned with the manner in which the speaker has expressed himself—his syntax, style, vocabulary choices, and the like. Lévi-Strauss examines all variants of a myth that are available, while Piaget poses as many questions, in as many forms, as is practicable. Like Freud, both men pay scant attention to the manifest content of the given message; they are interested not in who did what or how, but rather in the nature of the reasoning or operations at a level below overt language. In studying the responses of a child, Piaget picks out the significant underlying propositions, which he can then express in the logical parlance of p's and q's. The mental actions reflected in the protocol are a series of operations performed on words, which themselves represent actual or potential acts upon the environment. Piaget concedes that at the level of formal operations ordinary language is necessary, since such operations require expression in natural or logical language. The capacity to deal with possibilities and with hypothetico-deductive reasoning depends upon language use; and so, as one advances beyond concrete operations, language does come to play more of a determining role.

Lévi-Strauss, even more than Piaget, ignores the manifest message in his search for the principal propositions underlying it. These propositions are, of course, expressed in language but, as with Piaget, Lévi-Strauss is interested in the referent of the language—the experiences and actions reflected in it—rather than in the specific wording. The crucial aspect of the referent lies in the sensory perception of the speaker, the kinds of contrasts and dichotomies he discerns in the world, as well as the logical bifurcations he imposes on it. Such divisions of the experiential flux are fundamental in nature, being imposed by the intrinsic workings of the brain, while the specific discriminations made in a given culture are accidents of environment. Percepts are organized, *bricoleur*-fashion, into classificatory and mythic systems which are necessarily linguistic. Obviously, language is important in transmitting these systems to successive generations; but the language itself is a reflection of what the individual has perceived in the world of objects and persons because of psychological processes common to both perception and language. Language is attractive to the student of thought because of its universality and availability, rather than its uniquely faithful mirroring of the cognitive process. Thus, Lévi-Strauss's position is, at most, a diluted version of the Whorf-Sapir hypothesis, which would confer upon the actual categories of the language a determining role in the thought processes of individual speakers.

Examined more closely, then, the dispute over relationships between language and thought seems much less dramatic. Both men are really interested in a level beneath the language that is spoken or heard—in the actions or percepts reflected in language. These actions and percepts, in turn, are significant because the mind is constructed in a specific way. It is not surprising that Lévi-Strauss should have a less than total commitment to literal language, given his description of himself as thinking not in words but in impulses, feelings, tensions, and pulls. Furthermore, his relative de-emphasis of a linguistic model in his later work, in favor of a model constructed after music, may be viewed as a tacit admission that language cannot account for all of thought. The indicated conclusion, then, is that Lévi-Strauss's greater claims about the role of language in thought simply reflect a broader view of what might be considered "language," while Piaget's minimizing of the role of language in thought results from a stricter definition of language (as distinct from its underlying operations).

Ever since the travels of explorers and conquistadors first revealed a dispersion of humans across the globe, there has been an abiding interest in whether individuals from wholly alien cultures possess the same mental processes, follow the same pattern of mental development, attain the same intellectual level. While agreement on definitions has been infrequent, this has not stopped observers from speculating about the mind of Civilized Man, the mind of Primitive Man, the degree of disparity between these idealizations. Dating back to the Biblical rejection of the barbaric Philistines and reaching forward to modern controversies on race and I.Q., the question of commonalities of thought among different groups has continued to perplex and to fascinate. And the mind of the primitive has seemed a particularly attractive subject for study because, on the one hand, he appears to subscribe to outlandish customs and superstitions, while, on the other, he is capable of astonishing feats of navigation, calculation, and artistry.

In their views of the minds of primitive and Western man, Piaget and Lévi-Strauss once again appear to differ. In his early work, Piaget drew explicit analogies between the reasoning of children and of primitive peoples. Both, he said, exhibited in their thinking animism, artificialism, realism, and other irrational mergings between aspects of the environment and their own thought processes. This view, understandably enough, drew heavy fire from Lévi-Strauss in *The Elementary Structures of Kinship;* in it he maintained that the five-year-old's thought was qualitatively similar to that of the adult's, since both, for example, perceived the world in terms of opposition and contrasts. Just as Piaget had relied heavily on Lévy-Bruhl's view of the primitive, Lévi-Strauss drew extensively on the work of Susan Isaacs, a contemporary of Piaget's, who had found wisdom in the words and acts of kindergarteners. Lévi-Strauss argued that the content of what children say may reflect insufficient familiarity with the surrounding culture but that their *forms* of reasoning are like those of adults. The mind is programmed to reason in certain ways, but it takes time to become acquainted with the elements of one's environment, knowledge of which can not be preprogrammed. Lévi-Strauss drew parallels between the Western view of primitives as children, and primitives' view of Westerners as children—a comparison based in each case on the failure of both the strangers and the group's own children to have assimilated the culture of the adults. The inference, he indicated, is that for children as for foreigners this lack of assimilation is due to the strangeness of the environment rather than to intellectual deficiencies.

Again we appear to be witnessing a direct conflict between Piaget and Lévi-Strauss on the relationship between child, primitive, and adult thought. Yet, it is striking how both men have modified their positions since their early writings. Consistent with his de-emphasis of verbal expression, Piaget now declines to speculate about the relationship between primitive and child thought, though he hazards a guess that primitive tribes may not advance beyond concrete operations. He is content to leave to empirical research, however, the task of determining just how distinctive the primitive mind may be.

For his part, Lévi-Strauss no longer draws close analogies between five-year-olds and adults, and has allowed that there are two kinds of science, the science of the concrete and Western science. The science of the concrete seems to be roughly equivalent to concrete operations: the primitive is able to deal systematically with the objects and percepts of his environment but restricts his concern to their manifest, surface qualities. In this he is different from the Westerner, whose science focuses upon underlying structures and offers classifications and explanations at a more abstract level. Lévi-Strauss still claims that the two sciences differ more in content than in kind; he would probably deny the existence of intellectual operations which Western man but not the primitive can perform.

If we wish to test the notion that the primitive can reason like the Western formal operator, it seems sensible to focus upon the primitive's mythmaking, since his division of the natural environment into elements which smell or look alike seems like a manifestation of concrete-operational thinking. In making and relating myths, the primitive is dealing with verbal propositions rather than with concrete objects, and is operating entirely on the level of ideas, rather than with the physical manipulation of material reality. It should be possible to examine myths and to see whether one can find in them the same forms of logical operations as Piaget finds in the protocols and systematic actions of his adolescent subjects.

Once one starts to examine the myths, however, a serious problem arises. It may very well be, as Lévi-Strauss claims, that myths are replete with examples of hypothetico-deductive reasoning or illustrations of the logical calculus. The myths, however, are the products of thousands of years of telling, borrowing, and retelling: when an individual relates a myth, he is not constructing it on its own; he is transmitting a product gradually built by countless individuals over a long period of time. One must question whether these two activities—solving a problem by one-self in the laboratory or relating a myth which belongs to the culture—are at all equivalent as tasks, and the answer is clearly that they are not. Thus, an impasse is reached on the question of the intellectual level of primitive thought.

At present, the relationship between primitive and modern thought remains an open question, and numerous psychologists and "cognitive anthropologists" are in the field trying to get answers to it in the only conceivable way—by testing individuals from different cultures on various problems and tasks and noting their level of performance. So far, the evidence suggests that Piaget has a stronger case: concrete operations seem to take longer to develop in primitive than in Western cultures and are possibly not reached at all in certain of them; formal operations have been seldom studied and are difficult to find evidence for in the bush. But the difficulty involved in all such investigations should not be minimized. The testing situation is a familiar one to children in a technological society; it is part of their (concrete) reality. The materials used and the verbal interrogation methods pose no problem. On the other hand, the whole entourage of experimental personnel and equipment is alien to the more primitive tribes; radical adjustments may be necessary before a study can be regarded as a routine affair and before the experimenter, who almost always works through an interpreter, can convey what he is looking for.

Thus, social scientists still debate whether true cross-cultural tests on Piagetian tasks are possible, particularly in milieux where there is no schooling. It has already been found, for example, that primitives perform at higher operational levels when the materials and actions are familiar and meaningful. They can count potatoes more readily than poker chips; if they are farmers, they are more likely to exhibit understanding of the conservation of liquids if they can pour themselves than if the experimenters do the pouring. One easy conclusion is that primitives are restricted to "concrete" materials and hence not capable of higher forms of abstraction. But it is always possible that within their own society they do practice high-level abstraction; it is also possible that if tasks analogous to those of Piaget were put to Western children in a setting equally bizarre to them—an initiation rite, say—they might fail at those tasks. Still, before one concludes that the intellectual operations used by both groups are identical, it seems reasonable to demand that a primitive himself solve some logical problem rather than merely repeating a tale he has learned at his parents' feet.

In any event, it may safely be said that, from what may have appeared irreconcilable differences, Piaget and Lévi-Strauss have moved somewhat closer together. Piaget no longer draws unsupported analogies between children and primitives, while Lévi-Strauss allows that there may be more than one kind of science and no longer glorifies the abilities of five-year-olds. The situation here parallels that regarding the relationship between language and thought: Piaget notes that children and adults focus on different aspects of a situation and interpret events differently, and so concludes that child, primitive, and adult thought are different. Lévi-Strauss claims that what is crucial is the very capacity to perceive contrasts and to interpret events;

since this capacity is found in all human beings, he tends to minimize the distinctiveness of varieties of thought. Similarly, Piaget notes that children and adults have different theories of causality, while Lévi-Strauss stresses that both have adopted causal models of the world. In sum, as regards two classical problems on which they seemed far apart, Piaget and Lévi-Strauss may indeed evince a measure of agreement; and neither man has been proved clearly wrong on either issue. However, clear differences remain between them, most notably in their respective emphases on structure and development and in their treatment of perception and action.

Let us say that one is undertaking a study of the *Leitmotiven* found in the *Ring* cycle of Wagner. One approach would simply be to list all the prominent motifs, to say what they refer to, and then to note how they were sometimes combined. This method resembles the promulgation of a cast of characters, who can be defined before the work begins, and may be said to have an existence outside the work—so that one could, for example, recognize the Valhalla motif even if it occurred in a work by Arnold Schoenberg. How, though, does one come to know that a certain sequence of notes actually stands for Valhalla, when one is listening to the opera without a scorecard? Presumably what takes place is some sort of a gradual correlation process, where one recognizes a theme as having been heard before, and then discovers that it always appears when the scene is set in Valhalla or when some reference to Valhalla has been made. One's apprehension of the theme will also change, depending on the events of the opera and the way in which the theme is used; and if the same configuration of notes should appear in a totally alien setting—say, in a show tune or rock ballad—one would either assume that the use was ironic or that it was totally unrelated to the *Ring* cycle.

The first of these approaches to *Leitmotiven* frequently

characterizes the philosopher, who asserts some sort of a connection between two elements—let $x =$ Valhalla—and then honors this distinction consistently and unfailingly. In contrast, the psychologist, and particularly the developmental psychologist, is not interested in arbitrary connections posited independently of the normal functioning of an organism. Thus, x cannot simply be stated as equivalent to Valhalla; no perceiver can be expected to assume that some connection exists. Rather, the listener must slowly discover the relationship between the series of notes and a specific idea; nor will the relationship ever become frozen, for each fresh encounter with the theme or with the concept of Valhalla will occasion some adjustment in the correlation between the two. This latter approach is often termed the developmental or genetic one, while the approach adopted by philosophers may be thought of as an $a$genetic, structural one.

Piaget has eloquently argued that one begs the question merely by stating that a structure or relationship exists. True, for some definitional or philosophical purposes, this may be adequate; but comprehensive understanding of the nature of a structure can only come about through a careful exploration of its prior evolution and through an appreciation of the direction in which it will continue to evolve. Philosophers for centuries argued about the nature of number, yet came to no agreement. This was because, in Piaget's view, "number" is no single entity or construct, but rather a series of actions and operations, a few of which can be performed by very young children, but most of which await a coordination of schemes only possible at the age of seven or eight. An understanding of number is thus dependent upon an appreciation of its ontogenetic components and a mastery of the process by which they are joined. Similarly, Piaget believes that one cannot comprehend such entities as emotions, laws, or concepts unless one examines their history, which alone accounts for their present form, tentativeness, and flexibility. In an oft-cited formula, Piaget declares that there is no structure which lacks a genesis, and that the process of genesis can only be understood in view of the structure which exists at the beginning and the structures into which it will evolve.

In a sympathetic treatment of Lévi-Strauss, Piaget concedes that the ethnographer has been placed in an impossible position as far as gaining knowledge of genesis is concerned. The early history of primitive peoples is forever closed to him, and as a result he can never know what led up to their myths or customs as currently constituted (though he may be able to make shrewd guesses). But, Piaget emphasizes, the inability to secure developmental or historical evidence about primitive tribes is no license to claim, as some structuralists have been tempted to do, that the knowledge involved in customs or language is innate and that no learning or interaction with the environment is necessary for its unfolding. Such a view runs completely counter to Piaget's orientation, which emphasizes the active role played by subjects in the construction of knowledge and avows that development will not proceed unless various environmental conditions are present. Piaget concludes that the ethnographer had best leave open the question of how the customs he studies have come to develop; the lack of data regarding genesis dooms him ineluctably to an impoverished structural approach.

Piaget does feel, nonetheless, that Lévi-Strauss might receive one lead from the developmental approach: the concept of equilibration. Only a notion of this type, Piaget contends, will enable him to explain why a culture might choose one set of cultural systems rather than another; and the anthropologist should recognize that the collective intellect reflected in such products as myths or kinship systems is a form of social equilibrium resulting from the interplay of individual operations over the course of time. Such a reorientation would remove the ill-considered (to Piaget) bias toward the assumption that all cultural systems are innate—a set programmed into the mind from which each tribe makes its selection—and substitute instead the constructivist view of knowledge which Piaget feels has been shown to be correct.

Lévi-Strauss is understandably sensitive on these issues, since he has emphasized in his own writings the extraordinary difficulties involved in tracing the development of an institution. As a result of these difficulties, he has downgraded the historical approach in ethnology and, more fundamentally, has highlighted the relativity and tentativeness of all historical studies. In the dazzlingly obscure closing chapter of *The Savage Mind,* a lengthy and sharp attack on the dialectical materialism of his polemical rival Jean-Paul Sartre, Lévi-Strauss tries to show that the genetic approach to history is not free of mythmaking. The schoolboy may believe that there is only one account of the American Revolution; but the sophisticated historian must acknowledge that there are many myths of the American Revolution or the Civil War, each of which has maintained a tenacious hold on different segments of the population despite the passage of time. The mere listing of an event and a date is a value-laden act, for one must ask: why choose that event? and why that particular date in the midst of the event? While written records promise a more reliable link to the past than the oral tradition on which primitive tribes must rely, the existence of archives in no sense guarantees an unambiguous determination of what really happened. Indeed, Lévi-Strauss seems to argue that such a quest is inevitably doomed to fall short: we are all victims, to a greater or lesser degree, of various myths, of elements of the past which influence present thought, and the possibility of nonmythic history or histories is forever precluded.

Elsewhere, it is true, Lévi-Strauss does pay lip service to the importance of genetic studies, of investigating the foundations of institutions or societies, and alludes to studies of this kind that he himself has undertaken. However, it seems just to accept his insistence that he is not actually much interested in such explorations. As for Piaget's unsolicited advice, Lévi-Strauss would likely agree with the view that cultural codes reflect the coordination of individual actions; emphasize the technico-economic infrastructure's role in determining which set of codes is adopted; argue that the brain is programmed in a highly specific way with regard to the structures underlying the choices; and throw up his hands at the lack of historical evidence about primitives which might help to answer questions about the development of institutions and codes.

Lévi-Strauss, then, regards a society as a sum of codes, each of which captures the crucial elements of a cultural realm and which can be mapped onto other codes by a series of transforming laws. The forms of the codes are dictated by the structure of the mind, their contents reflect the elements in the environment—the particular flora and fauna, the view of the sky, the technology—and the make-up of man's perceptual apparatus. Lévi-Strauss sometimes calls primitive societies "cold": they are caught up in a timeless void, without history, repeating with predictable variations the same set of practices as their ancestors. They have reached a satisfactory equilibrium, and, so long as they are unaffected by external forces, they will see no need to change or to make a history. Their spot on the Mendeleev chart of codes is fixed. In contrast, modern Western societies are "hot," because they have made constant change a part of their structure and are wedded to such notions as history and progress. Lévi-Strauss leaves little doubt that he himself prefers to see a certain balance between Nature and Culture, the attainment of a state of relative equilibrium. Indeed, he might accuse Piaget of reflecting the Western bias toward change.

In marked contrast, Piaget views society as a group of actors who have reached various points in intellectual development and whose relationship with one another reflects these levels. He allows that a whole society may be moored at a concrete-operational level and would not be surprised to learn that adolescents in primitive societies often progress on their own beyond the level of concrete thinking, only to fall back upon it when their use of formal operations receives no support from their cultural environment. (This hypothesis, if confirmed, would make quick work of any claims that primitives are "innately stupid" or suffer from hereditary limitations preventing an advance beyond concrete operations.) Nonetheless, Piaget insists that man's final level of equilibrium is at the level of formal operations and that, given a supportive society, and the right kinds of questions and materials, a child will naturally equilibrate his thinking there. It may be that a society's reliance on formal thinking will preclude a "cool" culture, since applications of formal operations will lead to further progress or changes in the technico-economic system, and perhaps even to "post-formal" thought. Yet it is also possible that formal-operational thinkers may elect to reject this advanced mode of thinking or to resist its application in realms where it could lead to unwanted further progress (or to regress); such a trend may be discernible in certain pockets of contemporary society.

Piaget remains suspicious of any approach which denies the perpetually ongoing processes of assimilation, accommodation, and equilibration. He might well feel that primitive societies are only "cool" from a distance—that if one knew in which areas to look, one would turn up considerable change over time, both within individuals and within the culture. If there are structures in all societies, as Lévi-Strauss has shown, there must just as surely be geneses in all societies; the fact that dynamic changes are not as easily discernible is more likely a reflection of our own ignorance about where to look than a demonstration that these societies are in fact devoid of genetic evolution. Since continuities between individual and cultural development have already been demonstrated in Western society, we may well expect to find similar continuities in other areas of the world.

As a reflection of their different emphases on structure and development, Piaget and Lévi-Strauss embrace different root metaphors or core concepts in their thinking about thought. Piaget, of course, ties thought to action, and sees the level of thought as a direct reflection of the actions which the child is capable of, either directly, in the case of sensorimotor action, or implicitly, on the level of operational, or representational, thought. His guiding picture of the child attaining knowledge depicts a seeking, exploring individual; the child is continuously acting, and coordinating his actions, until they eventually coalesce into structures which allow reversibility of states and an understanding of these states. If Piaget wanted to study an individual, but could not gain direct access to him, he would ask to see a film of the individual, so that he could witness his various actions in relation to one another. Even in analyzing verbal protocols, Piaget is attempting to ferret out the actions, or the propositions which refer to them, in order to determine the relations of operations obtaining among these actions.

For Lévi-Strauss, the major facet of cognition is the perception of opposites or contrasts in the world. Perception is in a certain sense active, of course—a comatose organism does not perceive. But the physical actions upon the environment which play so central a role in Piaget's thinking are hardly treated at all by Lévi-Strauss. He appears to believe that, as a matter of course, and with little antecedent exploration, the mind will perceive oppositions and contrasts in the environment, and that these will be (and already have been) directly embodied in cultural systems and products. The mind does not "photograph" the environment, it dichotomizes it, building myths and other cultural systems out of the perceived oppositions. Lévi-Strauss does not require films of natives engaged in activity in order to assess their intellectual structures; records of their myths, examples of their artworks, accounts of their kinship systems (whether or not the regulations are in fact followed), snapshots of their village, form the bases of his analysis. In his less-guarded moments, Lévi-Strauss has even suggested that he can know the mind of any other person simply by exploring his own. This Cartesian conceit is epitomized in his remark:

> If the final aim of anthropology is to contribute to a better knowledge of objectified thought and its mechanisms, it is in the last resort immaterial whether the thought processes of the South American Indians take shape through the medium of my own thought or whether mine take place through the medium of theirs.

That he is far less concerned with the active "epistemic" subject is also borne out in his companion comment that

> I therefore claim to show, not how men think in myths, but how myths operate without their being aware of the fact.

Although one might be able to translate this view into Piagetian operational language, the intentions of both men would be distorted by so doing. The possibility emerges here that Piaget and Lévi-Strauss, despite their unmistakable continuities, on the one hand, and intermittent disagreements, on the other, are engaged in complementary rather than either identical or opposing missions. Piaget's route to the universals of thought takes him to the behaviors of individual subjects at different times in their developmental trajectory, whereas Lévi-Strauss's path is through the cultural (languagelike) codes of various primitive societies as they have functioned at a given moment in time or throughout human history. The kinds of thought in which the two theorists are respectively interested are also somewhat different, and should be specified if our comparison is to be comprehensive.

Piaget has deliberately restricted his investigation to

logical reasoning. He is interested in the development of science and in scientific thought; as for the creative imagination, he candidly remarks that "It is a magnificent subject which remains to be investigated." He views play, fantasy, and imitative role-playing as unintelligent, insufficiently adapted behaviors (play being the preponderance of assimilation over accommodation, imitation the preponderance of accommodation over assimilation) which gradually disappear as intelligent (read "scientific") thought gains in ascendancy. The content of the child's area of study is irrelevant: the task of exploring the principle of seriation or conservation involves identical mechanisms, whether it happens to be concerned with pebbles, rocks, balls, coins, or beads. Indeed, Piaget's aim in his experiments is, disregarding particular content, to focus exclusively on the form—the coordination of actions—of the reasoning process.

Lévi-Strauss, by contrast, is not particularly interested in scientific reasoning, except as it figures in the concrete classifications of the primitive. If anything, he wants to reduce rather than explore differences between what he and the myth-telling savage are doing. When he admits that he is attracted to primitive thought in part because he finds a generous dose of it in his own mind (and in the mind of Bergson), he is acting no differently in principle from Piaget, who has obviously identified from an early age with the scientific community. Although Lévi-Strauss might not explicitly acknowledge an interest in the structure underlying aesthetic perception, he clearly is intrigued by the logical aspects of the qualitative realm. Since he dwells on qualities—raw/cooked, hot/cold, noisy/silent, jagged, mossy, full—and on their interrelations, he finds himself in a paradoxical epistemological position. On the one hand, as an aspiring formalist, one interested in the discovery of laws of thought, he wants to probe beneath qualities to the logical algebra which governs their use. Yet, on the other, intent upon studying the particular configuration of qualities in each society, he cannot treat all qualities as interchangeable. To say that the mind contrasts qualities a and b, or that one myth is transformed into another by a negative operation, is to make a statement that is devoid of interest in qualitative terms. It is vital for Lévi-Strauss's theory that a primitive be found preoccupied with rawness and cookedness rather than, say, three-pointedness and six-pointedness; an interest in such dimensions as temperature and cuisine is symptomatic of those questions about, and qualities of, the nature of man and culture thought to be most central in all minds. Important as it is for Lévi-Strauss that the mind perceives oppositions, fortunate as it is that the operations can be described abstractly, it is equally crucial that the mind focuses on specific qualities such as heat and cookedness. Any comprehensive theory of mind, and certainly his theory, must not lose sight of either element.

Piaget's and Lévi-Strauss's notions of thought emerge most clearly in the formal models and diagrams which populate their works. Piaget reduces all the reasoning of his subjects en route to the stage of formal operations to sixteen propositions of binary logic and to a *Viergruppe* containing four operations. This forms the core of his demonstration, and whether it is based on problems involving billiards, chemicals, or pendulums is irrelevant. Lévi-Strauss nearly always includes in his charts the specific qualities discerned by the primitive. That is necessary, for the specific quality, as well as its logical relations to other properties, is of cardinal significance.

If, in response to one of Piaget's test problems, a child suggests the use of a knife to cut an apple into parts, the particular utensil recommended and the particular object cut are of minimal import. What Piaget focuses on is the action of cutting and other subsequent actions involving the materials, such as joining, clustering, dividing, adding.

The fact that a number of actions have occurred, and the nature of the relationships between these actions, are paramount.

On the other hand, if a character in a myth knifes another, it is insufficient merely to note that there has been an action involving one object. Nor can one equate these actions and objects with any other set and simply notate them with identical symbols; reducing experience to arbitrary signs results in too great an impoverishment. Rather, "knifing" has a set of associations quite distinct from shooting or burning alive and implies an instrument with a cold, metallic blade, a thrust, the subsequent shriek of pain, effusion of blood, feelings of triumph, betrayal, or loss. The effect, effectiveness, and significance of a myth or rite depend on the term "knifing" (or, possibly, on a synonym like "stabbing"), and its accompanying cluster of social implications, religious overtones, economic references, and secondary allusions to cuisine, technology, and magic. Exquisitely sensitive to this aspect, Lévi-Strauss has sought to include the numerous "distinctive features" of such terms in those intricate diagrams and equations which outline the structure of a myth. As the mere mention of "knifing" cannot always convey the qualities implicit in the word, explicit reference to its dimensions and an exploration of their possible permutations do much to vivify the concept. If Piaget's descriptions stimulate one to take out a paper and pencil in order to check the logical validity of the child's reasoning process, Lévi-Strauss's descriptions will more likely cause one to "relive" the experience of the primitive.

We may conclude, then, that for Piaget the form of reasoning takes clear precedence over the content, whereas in Lévi-Strauss's approach these two aspects of thought are more nearly matched in importance. The consequence of this difference in emphasis is that Piaget's viewpoint is well suited for analyzing scientific reasoning but of limited value for forms of thought which extend into nonrational domains; while Lévi-Strauss's formulation is less useful in the scientific realm, and generally inferior in formal power to Piaget's model, but highly suggestive in the realms of qualities, art, and intuitions. Lévi-Strauss's closeness to ordinary language is epitomized in this difference: just as he finds language a more appropriate model for thought than does Piaget, so, too, the kinds of analyses in which he engages are tied to the particular nuances of language. Myths are intimately involved with language, both the particular properties which characterize ordinary language (sets of opposites, distinctive features, a certain freedom in translation) and those features which distinguish it from formal mathematical languages (lack of precise denotation, unsuitability for translation into a different symbol system) and from action (lack of reversibility). Lévi-Strauss's analysis comes closer to capturing the distinctive properties of those forms of reasoning which are languagelike, while it is less germane to forms which do not depend upon natural language.

Our comparison above has pointed up differences between the theories of Lévi-Strauss and Piaget, though perhaps not in those areas where they might have been anticipated. Whereas a preliminary review indicated vast disagreement on the relationship between thought and language, and between primitive and scientific thought, a more careful analysis has suggested a fair degree of agreement and tentativeness on the part of both men. On the other hand, a surprising degree of complementarity of perspectives has emerged in two other areas: Piaget has emerged as a staunch defender of the structural-developmental approach, one whose root metaphor for intelligent thought is *action;* Lévi-Strauss is equally committed to an agenetic structural approach, and finds *perception* to be the most appropriate model for intelligent thought. An important question now arises: are these two approaches merely complementary, in the sense that one can put them together to make a whole; are they antagonistic to one another, one precluding the other; or is a productive synthesis possible? I find no reason to believe that the two approaches exclude one another. Indeed, from nearly every perspective except the most fine-grained analysis, Lévi-Strauss and Piaget appear as engaged in highly similar pursuits. The complementary nature of their positions is difficult to deny, but merely to say that they sum up to a whole is to reject the more challenging job of an attempted synthesis. One can say that Freud and Marx, or Freud and Darwin, or indeed, any other two great figures, are complementary to one another and that their approaches should be combined; but it takes effort and evidence, rather than exhortation, to bring about such rapprochements. I shall not pretend to execute the grand synthesis, but, picking up clues from recent work in linguistics, and drawing on my own research, I shall essay some proposals concerning possibilities for convergence of Piaget's and Lévi-Strauss's positions.

3. NOTES TOWARD A SYNTHESIS

Inasmuch as linguistics has traditionally served as both an impetus and an exemplar for advances in the social sciences, it is not surprising that the great linguist Roman Jakobson was one of the first individuals to sense points of contact between the structural approach and the developmental approach. In 1941, Jakobson published *Child Language Aphasia and Phonological Universals,* a comprehensive monograph in which he sought to demonstrate that the same laws describe both the acquisition of language by the child and its dissolution in the adult suffering from brain damage. He began by noting that in infancy every normal child will babble all manner of sounds, but that a time will come when his babbling will cease and future sounds will unfold according to the principle of "maximal contrast." (Explanation of this remarkable fact practically demands a structural orientation.) At the first stage of language development proper, the acquisition of vowels begins with a wide vowel, that of consonants with a forward articulated stop. In other words, *a* will be the first vowel and a sound produced by the lips, *p* or *b*, the first consonant, the contrast being the simplest and greatest possible—total obstruction, *p* or *b*, followed by unfettered openness, *a*, of the vocal apparatus.

The first consonantal opposition—nasal vs. oral stops (*mama/papa*) emerges next in child language, then the opposition of labials and dentals (*papa/tata* and *mama/ nana*), these comprising the minimal consonantal system for all languages of the world. These consonantal oppositions are followed in turn by the first vocalic opposition— a more narrow vowel being opposed to a wider one (*pipi/ papa*). Jakobson adds:

> . . . if we now consider those acquisitions of the child's consonantal or vocalic system which exceed the minimum already discussed, a fact of great importance comes to light—the amazingly exact agreement between the chronological succession of these acquisitions and the general laws of irreversible solidarity which govern the synchrony of all the languages of the world.

The evolution of sounds continues to follow universal "laws of solidarity": no child or language can have fricatives until it has stops. These laws of solidarity are also said to be panchronic—i.e., they obtain at every stage in all languages and dissolve in reverse order in cases of speech pathology ranging from dream talk to severe aphasia.

Jakobson's study is of particular interest because, unlike others in structural linguistics, it is oriented toward developmental and psychological questions. He comments explicitly on this connection:

> . . . this system is by its very nature closely related to those stratified phenomena which modern psychology uncovers in

the different areas of the realm of the mind. Development proceeds from an undifferentiated original condition to a greater differentiation and separation. New additions are superimposed on earlier ones and dissolution begins with the higher strata.

This development from the simple and undifferentiated to the differentiated and stratified, it will be noted, reflects a cardinal principle in the work of Piaget.

While it is unnecessary to follow here the full course of the evolution of child language, one issue raised by Jakobson has especial suggestiveness for our efforts at synthesis. On the basis of reports that speech sounds are perceived by many individuals as possessing, like visual sensations, degrees of lightness or darkness, chromatism or achromatism, Jakobson explores the relationship between the perception of sound and that of light. He suggests that the most productive way to view auditory stimuli in this context is to consider vowels as varying in chromatic quality and consonants in "lightness" and "darkness," vowels being analogous to the varied colors of the spectrum, consonants to the hueless gray series. Chromatism thus becomes the specific phenomenal feature of vowels, while consonants, without marked chromatisms, become the dimension of light and darkness, with labials (b, m) having a dark, and dentals (d, t) a light, quality. After reviewing a mass of supporting data, Jakobson concludes that persons capable of such synesthetic perception (phenomenal experience in a sensory modality other than the one stimulated) tend to make similar sound/light associations, so that synesthetic perception may be seen as nonarbitrary, regular, and consistent. The vowels o and u are linked to the specifically dark colors, and e and i to specifically light colors; further, more chromatic vowels are linked to variegated colors (a with red, for example) and u and i are connected to the least variegated colors. Jakobson closes by remarking that "the development of the color 'instinct' (and its pathological disturbances) provides striking analogies to the development and dissolution of the phonological system"—although he leaves it to Lévi-Strauss to cite another scientist's bold claim that "there probably exists in the human brain a map of colors, part of which is similar topologically to a map of sound frequencies there."

In addition to its intrinsic interest and argumentative force, Jakobson's discussion in *Child Language Aphasia* is relevant here for two principal reasons. First, he demonstrates the possibility for a developmental analysis in a complete, isolated system such as language. Indeed, his analysis of changes over time proves very revealing about language and thus belies reservations voiced by earlier linguists about the fruitfulness of such investigations. Second, Jakobson shows that language learning need not be considered in isolation from other kinds of psychological activity. In fact, he suggests that the same principles which appear at work in the perception of language also influence perception in the visual realm—and, by extension, in other sensory and cognitive domains as well.

Jakobson appears to have demonstrated, then, that structural and developmental approaches can be productively combined. From structural linguistics, he draws the approach of concentration on a specifiable code and analysis in terms of binary opposition and distinctive features; from developmental psychology, he takes the notion of differentiation and integration, the idea of structured stages, the notions of progression and regression according to specifiable principles. His concept of irreversible solidarity embodies an important principle of developmental psychology; that the attainment of an advanced stage necessarily implies that one has passed through the earlier stages.

Although Jakobson has clearly demonstrated the possibility for a combined structural-developmental analysis in a languagelike realm, a staunch Piagetian might still have reservations about the relevance of this work to cognitive development. It might be argued, for example, that the phonology of language is only a very limited area, whereas Piaget has attempted to ferret out principles which govern all of thought. This kind of argument loses its force, however, when two additional considerations are taken into account. First of all, as we have already suggested, it is misleading to suggest that Piaget has focused upon all forms of cognition; rather, he has taken as his preserve the realm of Western scientific thought, which, however crucial it may seem today, does not represent with any fidelity or comprehensiveness the forms of thought valued in other cultures or during other periods. (In contrast, human language is of course a universal phenomenon and, as Lévi-Strauss has shown, is integrally involved with forms of thought found throughout the globe.) In the second place, Jakobson has not in fact restricted his developmental analysis to the phonological realm of language. In later work, he has outlined the development of six forms of verbal communication, which range from the conative (language expressing wishes) to the metalingual (language referring to language) and the poetic (language which calls attention to itself). Jakobson argues that these, too, unfold in a systematic and regular order, with the later forms of communication dependent upon the stability of the earlier ones. He also allows the environment a far greater role in bringing out the later forms than is the case with phonological evolution, which seems more closely tied to hereditary and physiological factors. Although Jakobson has not, to my knowledge, elaborated on this point, it seems quite likely that these aspects of language depend upon an interaction of the child with other persons in the world, as well as with the codes of his culture, and that they reflect structures akin to those studied by Piaget (e.g., action upon the object, action upon the action, the decline of egocentrism). Whatever differences may remain between language, as broadly viewed by Jakobson, and cognition, as defined by Piaget,

the developmental analysis put forth by the former suggests the possibility of a meaningful synthesis between the
two branches of the structuralist school.

A second area of difference, and potential reconciliation,
centers around Piaget's stress upon actions and his concentration upon operational thought, and Lévi-Strauss's
reciprocal emphasis on perception and the role of distinctive features of objects. These emphases follow logically from the particular realms the two investigators have
respectively elected to explore—actions and operations
being more evident in children's behavior, perceptual
properties and distinctive features in myths and the arts;
yet I feel that each analyst could conceivably have couched
his treatment in the jargon of the other. A slight shift of
focus regarding the work of each man will illustrate the
potential for translation.

In studying the sensorimotor stage, Piaget focuses on
the various actions of the child which eventually coordinate with one another to produce the formation of the
object concept. It seems probable that sensitivity to contrasting qualities plays a constructive role in this stage of
development. The infant acting upon objects perceives
aspects particular to each object and develops schemes
appropriate to these distinctive aspects: edible/nonedible,
graspable/nongraspable. His ultimate definition of an
object may be viewed as a sum of the appropriate actions
which he may perform upon objects, and these in turn rest
upon his prior analysis of the distinctive features of an
object. Similarly, his identity or equivalence judgments—
whch Piaget finds crucial at every stage of development
—naturally involve the consideration of certain features
as defining and others as nondefining; such an analysis is
a perceptual task fixing upon similarities and contrasts.
(For example, at the concrete-operational level an identity
operation involves states identical or equivalent in distinctive features, whereas reversing and compensation
operations comprise permissible transformations or rear-

rangements of distinctive features.) And in regard to a specific domain such as conservation of liquids, the need for a distinctive-feature analysis becomes quite compelling. A child can only become aware that water remains the same in amount irrespective of the shape of its container if he is able to coordinate changes in such properties as the height and width of the water. He must realize that the change in height is compensated for by a change in width, which clearly involves an analysis of the relation of opposition obtaining between distinctive features. To discern features is certainly a sign of flexibility, but there is no reason to believe the flexibility is infinite; rather, the features to which an individual can be sensitive must reflect, in the last analysis, the structure of his perceptual system. Thus, even an analysis which focuses upon actions in the world of objects implicitly acknowledges the role of perception in the recognition and comprehension of these objects.

Correlatively, if Lévi-Strauss or Jakobson were to focus on the relationship of cultural systems to the individual's activities, or on the way in which an individual is able to proceed from one "transform" of a cultural system to another, they might well find an analysis in terms of operations a most appropriate and informative one. Any structural analysis of a scientific or mythic classification in terms of distinctive features would have to take into account, either implicitly or explicitly, alternative ways of classification, the psychological process by which the individual embraces one mode rather than another, the dynamic way in which features are combined and manipulated. Or, if the interest centered upon a kin relationship like the avunculate, the existence of such a system would seem dependent on the individual's capacity to adopt different attitudes toward other individuals and to fit himself into an overall system of attitudes. Such analyses seem most readily and profitably viewed in terms of developing operational structures. Even the naming and classify-

ing systems of primitives, which Lévi-Strauss often presents as if they were cultural givens, involve generative
activity on the part of an individual who is acquiring the
system or on the part of a culture confronted with a new
object or experience to name. Whether these activities
are constructive and open to conscious examination, as
Piaget prefers to view them, or a reflection of unconscious
mental activities, as Lévi-Strauss might describe them,
is less important than the probability that some active,
generative transforming mechanisms are involved in either
case.

The point I wish to make is not that the two approaches
need inevitably merge into one, but that they might well
be consistent with one another. In describing the operation of reversing, Piaget postulates states A and B; that
the person is able to take cognizance of A and B implies
some sensitivity to the defining and distinguishing characteristics of each. By the same token, in speaking of possible
combinations of distinctive features, Jakobson and Lévi-
Strauss suggest that different units may stand in a series
of definable relationships to one another. The way in
which the individual or the society negotiates these relationships may be appropriately formulated in terms of
such operations as identity, compensation, or reversibility.
(Compatibility of the notions of distinctive features and
operations needs to be further explored, but that technical
task is best laid aside until another occasion.)

While we have outlined above the possibilities for reconciliation between the overall approaches, genetic and
agenetic structuralism, and between the analytic terms,
operations and distinctive features, we are still left with
respective predilections for different root metaphors—
Lévi-Strauss committed to perception as central, Piaget
devoted to action as the prime mover. Some of my own
work with young children has suggested that, here as
well, there is much potential for agreement; I will briefly
review some of the evidence on this point.

If one performs a motor activity in front of an infant—
for example, opening and closing the mouth, protruding
and withdrawing a finger—any of a number of results can
follow: the child may ignore the behavior, reproduce it
completely, or reproduce selected aspects of it. A number
of studies of imitation have now indicated that the infant
is particularly sensitive to the "modal" properties of a
behavior. The child will seize upon such aspects as "opening and closing" or "extending and withdrawing," and
will imitate them even when he is still unable to match
the bodily zone appropriately. An open hand may elicit
an open mouth; rhythmic alteration of the finger may
stimulate matching tongue movements. Similarly, when
he views a spectacle in his environment, or hears an unusual sound, the child is likely to become involved with
the display in a bodily manner; he will settle upon the
display's dynamic, or "vectoral," properties—its force,
direction, degree of balance, penetration, rhythm, etc.—
and reproduce these vigorously in his behavior, even while
eliminating aspects closer to the physical properties of the
stimulus but differing in dynamic quality.

I would hypothesize that this sensitivity to "modal" and
"vectoral" properties of the environment, to generalized
aspects of force, direction, rhythm, and action, derives at
least in part from the child's own bodily experience of
these aspects, which reflects, in turn, the activities of which
he is capable. In the course of his daily life, the child
experiences fullness, emptiness, openness, closedness, penetration, withdrawal, regularity, imbalance, and various
degrees of pressure and direction. For reasons we do not
yet understand, he is able very early to extract similar
properties from the perceived environment, and to embody
these properties in his own spontaneous behavior. His
perceptions and actions come together through these distinctive *modes*, which form a bedrock of his experience
and his behavior. The sensitivity to modal/vectoral properties (which cut across sensory modalities and are mani-

fest in both the perceptual and the motoric realm) is, I would suggest further, a necessary antecedent for the use and the comprehension of symbols, and remains fundamental to our cognition in the adult years, though it may to some extent be superseded by more precise (and limiting) methods of classifying, perceiving, and acting. In other words, all of us perform an analysis of external events we observe in terms of their phenomenal openness or penetration, even as we assume analogous attitudes and perspectives in our personal behavior and activities. The scientist strives to eliminate these "subjective" aspects from his published reports, even though they may assist him in his preliminary investigations, while the artist seeks to preserve such general properties in his finished product.

The major structuralists have each made analyses of the sort described just above. In his discussion of play, dreams, and imitative activity, Piaget gives copious examples of the child's sensitivity to these general forms or properties; and, though he points out how they may interfere with operational thought, he recognizes them as a necessary factor in development. It is Piaget's greatest weakness, I believe, that he has not followed through on analysis of the development of these forms of perception and action. Lévi-Strauss and Jakobson, for their part, are centrally involved with such qualities, both as they are reflected in the language which the individual hears and speaks (open/ closed sounds), and as they are embodied in various cultural forms, ranging from social structure (balanced/ disharmonic) to works of art (empty/full, above/below). Indeed, the kind of synesthetic experience which they attribute to the operation of the nervous system may well depend upon a sensitivity to modal properties, which are by their nature cross-sensory, or "inter-modal."

Both branches of structuralism, then, would probably agree that the child processes information of a modal sort, and is sensitive to qualities and their opposites, from a very early age; that these properties are not limited to any particular sensory modality; and that there is some predisposition to retain this kind of bodily involvement in dynamic activity throughout the life cycle. Modal properties, I would submit, undergo a characteristic evolution (e.g., sensitivity to openness and closedness should develop before sensitivity to intrusion and introception) ; they are found universally; and they should emerge in characteristic configurations, depending upon the personal history of the individual and upon environmental influences in the given culture.

Through the concept of modes and vectors, a further synthesis of the work of Piaget and Lévi-Strauss should become possible. The mode may serve as a new "root metaphor" for thought, indissolubly linking the concepts of perception and action. Piaget's emphasis upon actions and objects and Lévi-Strauss's reciprocal stress on properties and features are both encompassed in this formulation. For modes (and vectors) , deeply embedded in the biological makeup of the young organism, constitute the basic developmental matrix out of which more refined behavior and thought evolve; specific qualities result from the combination and mixture of various modes, and operations are the possible relations obtaining among modes. Modes also cut across the division of form and content, for they are formal properties which nonetheless acquire significance and force in the person's subjective experience. Finally, modes serve as a transitional element in the child's development from a sensorimotor operator to an individual whose world is defined in terms of language and other forms of symbolic mediation. Modes serve as the initial referents for cultural symbols like words, and remain as principal referents for more personal kinds of symbols, such as those involved in subjective experience or in the arts. Even as the development of the object concept constitutes the pivotal event in the development of scientific thought, modal perception and activity form a leitmotif for the full range of human development, manifest in the earliest days of childhood, yet persisting in the most intricate and sophisticated encounters with aesthetic objects or with other persons. Standing midway between object and distinctive feature, between perception and action, between art and science, the concept of the mode may serve as a link, tying together principal orientations in the study of mind.

I have long felt that convergence of structuralist methods would be greatly facilitated if an area could be found in which units could be isolated and a clear end-state propounded. I have now proposed that "modes" may be the possible units for such an analysis, and have implied that the artistic development and mastery might be a suitable end-state. One can outline with some precision the end-state of artistic development, the kinds of skills and capacities a talented artist or performer—or connoisseur—must have. There should be stages en route to this end-state, for example, appreciation of the concept of representation or the capacity to ignore dominant "figures" in an array and attend instead to stylistic or expressive features. Piagetian methods could be brought to bear in devising tasks for children of different ages and in assessing their degree of comprehension and achievement. And Lévi-Strauss could make a singular contribution in this regard, for it is in his work, more than in that of any other contemporary thinker, that one finds clues as to the building blocks of aesthetic creation and creativity: the kinds of modal qualities, perceptual sensory aspects which are salient to all people and which assume a significant place in the myths, customs, and art objects of diverse cultures. Wedding Lévi-Strauss's sensitivity to these universal categories of phenomenal experience to Piaget's careful methods of clinical investigation offers hope for a structural approach which can shed light on the range of human intellectual power and creative activities in diverse cultures. The fact that it is so difficult to contrast the science and philosophy of different cultures, yet natural and suggestive to compare their paintings, music, or myths, gives further impetus to such an undertaking. As both men, dating back to their earliest years, have maintained an interest in humanistic studies, and have been intrigued by the operation of irrationality and affect in human life, while maintaining a steady commitment to scentific methods and procedures, such a study would help to achieve goals close to the hearts of both: the integration of the social sciences, the specification of characteristically human forms of thought, the inclusion of the full range of content to which they refer. Indeed, the intense curiosity which both men exhibit toward the "mysteries of musical creation" suggest that this domain would be a particularly promising one to investigate, one that might perhaps even lead to a synthesis of the structural and developmental approaches.

Both of our thinkers have revealed on occasion the full vista of their aspirations in the sciences. Lévi-Strauss has indicated his belief that structures are not merely the invention of the analyst, that they really exist in the culture, and in the minds of the members of that culture, because of the nature of man's nervous system and his genetic endowment. Indeed, Lévi-Strauss has, of late, even drawn the curtain which separated Nature and Culture, indicating that in the last analysis, Culture is also part of Nature and that the structural approach may eventually effect a merger of man and Culture into the larger realm of biological and physical Nature. The Finale of the *Mythologiques* includes a rhapsodic passage on the structuralist implications of DNA, animal communication, the relationship between protozoa and bacteria, the visual system of cats and frogs, and the related shapes of the brains of birds and men. Lévi-Strauss expects to find the same determining principles underlying the communication of apes, the reproduction of plants, and perhaps even in the beloved rocks of his childhood, as he discerned in

systems of kinship or corpora of myths; there may be a
single key to understanding the universe, after all.

Piaget, though usually more taciturn about the poetic
aspects of his vision, has also, in recent writings, indicated
his belief that in the search for structures one will arrive
at fundamental properties of the universe. Not only do
structures really exist in the mind of the operating child;
but, Piaget suggests, they are similar to the structures in
the world probed by the physicist, that is, in the world of
physical objects. Perhaps, he implies, it is because we are
built to interact with that physical world of physics—
matter, gravity, probability, and entropy—that our actions
assume their peculiar structures:

> There are physical structures which, though independent of
> us, correspond to our operational structures. . . . here we have
> remarkable proof of that pre-established harmony among
> windowless monads of which Leibniz dreamt . . . the most
> beautiful example of biological adaptation that we know of
> (because it is physico-chemical and cognitive at the same time).

Having discussed such matters with no less an authority
than Niels Bohr, Piaget recalls the physicist's warning:
"The analogy between operations and the physical world
is a suggestive one, but one that is perilous as well." However, it is with a twinkle in his eye that Piaget repeats
these words.

Despite, then, their concerted efforts to rid European
psychology and anthropology of idealism and unsupported
speculation, both Lévi-Strauss and Piaget themselves entertain grandiose thoughts at times about the implications
of the approaches they have developed. It is not surprising,
and it is somewhat gratifying, to discover this facet of the
program, since the ability to discover new intellectual ho-
rizons would seem closely linked to a strong imaginative
power which can perceive connections and syntheses where
others see only isolated particles of information. There is,
to be sure, an attendant danger in such creative efflores-
cence: one may claim unities in the absence of evidence,

or in the face of contrary evidence; one then moves out of step with the scientific credo, though one may with such boldness lay the foundation for a scientific break-through. Indeed, it is with regard to the scientific status of the two theorists, the relation to work being done by other persons, and ultimate claims to reliability and veri-fiability, that the strongest debates about the structuralist school have centered. It is to a review and assessment of structuralist claims, achievements, and problems, there-fore, that we now direct our attention.

6 Structuralism as a World-View

The human sciences will be structuralist, or they will not be at all.

—LÉVI-STRAUSS

Not Lévi-Strauss, not Piaget, but Marx, Mao, and Marcuse, were the heroes of the French students who marched through the streets of Paris in May 1968, throwing the regime of General de Gaulle into turmoil. The students, workers, and thousands of other Frenchmen who joined in these short-lived but epochal uprisings were protesting against grave injustices they found in their seemingly prosperous and peaceful country. While the reasons for these events were quite complex, and a subject of heated argument, there was considerable agreement that the balance of power among the French intelligentsia was altered by the events of May.

During the Second World War and in the immediate postwar years, the philosophy of existentialism (in its Marxist and phenomenological varieties) exerted a dominant influence on educated French youth. Sartre, Camus, de Beauvoir, Merleau-Ponty spoke of the importance of engagement, involvement, and passion; these intellectuals became involved in political and social conflict and made their stands known. By the 1960's, however, widespread disillusionment over the Algerian rebellion and the Cold

War had brought about a reaction against such political commitment, and a new intellectual style became popular. Among those who reflected this "cooler" style were the structuralists such as Lévi-Strauss, Jacques Lacan, and Michel Foucault, who, whatever their political persuasions, despaired of influencing events which they saw as under the control of remote and impassive forces. A retreat within, toward scholarship, analysis, objectivity appeared to be taking place: articles appeared chronicling the death of existentialism and the emergence of Lévi-Strauss as the principal intellectual figure in France.

Whether or not those heralding the demise of the "engaged intellectual" had pinpointed a genuine phenomenon, the uprising of 1968 signaled a new shift in intellectual allegiance among French students. Among French intellectuals, Sartre stood almost alone in publicly taking the side of the rebellious students; other members of the academic community generally took a dim view of the Guevarist tactics espoused by the militants, and tended to espouse a liberal, rather than a radical, critique of the French scene. "Structuralism is dead," cried the students; whether or not they had ever read a word of Lacan or Lévi-Strauss, they sensed a tie between the philosophy of these men and the establishment they had come to despise.

That there is at least a surface connection between trends in the social sciences and the French rebellion cannot be denied. The uprisings began in the new University of Nanterre, progressive by French standards, where contemporary sociology and psychology were extremely popular subjects. Indeed, Daniel Cohn-Bendit, one of the leaders of the movement, was himself a sociology student, knowledgeable about currents in the social sciences, and sufficiently convinced of their perniciousness to begin his published version of the course of events with a scathing attack on these sciences. For students like Cohn-Bendit, the evil of the French university and the French state consisted in their bureaucratization, their inaccessibility, their imperviousness to change. De Gaulle stood aloof from the masses and their problems, preferring to identify with the remote past, to which he attempted to subordinate the present situation. Other institutions were similarly indifferent to current pressures and forces, had not changed in centuries, and seemed even to glory in their rigidity. As one commentator put it, the French university was like structuralism: a language sufficient unto itself, devoid of goals or meaning. The cycle of studies was reduced to a pure code, to which the students could make no contribution; all had already been decided. The culture dispensed by the university appeared to be a class culture, as alien from today as a dead language. Structuralism was an effort to inject into the domain of ideas the patent immobility which characterized social structure during the present era. In short, the university was nonsense, meaningless.

The adequacy of this critique from the left will be taken up a little later, after we have introduced some of the criticisms of the work of Lévi-Strauss and Piaget made from within the academy, and chiefly from the right. What is clear to begin with is that for a variety of reasons, structuralism has aroused strong feelings both within and without intellectual circles and has even been implicated in the most dramatic event in recent French history. Why structuralism has merited this attention, what there is in the analyses of Lévi-Strauss and Piaget which can engender such debate and bitterness, is an intriguing question which may reveal something about the status of scientific inquiry in the contemporary world.

1. CRITICAL REACTIONS TO STRUCTURALISM

Piaget's early studies of children's reasoning were widely acclaimed by psychologists as pioneering attempts to chart the world-view of the young child. In contrast, his subsequent works on infancy and on the development of concrete and formal operations were largely ignored for several decades, except by scattered cognoscenti. It was only in the sixties, due in large part to the Sputnik-inspired resurgence of interest in intellectual development, that Piaget's work of the intervening years came to be recognized.

By and large, reaction to his work has been favorable from those who have studied it carefully. His disdain for statistical methods has been criticized by nearly every American commentator; but as replications have verified most of his findings, these critics have been disposed to write off Piaget's "sloppy" reporting methods as a Gallic idiosyncrasy. Relevant criticisms and modifications of aspects of Piaget's theory have come chiefly from those within the general structuralist camp—from psychologists like Jerome Bruner, who questions the need for the terms "operations" and "equilibrium," or from researchers like Thomas Bever and Jacques Mehler, who find evidence for understanding of conservations of number far earlier than does Piaget. For the most part, such criticism has been couched in respectful terms

Outside the group that agrees with or has been convinced by his approaches, however, Piaget has not been much discussed. He has proposed a new approach or "paradigm" for research in psychology; he assumes the subject can reveal interesting things about himself and that the subject is perpetually and actively constructing knowledge about the world; he views behavior as an interaction of present structures with assimilable aspects of the environment, rather than as a series of responses to independently definable stimuli. The dominant behaviorist tradition, in contrast, subscribes to the notion that a subject's testimony or interpretation provides no clue to psychological processes, and that the subject acquires knowledge or "learns" by merely reflecting what is present in the environment, rather than by actively transforming it. Since behaviorists and Piagetians speak different languages and proceed from different assumptions, there can be (despite some valiant attempts in this regard by "neo-behaviorists") no "meeting of the minds" between these two approaches. The Gestalt school, so revolutionary and promising when Piaget began his work, is no longer active as a separate force, and its most enduring contributions have long since been absorbed into general psychology. The battle for the loyalty of the new generation seems to be between the constructive, cognitive Piaget school and the behavioral learning tradition; the outcome is as yet uncertain.

The reception given Piaget beyond the borders of psychology—among philosophers, mathematicians, and biologists, among others—resembles that accorded Lévi-Strauss within the field of anthropology. Both men have been viewed as taking revolutionary leaps in thought, stating them boldly, but providing insufficient documentation. In the frequent and heated disputes over the merits of their ideas, they have been regarded as either designers of a new science, incorrigible and destructive iconoclasts, or mysterious and suspect characters whose opaque writings obscure as much as they reveal. Lévi-Strauss is recognized for having charted new areas for study, and as having had a stimulating effect on ethnography, but he is seen as having proved few of his key assertions satisfactorily. A practice has developed—and indeed become something of a minor industry—of an anthropologist aspiring to publication writing a brief, devastating article either refuting a theoretical point of Lévi-Strauss's or introducing an empirical counterexample to, say, the latter's interpretation of the bull horn among the Indians of central Brazil. These critics are conspicuously united in their lip service to the grandeur of Lévi-Strauss's scheme and in their claims that one must, nonetheless, take one's time in going from hunch to scientific generalization.

Whatever the disagreements over the nature and extent of Lévi-Strauss's positive contributions, it is clear that his critiques have helped significantly in effecting the downfall of the principal schools of earlier theory: Malinowskian functionalism, Radcliffe-Brownian structuralism, and the lingering vestiges of evolutionism, diffusionism, and historicism. Many investigators have been content just to write out their detailed ethnographies of individual peoples, while those concerned with theory have tended either to embrace a kind of anthropologically viable Marxism or to join the rapidly growing school of cognitive anthropology, or ethnoscience. Ethnoscientists examine the classifying, naming, and kinship practices of diverse cultures in an effort to draw semantic maps of the structure of such domains and to find parallels between domains in disparate societies. While the goals of this movement resemble Lévi-Strauss's program, its methods tend to be quantitative rather than qualitative, its focus narrow, and its results disappointingly thin when weighed against those achievable by the simple exercise of common sense. Yet the hopes of American (and perhaps also world) anthropology seem pinned on this movement, which is less dependent upon the imaginative flair of a unique "great man."

As is all-too-customary in academic circles, some of the attacks on Lévi-Strauss and Piaget have been quite vicious, particularly those from representatives of the earlier traditions which the structuralists are, more or less explicitly, rejecting. These opponents have tended to focus upon the validity of positing "basic units and structures," the status of such terms as distinctive features, operations, or kinship structures, or the abandonment of such widely accepted notions as drive reduction, imitation, and empirical learning in favor of "constructivist" or "mentalistic" noting of how behavior is caused and how it unfolds. Since none of the leading structuralists is disposed to shy away from a good fight—indeed, they seem to relish one—the learned journals have come to feature generous doses of personal aspersion as the two sides repeatedly square off. In a personal communication to one such combatant, Lévi-Strauss explicitly referred to the exchange as a potlatch, and hinted that, as in that form of ritual exchange, the greater prestige would accrue to the more destructive participant. Piaget has an interesting way of handling *his* opposition: he is likely to invite a worthy adversary to spend time at his center, and to seek to win him over to the truth of genetic epistemology. As if they were trophies of battle, Piaget now proudly lists in his books the names of former antagonists who have since subscribed to the worthiness of his enterprise. It is said, however, that some of these reconciliations have been more personal than intellectual, and that some of the collaborations to which Piaget proudly points exist, as in some joint diplomatic communiqués, more in name than in spirit.

Both men have had their problems, not only with their detractors, but even at times with their admirers and disciples, of which each has more than his share. Although both have repeatedly emphasized their distaste for the role of founder of a school, and there is little reason to doubt their ambivalence about an enthusiastic yet uncritical following, each is burdened with sycophants willing to defend every quotation, aside, and comma (even when the Master has already changed his mind). These disputes and apologies will not concern us here, since they so often deal with specific points of detail and are linked more to pride than to substance. It does seem relevant, however, to mention some of the more general criticisms leveled against the structuralist movement.

On the methodological level, Piaget and Lévi-Strauss are both criticized for careless reporting of data, lack of statistical tests, failure to specify the way in which examples were chosen, and excessive reliance upon one, two, or three cases. The issue of care in reporting seems to reflect, to some extent, different scholarly practices in Continental

Europe and America: scientists in the United States are far more preoccupied with sample sizes and tests of significance than their European counterparts. As for the use of a small population, both Piaget and Lévi-Strauss subscribe to the notion that one case scrupulously investigated and thoroughly understood is far more valuable than scattered data collected on a variety of subjects. Both, nonetheless, have encouraged their associates to document their findings with further examples and have themselves taken the criticism of limited sampling more fully to heart in later work. In this regard, at least, the pressures exerted by a skeptical scientific community appear to have engendered a positive result.

As spiritual descendants of Descartes, however, both men are prone to place great trust in their own insights, intuitions, and formulations. What seems clear to them tends often to be treated as self-evident in their books, and many terms in need of careful definition are casually adopted without comment. In addition, the overtones of idealism which we have discerned in their more recent writings—the suggestion that structuralism may prove the key to the ancient mysteries of life and the world—are an irritant to more prudent or pluralistically disposed thinkers. All these factors serve not only to make reading of their works difficult, but also to suggest the possibility that the structuralists are not themselves aware of all the problems raised by certain of their positions. However, their practice of "thinking aloud" is at least understandable, in the light of both men's constant attempts to map out new areas; in their fervor to communicate principal points, they inevitably forgo the infinite care which individuals working in more traditional and delimited areas can take with their work.

The positing of constructs and entities for which there is little or no direct evidence is a practice for which the two men have been subjected to heavy criticism. There is a persistent (and undeniably praiseworthy) tendency in

contemporary science to rid reports of metaphysical terminology, of constructs which do not lend themselves to
operationalization and disproof. That Piaget and Lévi-
Strauss rely so frequently on metaphor and unhesitatingly
introduce new constructs or analogies rankles even sympathetic readers and calls the rigor of their approach into
question.

The grand assurance with which structuralist claims are
often put forth is also a bone of contention. Many individuals, while impressed by Piaget's and Lévi-Strauss's
observations and their resulting middle-level generalizations, resent structuralism's pretensions to be a new world-
view or academic ideology. Such critics argue that the
structuralists' findings can be satisfactorily subsumed
under the currently established paradigms of psychology
and anthropology—i.e., behaviorism and functionalism.
It is here that we touch on the real crux of the dispute
over structuralism. Every social scientist implicitly or explicitly assumes a certain perspective toward knowledge
in his work and adopts a certain picture of how organisms
function. For many years, an image of man as a struggling
biological organism with strong drives which govern his
behavior, and a view of knowledge as a reflection within
man of the "real" contents of the environment, have held
sway in Anglo-American social science. Structuralism
threatens this outlook, for it attributes to the individual
more innate mental structuring and functioning; regards
the subject as playing an active role in the construction of
his knowledge; stresses the universal similarities among
men, regardless of differences in their social organization;
finds no need to posit "needs for" or "functions of" structure; and, in its Piagetian variant, asserts that children
pass through qualitatively distinct stages which can be
understood in their own terms. As these views have received increasing support from structuralist (and some
non-structuralist) research, the findings have become more
and more difficult to assimilate into the traditional frame-

work; conventional accounts of learning, of social structure, of cultural products become undermined, and the possibility arises that behaviorism and functionalism must be abandoned as viable theoretical approaches. Many scientists, particularly those who have established reputations within the behaviorist-functionalist tradition, have a vested interest in the older paradigm and, rightly or wrongly, are not going to surrender to the approaching structuralist troops without a prolonged siege.

Objections to the structuralist approach have not, however, been restricted to attacks from the academic rear guard concerning the merits of applying its perspective to specific problems in psychology and anthropology; its entire implicit world-view has also been assailed as pernicious by various articulate critics of a different persuasion. The most notable (and notorious) of these attacks has been that of Jean-Paul Sartre on Lévi-Strauss's program, in his *Critique of Dialectical Reasoning*. Proceeding from a Marxist-Hegelian view of society, which is rooted in history and which contrasts opposing viewpoints in order to achieve a "higher truth," Sartre denigrates Lévi-Strauss's analytic approach for restricting itself to classification, as well as his "objective" perspective, in whose terms man is treated as an "ant" and his unique human values are denied. Sartre's own philosophy is firmly rooted in politics and history: he adheres to the Marxist eschatological view that the proletariat will overthrow capitalist society; the anthropological proposition that primitive man, having rejected history, is forever distanced from civilized man; and the philosophical claim that man can determine his own fate. These perspectives are directly threatened by Lévi-Strauss, who views each society as possessing its own integrity, Western man as in no way privileged, and men as controlled by the structure of their brains, which permits them only a quite limited range of cultural and intellectual options. While Sartre considers structure in dialectical reasoning to be a product of men's activity in the technological world, Lévi-Strauss reverses the argument, claiming that all practical activity presupposes a structure.

Although to many outsiders this debate may seem a bit like a tempest in a teapot, raging only within the narrow confines of French intellectual circles, it is in fact of considerable consequence. At stake may be the traditional humanistic view of man, or more precisely perhaps, of the special status of literate man and of his capacity for self-definition, free will, and infinite creativity—not to mention the Marxist critique, which, in its Sartrean variant especially, demands·that one choose sides in the class struggle. Lévi-Strauss remarks coolly that it is Sartre who is being inconsistent, for if he believes in economic determinism, there should be no free choice anywhere; and if he believes in the purity of history, why should he subscribe to one particular mythic version of history—that of Marx? His own viewpoint, he argues, is much less ethnocentric than Sartre's, since he recognizes the dignity and individuality of non-Western men, whereas Sartre seems to be saying that *he* knows what is best for *them*.

A corollary of Sartre's position, and one often propounded during the May events, presents structuralism as a reactionary force which does not recognize the possibility of or need for change and therefore supports the status quo. To such charges Lévi-Strauss, who signed the intellectuals' manifestos of protest during the Algerian conflict, responds with some anger. He denies that structuralism has any political relevance whatsoever; it is simply a scientific procedure for studying behavior and can be applied indifferently by Maoists, liberal democrats, or royalists to studies of communism, fascism,· or anarchism. He also alleges that existentialism is itself counterrevolutionary, since it is a misguided and anachronistic attempt to preserve philosophy as a humanistic reserve, man as a hallowed vessel.

One can agree with Lévi-Strauss that structuralism need

not necessarily imply a single world-view, and recognize that men who call themselves structuralists have widely different political views, while still allowing that there may be a connection between ideology and politics, and questioning whether Lévi-Strauss himself is completely free of ethnocentrism or "humanistic" feelings. In the first place, ideas seem never to have developed in total isolation from the extant forces in a social system; sociologists of knowledge have little difficulty linking the intellectual and cultural scene in the early part of the twentieth century with the reaction against a behaviorist hegemony and the development of the structuralist perspective. With hindsight, indeed, these parallels become obvious: the desire to avoid favoring one society over another, curiosity about cross-cultural comparisons, respect for mathematical formulae and models, suspicion of overly simplified, atomistic, reflexive, and environmentalist positions, interest in the properties of mind for their relevance to the education of children and the development of superior technology. Individuals do, moreover, embrace philosophical positions for personal and temperamental reasons, philosophical assumptions do influence personality, and it is easy to see how the views of Piaget and Lévi-Strauss fit in—indeed, merge—with their personalities: Piaget, the serious ascetic observer of man and animals, deeply interested in the source of his own precocity, somewhat uncomfortable with disrupting affective factors, desirous of a grand synthesis of all the multifarious areas which he has been able to master, living in a country where the mind can afford to explore freely since it is less susceptible to political or social turmoil; Lévi-Strauss, the romantic adventurer turned cool savant, disaffected from the superficialities and games of his own society, cultivator of sensory experiences and qualities, pursuing the essence of man as he finds and knows him, a sometimes irrational but ever comprehensible creature who receives his deepest confirmation from spiritual flights into poetry, music, nature, and art. Certainly structuralism is a theory and a method of its time, and its magnificent creators are themselves unable to step completely outside the period, although both—in this, too, consistent with their personalities and ideologies— have been extraordinarily successful in freeing themselves of parochial biases.

As Piaget's work is less directly connected with issues of social structure and change, he has avoided conflicts with sociologists and political theorists, but has become instead the whipping boy of meliorists in the educational realm. Piaget has concluded from his work with children that development has an optimal rate, which is peculiar to each individual and is tampered with only at its peril. He is opposed to attempts to "speed up" development and has a somewhat fatalistic attitude about the possibilities of radically altering intellectual level through quick "enrich- ment" programs. Consequently, those eager to improve the lot of "disadvantaged" groups through "head starts" or "leaps" consider Piaget an ominous figure (much as feminists attack Freud and Erikson), seeing the drift of his approach as an insistence that things are the way they have to be. Actually, however, Piaget's position is more subtle than some of these opponents imagine, for he does allow substantial variation in developmental rates depend- ing upon the amount and kind of organism—environ- ment interaction. Identical twins raised, respectively, in Newton, Massachusetts, and on the hills outside of Rio, will proceed at markedly divergent rates and reach different intellectual levels because of their dissimilar stimulation and environments. Piaget is not at all opposed to enrich- ment of the total environment—indeed, he recommends just that in his essays on teaching, which together could form a bible for proponents of the open classroom. What he inveighs against are attempts to teach a particular task more rapidly or to give undue emphasis to one skein of intellectual development, such as painting skill or lan- guage learning, rather than on the mental structures of the child as a whole. Since development involves structured wholes, which integrate diverse components, speeding up the development of one or two components will only interfere with the process of equilibration, not result in more rapid growth. Furthermore, as Piaget has often remarked, cats reach the fourth stage of object permanence much more quickly than do human infants; they also remain at that stage for the rest of their lives.

Piaget and Lévi-Strauss, then, both appear to believe that organisms (and societies) have an "inner wisdom," an intrinsic rhythm or equilibrium which is best left undisturbed; this point of view, to some extent reflecting residence in older and more established societies, is difficult for those who live in unstable, rapidly changing milieux to comprehend. Inasmuch as change is slower and more difficult to bring about in the former societies, those who criticize the structuralists for pessimism and rigidity are wrong as far as Switzerland is concerned, but more relevant in societies in which the rate of change has been accelerated. And, as Piaget himself is fond of pointing out to students who would identify his structuralism with a distinct political position, he has devoted his intellectual career to opposing, with equal fervor, American behaviorism and Soviet reflexology, the highly similar psychological approaches of two countries who have been at ideological odds for a quarter of a century.

Even if Piaget and Lévi-Strauss have faint tendencies toward a static view of society, they most certainly have an active view of scientific progress. Both men follow new research in the social and natural sciences with keen, almost fanatic interest and continually attempt to relate their own work to biological and mathematical findings, applying techniques from these disciplines to their anthropological and psychological discoveries. While they have often made judicious use of such discoveries, both have a certain tendency to accept uncritically findings from "harder disciplines." Thus, the writings of Piaget and

Lévi-Strauss are occasionally top-heavy with references to (and the jargon of) information theory, topology, algebra, modern logic, such recent postulates in physics as indeterminacy and complementarity principles, such contemporary interests of biologists as the genetic code and the chemistry of the nervous system. Naturally one cannot expect social scientists, even such brilliant generalists as Piaget and Lévi-Strauss, to have mastered the subtleties of all fields of knowledge; yet the impossibility of being a Renaissance *bricoleur* gives them no license to treat tentative findings from other fields as if they were established facts, or to take a term with precise technical meaning and give it a broad metaphorical application in another domain. It appears fair to say that both leading structuralists are a bit too infatuated with seemingly "hard-nosed" methods and results, and that their presentations would sometimes benefit from a simple, unadorned description of their findings, bereft of references to recondite mathematical structures or spectacular biological discoveries.

One criticism of Piaget and Lévi-Strauss which has not yet been much voiced, but which will probably surface in coming years, concerns the great emphasis both men place on the primacy of intellect. While this emphasis is quite understandable—considering the Cartesian tradition to which they belong, the general interest in intellect characteristic of this century, the inevitable reaction against the affect-laden approaches of Pierre Janet, Malinowski, and Freud, as well as the economic determinism of Marx —the recent focus upon reason, or upon a rational approach to the emotional and intuitive life, may be on the wane. Signs of a freshly risen counterculture, or new "consciousness," are becoming more frequent; one encounters evidence that many young adults and students are rebelling against the overly intellectualistic and academic interests of their elders, retreating in some cases into a life of sensibility where experience is cultivated for its own sake, and analysis is decried as unnecessary, disconcerting, or downright pernicious. To the extent that this trend accelerates, one may anticipate dislike of the Piaget–Lévi-Strauss approach on two planes: those who totally reject the analytic approach will consider these writers as irrelevant as all other theoreticians; those who are still wedded to analysis, but want to understand the contemporary scene, will turn to social scientists more attuned to the affective aspects of life and experience— to men like the psychoanalyst Erik Erikson and the existentialist Rollo May, who focus on the identities and anxieties of contemporary youth; or to such anthropologists as Erving Goffman and Harold Garfinkel, who study the casual behavioral patterns and everyday rituals of communities ranging from establishment corporations to hippie communes.

2. APPLICATIONS AND IMPLICATIONS

A phenomenon somewhere between an antistructuralist revolt and the intellectual vogue for structuralism perhaps heralds an imminent trend away from structuralism. I refer to the adoption of structuralism by the mass media in France during the middle sixties. "We are all structuralists," the intellectual and popular magazines declared as they gave two-sentence wrap-ups of the movement and then attempted to apply structural analysis to all available phenomena: James Bond movies, 180 comics in a French daily, meals at le drugstore, informal encounters at the Eiffel Tower. The absurdity of the situation is well illustrated in Sanche de Gramont's quip about a structural analysis of the French flag: "It will show that it is made of three vertical fields of color of identical width which follow one another, according to their normalization function, in the sequence red, white, and blue." Lévi-Strauss, horrified by this trend of "structuralism-fiction," has declared bluntly:

In the sense in which it is understood today by French opinion, I am not a structuralist. I am very much afraid that in France there is a total lack of self-criticism, an excessive sensibility to fashion, and a deep intellectual instability. The best way to explain the current infatuation with structuralism is that French intellectuals and the cultured French public need new playthings every ten or fifteen years.

While such excesses are amusing where they are not scandalous, they should not obscure the fact that humanists and social scientists working outside their respective specialties have put structuralist principles to interesting use. The most notable studies have been in the literary realm, where Roman Jakobson has undertaken studies of folk tales, poems, and the principles of poetry, Harold Ehrmann has explained structures in Corneille's play *Cinna*, and Lévi-Strauss and Jakobson have collaborated on a detailed analysis of Baudelaire's *Les Chats*. These efforts have sought to account in an exhaustive way for the plan of the artistic work, the balances and undulations between motifs, sounds, rhythms, and ideas, and the varying treatments of crucial elements, the directionality and final synthesis in the work. The strength of the best analyses, including those of Lévi-Strauss, is that they resist summary; indeed, those structural analyses of works of art which are most suspect are those in which the conclusions are listed in a line or two or in a simple formula or chart. Such précis are only relevant at so general a level that they do not differentiate between particulars and thus leave no room for making judgments and evaluations of individual works.

The foremost practitioner of structuralism in the literary realm is Roland Barthes, a widely respected French critic, who has formulated a theory of structural analysis in literature and has applied his techniques to a variety of literary documents, among them the works of Racine and the histories of Michelet and Machiavelli. Barthes has sought the application of structural methods to realms outside of literature, and his effort is worth describing here, provided that its playful and provisional character is acknowledged.

Barthes begins by introducing two aspects of any linguistic-structural analysis: the *system* (the parts of speech; the paradigmatic elements) and the *syntagm* (the arrangement of these elements in a syntactic sequence). He then suggests that the realms of clothing, food, furniture, and architecture can be thought of as analogous to linguistic code:

(1) Components of the *system of clothing* are the sets of pieces designed to be worn on the same part of the body, whose variation changes the meaning of the clothing—a winter hat, a bonnet, a racing cap. The syntagm of the clothing is the juxaposition at the same moment of different parts of the system—e.g., a skirt, a blouse, and a jacket.

(2) The parts of the *food system* are sets of foodstuffs from which one chooses a dish: i.e., for an entree one may have roast or fowl; the syntagm is the actual sequence of dishes during a meal, or the menu. (Both syntagm and system are highlighted in a restaurant, whereas only the syntagm figures in the typical home meal.)

(3) The parts of the *furniture system* are the stylistic varieties of a single piece of furniture (for example, kinds of beds); the syntagm is the juxtaposition of different pieces of furniture in the same area—as a set consisting of a bed, table, chair, and lamp.

(4) The parts of the *architectural system* are the possible variations in style of a single element in a building: the types of roof, balcony, wall; the syntagm is the sequence and arrangement of these parts within an edifice.

While this exercise is only tentative, it might well lead to productive findings. For example, Lévi-Strauss has found remarkable regularities in the components of different kinds of meals and the function of elements in each, while Alfred Kroeber has demonstrated repetitive cycles in the changes in fashion over the years. Neither of these analyses was dependent upon Barthes' scheme, but to the extent that such a framework facilitates discernment of the elements and their arrangement or the parallels across furniture, architecture, food, and clothing, it will have proved a useful adjunct to cultural analysis.

Barthes is also a contributor to structuralist theory and has made the interesting proposal that the sciences as well as the humanities are wedded to the language employed by practitioners. Typically, the writer of novels or poems is viewed as using language in a special way, with each word contributing to the overall effect, whereas the scientist has freedom to use any number of equivalent languages to make his point. Barthes, however, views language as a system which can be put to a variety of uses, and claims that none has a logical or practical claim over the others. Thus, the choice of scientific "jargon," with its tables, equations, and logical propositions, is a determination as loaded, consequential, and irreversible as the decision to write in iambic pentameter. Such a critique has implications for structural analyses of the Piagetian variety, for it suggests that in reducing thought to the logical calculus, Piaget is making strong assumptions about the generality of this "language." At the very least, Barthes challenges the easy assumption made by many scientists that the language they use is irrelevant: he reminds us that each code has its own powers, limitations, and implications.

Certain schools of literature and art have also been viewed as notably attuned to structuralist principles. For example, Samuel Beckett has been touted as a structuralist writer because his characters unfold as victims of a pre-ordained fate which they can neither control nor know— "I am made of the words, the words of others," says a character in one of his plays, which would seem to reflect the structuralist credo that codes within the culture make a central, perhaps determining, contribution to knowledge and self-definition. In postulating such affinities between structuralism and art, it is important to note whether the artist is actually employing structuralist techniques or is merely expressing some ideas common in structuralist writing. While concern with the unconscious models which underlie mundane experience does not seem a prominent part of the present art scene, emphasis on the potency and immutability of forces outside oneself does seem a recurrent theme in much contemporary art.

Still, some of the more explicitly formulated procedures for modern musical composition—notably, twelve-tone composition—do appear to have strong affinities with structural techniques. The composer introduces a tone row (the basic constituent units) and then imposes various transformations which can be defined formally, applied exhaustively, and ordered in various sequences. This technique is quintessentially structural and confirms Lévi-Strauss's belief in the strong links that exist between music and other structural codes. Of course, in the case of both the artwork and the cultural code, the structuralist principles involved need not be explicitly appreciated by the perceiver; at best, there is some match between his cognitive structures and the structure of the work, which it is peculiarly the analyst's task to elucidate. And Lévi-Strauss cautions that a structure explicitly placed into a work by an artist does not have the same status as one which is a product of the unconscious processes of the mind.

Though both Lévi-Strauss and Piaget are aware of all such recent applications of structuralism, and may well constantly ponder the implications of the movement they have launched, their public statements deal only with the scholarly goals they have perennially pursued. Where various commentators have speculated on the possibility of new cognitive structures, Piaget and Lévi-Strauss stress the weight of evidence indicating that man's cognitive capacities are, at least in the short run, relatively fixed. As committed rationalists, descendants of Descartes and the Enlightenment, both men judiciously evaluate the evidence which bears on their positions and have little sympathy for those whose analytic interpretations are guided by their personal wishes and aspirations. No doubt they have their own scenarios for the future salvation or damnation of man; but they resist commenting on them publicly. Their dominant fears, if any, may well revolve about the possibility of a reaction to the current emphasis on mind, in which spokesmen for knowledge and moderation will be swept aside in favor of leaders who will exploit the more affective and emotional aspects of their fellow men.

While the political implications of structuralism would seem much less potent than either its most vocal critics or most fervent supporters would have us believe, it seems likely that, like other .influential social-scientific theories, structuralism will eventually have an impact on the social and cultural aspects of the society. Recognizing the risk involved in such prognostication, I will here speculate on a few possible consequences of the absorption of structuralism into contemporary civilization.

Applications of structuralism within the scholarly community are perhaps easier to anticipate, because some have already emerged and because structuralism, by its nature, is a rather cerebral school. Study of the relations between various disciplines should receive a strong impetus from structuralism, given its doctrine that there are certain basic mental configurations which can be discerned across a range of diverse content. Indeed, the isolation of disciplines from one another is already under attack, and the acceptance of structuralism will probably hasten the demise of this practice. Efforts to find substantive relationships among diverse fields, such as those dealing with the organism as a biological entity, the world as a physical object, and man as a logical and aesthetic creature, will likely be fostered as well.

The structural and developmental approaches are already having an impact on the education of young children. New approaches encourage the presentation of material at the child's particular developmental level (or slightly above it) rather than in one invariable form, and call for recognition of the child's tendencies to structure and comprehend material in characteristic ways. Teaching of particular content areas and "school subjects" is also being replaced by attempts to convey the common framework underlying diverse fields and examples.

The advent of this new methodology will also influence the course of future research. Biologists and physiologists may attempt to locate the structures (or their analogies) which Lévi-Strauss and Piaget believe to exist in the nervous system. New mathematical and logical conceptions which more faithfully reflect the true range of human capacities, rather than idealization of those capacities, should be forthcoming. Translation between languages, both ordinary and formal, may proceed along novel lines, as linguists and computer engineers attempt translations on the level of cognitive structures rather than word-for-word or phrase-for-phrase.

Some less profound, and less palatable, applications can probably be expected. Once it becomes widely believed that the basic structures of thought have been discovered, those involved in influencing public attitudes will likely attempt to exploit these fundamental intellectual proclivities. Similarly, the documentation of different intellectual levels may be used by some as an excuse for denigrating those individuals or groups which appear moored at a less-developed level.

Yet, on balance, I would expect the influence of structuralism to be a liberating and unifying one. Once the point is conveyed that the diverse content of various cultures masks underlying similarities, apparent differences between peoples and groups may seem less vast. Structuralist pronouncements concerning the nature of thought will be widely disseminated and may provide individuals with better insights about their own thought processes and those of other persons. The study of methods of structural analysis will also contribute to a generally fuller understanding of phenomena—provided a tendency to debunk, through "laying bare" the essentials, is resisted.

One final point, even more speculative, merits mention. It is possible that individuals, once they have assimilated the structuralist analysis of the limitations of thought, will be content to "rest on their laurels" or to turn to non-intellectual pursuits. On the other hand, it is just as likely that knowledge of such "limitations," and the very fact of being conscious of one's own thought processes, will ultimately spur both individuals and cultures to undreamed-of intellectual heights—even, perhaps, lead to improvement in the genetic pool. Paradoxically, Piaget's own establishment of the limits of thought could be contravened by the creative tendency in human evolution which he has been among the first to consider.

3. STRUCTURALISM AND SCIENTIFIC INQUIRY

In speculating about future changes in man and in his mind, we reach beyond the bounds of structuralism's current achievement and look to its future. We must be careful here, I believe, not to confuse two independent trends. As an intellectual vogue, structuralism seems clearly on the decline in French-speaking countries, and probably will experience shortly the same fate in Anglo-Saxon lands. As a new force in the social sciences, however, structuralism—despite the various promising indications discussed in the preceding section—has yet to achieve its full impact. While many younger scholars are "in tune" with its principles and implications, most scholars and teachers of an earlier generation either actively oppose the movement, ignore it, or at the very least are strongly ambivalent about it. The social sciences have yet to embrace structuralism wholeheartedly. Yet my own feeling is that, whatever its fate as a popular fad, whatever its implications for the larger society, structuralism will not be ignored or rejected by the psychological and anthropological sciences. Rather, it will become part of the conventional wisdom in these fields, and, indeed, will be gradually assimilated into the theoretical foundations of the overall scientific enterprise.

Certainly this is Piaget's belief. Since the founding of his Center for Genetic Epistemology, he has collaborated in increasing measure with individuals from various sciences, and in particular with logicians, mathematicians, biologists and physicists, in an effort to determine the kind of mental structures utilized in work in each of these fields. "Genetic epistemology" has a dual meaning, since it refers not only to the origin of scientific thought in the young child but also to its evolution over the course of history. Exploring this uncharted domain, Piaget has made the intriguing discovery that in some respects the evolution of scientific thought has followed the evolution of thought in the child; thus in physics, belief in animistic or artificialist explanations of how the world works preceded the positing of invisible elements of matter which interact with one another because of physical forces. On the other hand, cultural history does not always recapitulate individual psychology; in the case of geometrical thinking, for example, the young child begins with a topological view of spatial ordering, next moves on to a projective view, and only at adolescence comprehends Euclidean space. Historically, however, the Greeks constructed Euclidean geometry, projective geometry was a product of the nineteenth century, while topological geometry is only a development of recent decades.

Through the concept of genetic epistemology, Piaget hopes to be able to unite the various sciences with one another in an integrated whole. He envisages this union in terms of a circle, with logic and mathematics at one point on its circumference, chemistry, physics, and biology next, sociology situated opposite to logic, with linguistics, psychology, and economy completing the circle; epistemology occupies the center of the circle. Piaget stresses the important role played by psychology in the circle of sciences:

> I cannot prevent myself from feeling a little proud of the master position held by psychology in the system of sciences. On the one hand, psychology depends on all the sciences . . . but the apprehension of reality is only possible through activities of the organism with respect to the object in question, and psychology alone permits the study of these activities and their development.

In his recent writings he has addressed an increasingly interdisciplinary audience, elaborating his vision of a unified though differentiated science built upon the doctrines of structuralism. To the humanistic strain in philosophy which embraces wisdom (which is not subject to disproof) he opposes the scientific tradition (which employs experimental controls) ; he also twits those who claim membership in the structuralist movement without adhering to its principles as set forth by Piaget.

Yet, if there is a discipline to which Piaget feels closest, it is biology. After more than forty years of benign truancy, Piaget returned to his first love and wrote a theoretical essay which he appears to regard as his most important general work—*Biology and Knowledge.* In this book Piaget tries to establish the biological nature of all knowledge and action, ranging from the primitive conditioning possible in a flatworm to the rarefied stage of formal operations of which only adolescent and adult human beings of the modern age are capable. All forms of knowledge, he argues, are illustration of the same functional mechanisms: assimilation, accommodation, and equilibration; it is the species membership which determines the extent to which knowledge can unfold in each organism. Piaget's goal is to demonstrate that the principles which govern biological evolution and embryological development are also operative in the functioning of man's most precious possession—his cognitive capacities.

As befits a fledgling elder statesman, Lévi-Strauss has similarly paid much attention in recent years to the relationship between ethnography and other forms of science. He has gone back to those scientists and philosophers of a synoptic bent—to Rousseau, Vico, Bergson—and has also made forays of his own into philosophy, literary criticism, and musical analysis. Though he may identify more with humanistic studies, while Piaget feels closer to the natural sciences, it appears that he, too, feels a special tie to the methods and findings of biology.

On February 19, 1968, at 10:30 in the evening, viewers of the First Program in France were treated to a rare spectacle: Claude Lévi-Strauss and Roman Jakobson engaged in a discussion with two biologists, François Jacob and Philippe L'Heritier, on the subject of "Living and Speaking." These men had assembled because of their common belief that the biological sciences and the communications sciences were moving closer together. Perhaps the most intriguing suggestion to emerge from the lengthy colloquy was Jakobson's speculation that the rules governing the use of DNA reflect, in a deep sense, the same rules which govern language use. Genetic information is inscribed in chromosomes through innumerable variations of four units or elements which are in themselves meaningless (adenine, guanine, purine, and pyrimidine). All the information needed about the development and functioning of life processes is simply "read off" from the chromosomes, where the relevant message has been inscribed in the genetic code. Just as in language, meaning inheres in the arrangement of meaningless elements; there is organization at each level of the organism: languages as well as organisms are subject to definable evolutionary principles—in Jakobson's words, "the same architecture, the same principles of construction, a totally hierarchical principle." The code is an alphabet with discrete words, and even markers for the beginning and ending of "utterances." It is perhaps inevitable that language, itself a product of natural evolution, should embody this same principle of genetic construction.

The biologists did not uncritically embrace Jakobson's analogy, pointing out, for example, that language permits the inheritance of acquired characteristics—i.e., the passing on of new knowledge to subsequent generations—whereas in genetics, for all but a few biologists (such as Piaget), such an idea remains total anathema. Jakobson conceded differences between biology and language, indicating that the realm of biology includes noncommunicative aspects. Yet the recurrent theme was one developed by Lévi-Strauss: that the notion of communication can be extended not only throughout the social sciences (communication of words, messages, and economic goods) but also throughout the biological realm. Language serves both as the instrument and as the model for other forms of cultural communication, and as an example and model for biological communication. In both realms, one encounters programs of action, goals, and meaning—the latter being viewed as a structural homologue between two codes. Lévi-Strauss concluded the discussion by noting that, in the biological sciences, you can have a structure resembling language which implies neither consciousness nor a subject. This gives hope for a unification of science, without the unpalatable prospect of dependence on the vagaries of phenomenal experience; though one's subjective impressions may sometimes be necessary as a point of departure in scientific investigation, they must ultimately be supplanted by an objective and explanatory analysis.

While Piaget finds his central link among the sciences in the logical capacities manifested in concrete and formal operations, Lévi-Strauss looks to the mechanisms of language for a common core. Though this adoption of a different model may appear to weaken the chance for a meaningful synthesis, recent work in linguistics indicates that the gap between logic and language may be illusory. In the years following the revolutions inspired by Saussure and Jakobson, a second revolution of equal breadth and significance has come about, owing to the work of Noam Chomsky. Chomsky, a linguist at Massachusetts Institute of Technology, has put forth a novel conceptualization of the nature of language, detailed models of the grammatical and phonological systems, and principled reasons for rejecting earlier formulations about the comprehension and production of speech.

Although a detailed account of Chomsky's linguistics is not possible here, the implications of his theories for studies of the mind should be discussed at least briefly, particularly in view of Chomsky's increasing preoccupation with the relationship between language and mind. Taking a lead from Descartes and his followers, Chomsky has argued that linguistic capacity is a distinctively human function, which reflects the natural logic or rationality of the mind, a creative capacity immanent in the brain and not dependent in any significant way on experience of the environment. Chomsky is very sympathetic to the notion of innate ideas, the Cartesian and Leibnizian belief that man comes equipped with specifically delineated hypotheses about what the world and the environment will be like. In the case of language, for instance, the human brain is thought to possess a series of universal rules that characterize all languages; the child's task in learning language is not to imitate those he hears about him but rather to eliminate from his set of rules and hypotheses those language systems which do not correspond to the one(s) he hears; with relatively little effort he will be able to speak accurately and creatively, producing novel utterances in whichever languages are spoken in his presence. The most powerful evidence supporting Chomsky's controversial position is the incredible speed with which normal children can pick up one or more languages, at an age when other cognitive capacities are still quite immature; and the fact, as well, that children sometimes make syntactical distinctions which are not found in their own language, but appear in alien languages which they could not possibly have heard. Chomsky thinks these phenomena can only occur in an organism possessing such extensive inborn structures in his head that the learning of language becomes as unproblematic as a duck's following his mother or a squirrel's burial of nuts.

Needless to say, such boldly stated claims have aroused virulent opposition among many psychologists and linguists, who have customarily viewed language learning as a painstaking process involving the combination of simple units—basic sounds and words—and reflecting the reinforcing and nonreinforcing properties of the environment. Chomsky has been even more disdainful concerning the behaviorist position than his fellow structuralists, claiming that it is either intolerably vague—what is a stimulus? a response? a reinforcer?—or simply wrong—no theory of imitation can account for the systematic mistakes made by a child in language learning: "little mouses"; "I goes downtown"; "Where the cup is?" He, in turn, has been challenged to give evidence for the existence of "linguistic universals" and for the close relationship he describes between language and logic. Chomsky has in fact proposed certain linguistic universals, both formal and substantive, but proof of these would be extremely difficult, for any new language discovered without these properties would vitiate the claim. As for the imputed link between logic and language, on which a synthesis between the views of Piaget and Lévi-Strauss may depend, Chomsky has suggested some general guiding principles, and put forth interesting interpretations of a few psychological experiments. No real demonstration of this hypothesis, however, is in the immediate offing.

Many individuals, including the three concerned, have sensed affinities between the programs of Lévi-Strauss,

Piaget, and Chomsky. Each of these scholars focuses particularly on Man, seeing him as a constructive organism, with generative capacities, who nonetheless is preordained to follow certain paths in his intellectual development and achievement because of the structure of his own brain and the regulating forces in the human environment. To be sure, there are significant divergences. Piaget and Lévi-Strauss differ, as we have already seen, in their assessment of the relative roles of action and perception, in their respective emphases on structure and development, in their formulations regarding language and logic. (Some links, as in Jakobson's analysis of language development and my own modal hypotheses, have already been proposed.) Chomsky assumes an intermediate position in that, like Lévi-Strauss, he emphasizes the determining role of language, and the possibility of innate knowledge of codes, while in his interest in basic mechanisms of reason, belief in the generativity of behavior and thought, and search for formal models of unconscious processes, he is more reminiscent of Piaget.

Piaget criticizes Chomsky for his belief in innate ideas and his spurning of the developmental perspective, though he allows that a purely linguistic analysis might proceed agenetically. Lévi-Strauss is comfortable with Chomsky's transformational approach to linguistic analysis, which is anticipated in his own writings, but has little patience with the latter's implicit picture of man as a creature of infinite capacity for original thought. For his part, Chomsky, while conceding the impressive efforts of Piaget and Lévi-Strauss to pin down mental structures, apparently has reservations about the modes of proof they adopt. More committed to operational definition, to the logical specification of each step in an argument, he is uneasy with the absence of crucial tests for many of the two older men's conclusions. These various disagreements are in a sense intramural, however; the doubts Chomsky raises about Piaget and Lévi-Strauss are reminiscent of the ones which more traditionally oriented scholars have introduced against Chomsky's own work. Except within the camp of the structuralists, Chomsky, Lévi-Strauss, and Piaget may be regarded as engaged in similar activities and in fundamental agreement on central issues. Indeed, Chomsky's assertions that language reflects the unique logic of the human mind and that ordinary language use is permeated by creativeness may portend the imminence of a meaningful synthesis of the major structural approaches to cognition.

Any forthcoming, let alone any final, synthesis concerning Mind will naturally draw upon a range of theories and findings, including some from individuals who have never heard of structuralism or who have only disdain for it. To mention but a few current investigations which seem particularly promising: the attempts of ethologists and of psychoanalysts to comprehend the instinctual and affective aspects of human nature; models of cognition devised by those working in computer simulation; findings concerning animal learning, particularly the recent attempts to teach chimpanzees to employ a variant of human language, using either sign language or reading; studies of symbol use or problem-solving in men or animals who have suffered various kinds of brain damage. The latter group of investigations are of potentially great interest for structuralists, who, while committed for the most part to a "dry" method, express belief in the existence of structures and structural mechanisms inside the human brain and nervous system. To be sure, failure to gain direct physiological or neurological support for structuralists' claims should by no means be taken as evidence that their formulations are wrong. Psychology, anthropology, and linguistics operate on a plane apart from the biochemical and neurological sciences, and it may be that functions discovered by structuralists are so linked to the interaction of neural mechanisms that any attempt at localization is doomed to fail. All the same, the structuralist case would be enormously bolstered if direct brain correlates for the perception of distinctive features, the principles of operational thought, or the knowledge of linguistic rules could be demonstrated. Indications that linguistic, logical, and intermodal capacities apparently break down along specifiable lines among brain-damaged individuals is an encouraging sign for those who would look to the brain for evidence about mind. Similarly, recent discoveries of receptors which respond to particularistic aspects of sensory stimulation provide support for the theory of distinctive features, even as findings about the breakdown of logical reasoning and spatial perception in various forms of brain damage suggest that logical operations are more than the figment of a structuralist's imagination. Not surprisingly, each of the major structuralist thinkers has found support for his general position in these recent epochal investigations in the natural sciences.

Before some genius (or madman) ultimately succeeds in fitting together all the pieces of the puzzle, new positions and findings will emerge and many tenets will be eliminated as misleading, unproductive, or simply wrong. It is my own view, one I have tried to argue in this book, that the contributions of the structuralists, in particular Piaget's reorientation to psychology and Lévi-Strauss's revolution in social anthropology, will be prominent in such a synthesis. Progress in the sciences involves a Dionysian as well as an Apollonian phase. Controversy and uncertainty are as necessary as calmness and consensus to the evolution of thought. There must be individuals who will generate new hypotheses, shake up a complacent or misguided scholarly enterprise, redirect future studies; there must be others, always a numerical majority, who will patiently and critically evaluate the evidence for the Dionysian hypotheses, retaining those which can be supported, reformulating or discarding those which are disproved or impossible to examine in a systematic manner. Clearly, Piaget and Lévi-Strauss—and Jakobson and

Chomsky as well—are closer to the Dionysian pole of science, and this may be one reason why they are more interesting, exciting, and controversial than many other equally gifted scientists, who work on more narrow or established problems, shun rhetoric and disputes, are devoted to careful data collection and rigorous analysis of each assumption; such Apollonian spirits are prone to disregard an interesting idea because it lacks support rather than to toss it into the water and see whether it will swim.

In view of the revolutionary zeal of the leading structuralists, it is ironic that, as noted earlier, the message of the school has been viewed as reactionary by certain critics and students. That the identification between structuralism and conservatism is at least a doubtful one, is demonstrated by the political militancy of the youngest of the leading structuralists, Chomsky, as well as the positions taken in the past by other individuals identified with the structuralist movement. My own view is that structuralism as the central intellectual force in France may well have seen its day, not because of its weaknesses, but because no school—be it psychoanalysis, existentialism, or structuralism—is likely to hold the public's interest indefinitely. Certainly there are areas which the structuralists have neglected—for example, affective development or the dynamics of apocalyptic change; but these omissions have indirectly reflected the particular interests of the principal structuralists, rather than constituting an endemic defect of the method. I feel that the imbalances discerned by certain critics can be compensated for in future work, while the critiques of those opposed to any sort of dispassionate or objective analysis cannot be answered in any case.

Even if conservative from some viewpoints, the structuralist school has, within the academic community, been strong on Dionysian spirits and Dionysian spirit; for this reason, it has created much controversy and excitement. When the smoke of battle has cleared, it will be necessary to examine it from a more Apollonian perspective and assess whether its performance is as impressive as its promise. Lévi-Strauss has remarked that "the human sciences will be structural or they will not be." I believe that this statement is correct, though perhaps not in the precise sense Lévi-Strauss intended. The contributions of structuralism are genuine and will be absorbed into the continually expanding scientific canon. In particular, the recognition that underlying surface phenomena are structures and types of organization which can explain relationships among disparate forms; the complementary nature of the developmental and structural approaches; the search for an explanation of behavior and institutions which is consistent with biological organization, capable of expression in logical form, and oriented toward crucial questions in the social sciences; the creation of methods which facilitate the discovery of structure and which can be practiced by trained investigators, are all contributions which should have a secure and important place in the social sciences of the future. Yet to be determined is which of the analytic units proposed by the various structuralist investigators will prove the most useful and powerful tool for subsequent analysis and synthesis.

Structuralism as a distinct and controversial school may well disappear, of course, as succeeding generations come to assimilate its basic tenets. For in my view, structuralism is simply the most imaginative and suggestive current statement of the professional code of any thoughtful and synthetically oriented scientist: finding the relationships between disparate phenomena, formulating them in a communicable and testable way, discovering the overall organization between parts and wholes, moving from mastery of a particular area of inquiry toward interdisciplinary syntheses which converge upon the same underlying principles. The crucial contributions of Piaget and Lévi-Strauss have lain in prodding the social sciences toward an acceptance of methods currently used in the "harder" sciences, and an application of recently developed logical and mathematical structures to analyses of thought and behavior. If this claim—that structuralism is simply an updated version of the scientific credo—stuns both structuralists and antistructuralists alike, it may be because scientific progress is in part dependent upon the bold overstatement of positions; as differences have been magnified in the controversy surrounding structuralism, it has become difficult to discern its continuities with past (and future) efforts in the human sciences. Dionysus apart, it is my feeling that new positions and revolutionary paradigms have characteristically seemed "structuralist" to the old guard and that they gradually become accepted in part and superseded in part as a generation reared upon them begins to articulate its own ideas.

Afterword:
Structuralism in the 1970's

In the ten years following the preparation of *The Quest for Mind*, structuralism has ceased to be a rallying point in contemporary social science. This is due less to problems in its basic assumptions than to the state of affairs predicted in the preceding pages: The major assertions of structuralism and the kinds of issues addressed by the first generation of structuralist thinkers have become part of the working assumptions of a large number of social scientists throughout the world today.

But if structuralism no longer exists as a rallying point, the work of the major structuralists certainly has gone forward. Until his death in September of 1980, Jean Piaget continued to work tirelessly on the numerous issues that had concerned him for over sixty years. Claude Lévi-Strauss continues his anthropological research in Paris, and the other figures mentioned above, including Roman Jakobson and Edmund Leach, have remained true to the credo outlined in this book. Noam Chomsky, a generation younger, has in my view become the chief contemporary practitioner of structuralism in the social sciences today.

Preparation of this Afterword was aided by a grant from the Sloan Foundation.

Even as the work of these individuals continued during the seventies, so, too, the issues that they addressed remained important foci for discussions in the social sciences. Yet there were new impulses as well, the chief of which has come to be called the cognitive sciences movement. Much of what Piaget, Lévi-Strauss, and Chomsky were concerned with in years past has now become central to the cognitive sciences. In this After-word, as I trace the course of structuralism through 1980, I will review the activities of the three principal contributors to structuralist thought as well as a number of concerns that have become part-and-parcel of the highly productive cognitive sciences movement.

1. JEAN PIAGET.

Piaget continued to work unabated through the 1970's, turn-ing out approximately a dozen major monographs. While none of the topics touched upon would surprise a student of the Genevan scene, Piaget and his numerous associates at the International Center for Genetic Epistemology did open up several new areas of inquiry. I will touch here briefly on certain novel themes in his studies of child development and also on various theoretical issues in biology and epistemology which continued to occupy him until his death.

The major empirical efforts undertaken by the Piagetian school in the late sixties through the middle seventies were the approximately one-hundred studies of the child's understand-ing of causality in the physical realm. Causality had long been an interest of Piaget, but his most recent work focused more directly on the limitations imposed by the *nature* of objects involved in various interactions in the physical world. Rather than simply treating the subject's operations per se, Piaget now paid greater attention to the actual laws of physics that govern pulleys, gears, billiard balls, and the other impedimenta used in his studies. The operations obtaining within and across these inanimate objects became a fresh area for study. Here was a "reaching out" to the environment, to the contributions to knowledge made by the "physics" of real objects, which had not previously been evident in genetic psychology.

The considerable attention directed to the subject's understanding of his own operations in the world marked a second shift of focus. Particularly in *The Grasp of Consciousness*, but also in other monographs and essays, Piaget probed the child's own reflections about his activities, his emerging capacity to think about and put into words those understandings that had previously been expressed only through sensorimotor action. The nature of this inquiry is suggested by an anecdote Piaget was fond of relating. One of his tasks required subjects to put into words the way in which one crawls: according to Piaget, mathematicians and philosophers (with their heads in the clouds) usually fail this test, whereas the more empirically oriented physicists and psychologists are able to grasp their own consciousness and offer a veridical step-by-step account of how they crawl.

A third area which occupied Piaget's associates, particularly Bärbel Inhelder and Hermine Sinclair-de-Zwart, concerned children's learning about new areas of knowledge and the steps through which they pass in advancing from one level of understanding to the next. This study featured a kind of microscopic examination of the processes of training and learning which had hitherto not taken place within the Piagetian corpus and which led to productive interchanges with Anglo-American workers.

Piaget continuously integrated the results from these new lines of study into his general account of development. Nonetheless, the description remained similar to that advanced in earlier decades. I have been struck by two emphases in his final writings on psychological development. First, there is the attribution to the young child of more "semilogical" knowledge than was granted before: for example, the child is now credited with appreciating certain principles of causality even during the preoperational stages. Second, I have noted Piaget's increasingly frequent return to some of the concepts he had picked up early on from the American psychologist James Mark Baldwin—concepts such as assimilation, accommodation, imitation, and the variety of relationships which can obtain between "subjects" and "objects." Clearly, those themes on which Piaget had become imprinted in the first part of his career continued to dominate *his* consciousness.

Even to list Piaget's other studies, and those of the numerous students whom he influenced, would take us too far afield. But it must be said that the rest of the field of developmental psychology was looking more critically at Piaget's view of the psychological development of the child. Essays by numerous influential students of development, including Thomas Bower, Charles Brainerd, Peter Bryant, and Rochel Gelman, challenged with increasing vehemence nearly every one of Piaget's major assertions. The quarrels were rarely with the phenomena themselves: rather, the critics challenged Piaget's belief in discrete, qualitatively different stages; his explanations for why children are unable to accomplish certain tasks; his claims that many basic abilities, such as decentration, conservation, and propositional thought, do not emerge until relatively late in childhood; and his image of the adult as a basically logical thinker.

These criticisms have now been brought together in numerous symposia, innumerable papers, and several important books by the aforementioned authors. I would put the present assessment of Piaget's work this way: Not even his severest critics challenge Piaget's position as the preeminent developmental psychologist of his time. Moreover, most individuals continue to address the issues he raised, and several researchers, for example, Lawrence Kohlberg in his work on moral judgment and Howard Gruber in his work on scientific creativity, have extended Piaget's ideas in ways that are congenial to the Genevan school. However, the field as a whole now views development as both more gradual and less homogeneous than did Piaget. If there are stages at all, they develop more smoothly and involve quantitative rather than qualitative shifts; and if there are structures, they are far looser, tending across some, but by no means all, behaviors. Logical cognition is still central, but there is far more interest in uses of mind. In the developmental psychology of the future, the chapter headings may well be the same, but the particular claims made about what children can and cannot do will be very different.

Paradoxically, however, this lessening of influence may well have been of little concern to Piaget. The Piaget of later years moved away from the data and from children toward more abstract conceptualizations on the nature of and relations between biology and knowledge. Clearly, he was searching for a formulation sufficiently general to encompass numerous issues in organic evolution across the range of the species and sciences with which he was familiar: to do so, he had to embrace concepts of ever greater generality and, some would say, ever greater vagueness.

Piaget's work here fell chiefly in two areas. On the one hand, pursuing a life-long interest in biology, he devoted a great deal of attention to his notion that development is progressive and that changes which occur in the lifetime of an individual organism can, within a reasonable span of time, affect the development of the species. Piaget took great care to disassociate himself from strict Lamarckians, and he was eager to identify relatively mainstream biologists like C. H. Waddington, who also had sympathy with the notion that the events in the life of the organism may rapidly bring about differences in a population.

It seems clear why Piaget's notions about biological development were so important to him. He wanted to explain the emergence of novelty, of originality, of new levels of thinking, and he wanted to give an explanation of how these innovations, once they had emerged, could become part of the human genome. Many of his explanations were extremely learned and ingenious, and various recent events in evolutionary biology—for example, the increasing acceptance of "jumps" in evolution—give some comfort to Piaget's iconoclastic biology. Nonetheless, I can only concur with Margaret Boden's prudent conclusion that very few biologists pay attention to Piaget's notions in this domain, and that within psychology, the notions are at best metaphoric or suggestive.

Perhaps the most central preoccupation of Piaget in the final decade of his life was his concept of equilibration—the model that he was constructing of how changes occur in the mental life of the organism. Piaget introduced a whole army of new concepts and refurbished many of his old ones in an effort to provide a satisfactory account of what causes perturbations in an organism, returns to equilibrium, further perturbations at a more advanced level of organization, and so on.

Once again, the reasons why Piaget focused on this concept were clear: his dogged efforts to provide a logical and scientifically tenable notion of processes of change and equilibrium can only be marveled at. But, alas, Piaget was able to establish a dialogue on the questions of equilibration only with individuals within his own research team. Very few outsiders took the time to read the several volumes on "contradiction" and "equilibration" or to criticize them seriously. While many researchers feel intuitively that Piaget was on to something, his abstract writings were simply too far removed from most researchers' quotidian concerns to stimulate the kind of careful attention that his claims within psychology have received over the last half century.

In sum, then, Piaget continued to work at a Piagetian rate on his trio of concerns—psychology, biology, and genetic epistemology. Moreover, he continued to integrate his conclusions in these disparate areas and to relate them impressively to efforts in other laboratories and disciplines. By the time of his death, his output was even grander than it had been ten years before, and there were discernible shifts of emphasis and attention. But by and large, Piaget's fundamental concerns were those apparent throughout a lifetime graced by a very wide network of enterprise. We must await Howard Gruber's intellectual biography to understand how these concerns originated and developed.

2. Claude Lévi-Strauss.

With the publication in 1971 of the final volume of his *Mythologiques*, Lévi-Strauss clearly declared the completion of his magnum opus. One does not have the feeling, as one did with

Piaget, of a compulsive race against time to complete every facet of an impossible, lifelong pursuit, but rather of the tidying up of various loose ends and the exploration of one or two relatively new areas of concern. Still, like Piaget, Lévi-Strauss has continued to work and write at an admirable rate on the issues of concern to him, and as with Piaget, the work of the past decade has helped clarify the nature of the enterprise in which he has been engaged throughout his scholarly life.

The largest undertaking in which Lévi-Strauss was engaged in the seventies was a study of ritual masks from a limited set of Northwest Indian tribes. With characteristic flair, Lévi-Strauss claimed that no individual mask had any decipherable meaning in itself and that the meanings borne by the masks could only be discerned by taking into account the masks produced by other groups—groups from the same region, but differing from a specific tribe in terms of time, geographical location, and/or social situation. Borrowing one of the chief tools of structural linguistics, Lévi-Strauss boldly decomposed the masks into component features (e.g., facial features which are protruding or involuted) and "scored" each mask in terms of its "value" for that feature. Devising one of his characteristic formulae, Lévi-Strauss concluded that if the form of a mask remains the same across groups, its semantic function will be altered; whereas, if the form of the mask changes (with respect to certain features), its semantic function will remain the same.

As this formula suggests, Lévi-Strauss applied to ritual masks the same kinds of analytic techniques and terminological analyses that he earlier employed with kinship, social organization, and myth. Above all, the myths play an important— perhaps too important—role in Lévi-Strauss's interpretation of ritual masks. We see sets of contrasting masks—for example, convexity vs. concavity—expressing the culture's "position" on such classic Lévi-Straussian dichotomies as nature/culture, heaven/earth, male/female, animal/human, and excessively close (incestuous)/sufficiently distant (exogamous) ties.

As always, Lévi-Strauss's demonstration about masks is a tour de force, graced by the kind of detailed analysis and understanding of each culture, and the enigmatic allusions to his own culture, that are impossible for anyone other than a polymath to evaluate. What I found most suggestive were Lévi-Strauss's incidental comments about the meaning of style, and by implication, the origin of art. In his view, the individuating features of a work of art or a craft arise because of the deep need of each clan or lineage to define itself in relationship to other ones. Lévi-Strauss ends his discussion of this set of masks with the assertion that the entire Western belief in individual creativity is an illusion. However liberating and stimulating this illusion may be to the practicing artist, one cannot follow the path of creation alone: one is inevitably declaring oneself in relationship to other users of the languages of an art.

While the study of masks opened up a rich new area of research for Lévi-Strauss and his colleagues, much attention was also paid to the deeper burrowing into areas which had been opened up earlier. For example, several years of lectures at the College de France were devoted to controversial issues of kinship that had arisen in the decades since *Elementary Structures of Kinship* had been published. In this sense, like Piaget, Lévi-Strauss was revisiting the issues that had originally exercised him in his study of ethnography. More than a little energy was also devoted to asserting his point of view vis-à-vis those of other critics. While Piaget tended to build bridges to his critics even at the cost of a certain degree of distortion, Lévi-Strauss seems more bent on defining those areas in which he disagrees with commentators. These include individuals whose work is at least superficially close to that of Lévi-Strauss, such as his longtime structuralist colleague Edmund Leach, as well as structuralist authors working in the humanistic tradition, such as Jacques Lacan. The list also includes individuals who represent other areas of French intellectual life—painters, writers, and philosophers—perhaps chief among them his phenomenologist colleague Maurice Merleau-Ponty, with whom he had much sympathy, and Jean-Paul Sartre, with whom he had none at all.

Lévi-Strauss has always been a man of (and for) occasions. Most prominent was his election to the French Academy, a unique and hitherto unprecedented achievement for an

anthropologist. He has received honorary degrees at numerous universities around the world and has given plenary
addresses at several convocations. As usual, he has marked the
receipt of honors with timely and often poignant remarks:
among the most moving is his address to a French-Japanese
circle of scholars in which he described the impressions and
revelations of a short visit to Japan and suggested that the
Japanese, unlike other modern technological societies, have
managed to maintain something precious from their past.

What stands out increasingly in Lévi-Strauss's writings of the
past decade is an impression that it is the life of the senses, of
sensory qualities, particularly of this sensibility as it figures in
the life of the artist, that looms largest in his own mind. We see
this in his reviews of works of art, in his strongly held (and
often critical) opinions about contemporary art, in his essays
on the concreta of life, which include a several-page disquisi-
tion on the meaning of the bean in classical Greek times and
throughout the preliterate world. We see it too in the extraordinary artfulness with which Lévi-Strauss's own writings are
executed, his sense of style and composition, which makes
contact with certain dominant traditions in French literature—
with the writings of the symbolist poets, of Proust, and,
perhaps foremost, of his "master," Jean-Jacques Rousseau.

In his most programmatic writings, Lévi-Strauss cries out
for a science that is large enough, qualitative enough, deep
enough, to include within its envelope the activities and the
products of the human senses. He finds hope in recent neurobiology, for example, in the discovery of cortical cells which
respond to particular qualities of experience. Now that science
has exorcised itself of misleading spirits, it can once again
broaden, so that it can incorporate not only abstract entities but
also sensory data—experiences that he feels are most important to human beings and are certainly most important to
Claude Lévi-Strauss.

3. NOAM CHOMSKY.

At the time that *The Quest for Mind* was written, it was already
clear that Noam Chomsky's contributions in linguistics would

be an important factor in contemporary social science. It was also apparent that Chomsky was a bona fide structuralist in the sense set forth in these pages: he shared the strategic, formalistic, and biological bent of the first generation of structuralist workers. What I did not anticipate was the extent of Chomsky's ambitions in the general areas of social science and humanistic scholarship and the enormous influence he would exert in the 1970's—an influence that would have earned him a place as an equal of Piaget and Lévi-Strauss in a reformulated version of *The Quest for Mind*. It is not possible to summarize Chomsky's work in this brief essay, but I will seek to relate it to the efforts of Piaget and Lévi-Strauss.

An event of historic significance occurred in October of 1975, when Piaget and Chomsky engaged in an informal debate over several days at the Abbaye de Royaumont outside Paris. As I understand it, Lévi-Strauss was also scheduled to attend but, perhaps characteristically, chose not to engage in this highly public confrontation. Elsewhere I've told the interesting, if somewhat disappointing, saga of the only meeting of these two modern masters.

To be sure, the meeting achieved symbolic importance in bringing the men together; it was also important substantively, in view of the number of pivotal investigators within the social and the natural sciences who attended, listened seriously, and participated actively in the discussions. However, the gathering was not in a deep sense a meeting of minds because, despite the several "set" pieces each addressed to the other, Piaget and Chomsky were not able to communicate. Piaget tried for a rapprochement, or at least for détente, but Chomsky withdrew when possible points of conciliation seemed to emerge. And perhaps this behavior was appropriate: in fact, Chomsky and Piaget did have deep and possibly irreconcilable differences in their views of social science, as well as in their conclusions about the nature of the human organism and its development, learning, and language.

Over the past ten years, Chomsky has made his views very clear. He believes that the human being is born possessed of (innate) knowledge of principles that govern many important aspects of his life. The clearest example is language: Chomsky claims that the child could never master its complex and highly abstract structure were he not already equipped to do so by his genetic endowment. Chomsky has argued vigorously in publications and in lectures that the same model should apply to other areas of life ranging from relatively circumscribed domains like music or mathematics to the whole area of culture. He feels that cultural knowledge consists of a set of categories and behaviors, and it is just these categories (and not others) that individuals are innately equipped to master. As in language, the child's task is simply picking out *which* of the species' potential artifacts and practices happen to be favored in the culture in which he lives.

Indeed, in his approach to language, Chomsky signals his principal message to all social scientists: define in as formal terms as possible a limited domain of knowledge; sketch the end point of adult competence; and determine the minimum amount of knowledge with which an organism must be endowed in order to acquire this adult competence, given the contradictory and fragmentary information available in its environment. As far as Chomsky is concerned, the answer to these questions will come ultimately from an understanding of the human nervous system. If this turns out not to be the case, we should all become physicists or ecologists and study the environment, not the organism; for all answers of importance would then inhere in the physical (and not the organic) world.

4. POINTS OF CONTACT.

In the first edition of *The Quest for Mind*, I began the task of comparing the views of this trio of structuralists, and I can only pursue this needed exercise a bit further here. Certainly, there are points of contact among the three men, the kinds of consensus that would also extend in large measure to the new and rapidly growing cognitive sciences movement: a belief in the importance of mental representation, an impatience with the traditional notion of learning, a faith that the similarities among individuals are far deeper than the differences, a conviction that much of the explanation of cognition derives from human biology, a sympathy with formal representations of behavior, and an antipathy to various "isms," including behaviorism, empiricism, and functionalism.

But, for our present purposes, the differences are more germane. As I've already noted, the disagreements between Piaget and Chomsky are profound. Piaget sees development as a constant interplay of the organism and its environment, with the organism playing an active, structuring role. Moreover, he sees all areas of intellect as being closely intermeshed with one another, even as he plays down the importance and uniqueness of language. In contrast, Chomsky regards the mind as a series of discrete mental "organs": each of these organs is preprogrammed to unfold in a certain way, in some cases given but minimal stimulation from the environment. Chomsky views language as a special case, radically cut off from other modes of cognition, though (perhaps paradoxically) central to illuminating the nature of the human mind.

The flavor and spirit of the two men are also distinctively different. Chomsky favors a use of mathematical reasoning and models which are precise and logical, whereas Piaget is content very frequently to use mathematical and scientific concepts in a much looser fashion. Though hardly without its critics within and outside the field of linguistics, Chomsky's formal treatment of language has been laid out with sufficient clarity that it can be employed by any researcher who masters its procedures; and through the citing of examples which are realizations of or exceptions to a rule, it is clear when a Chomskian formulation about syntax has been supported or disproved. Piaget's formalisms harbor grave difficulties in themselves, and it is virtually impossible to figure out just when and how they should be brought to bear on a body of data. In another vein, while Piaget studiously avoided comment on most political and societal issues, Chomsky feels this a proper role for the scientist and has implied on more than one occasion that there may be connections between an individual's scientific epistemology and his political beliefs.

It is more difficult to specify areas of disagreement between Lévi-Strauss and Chomsky. Lévi-Strauss has expressed admiration for certain of Chomsky's works; he should have no difficulties with Chomsky's belief in highly structured innate knowledge or with his skepticism concerning qualitatively discrete developmental stages occurring in an active learning organism. In fact, Lévi-Strauss often intimates that organisms are simply receptacles in which ideas impersonally unfold, and this conceit has a curious affinity with Chomsky's notion of preprogrammed mental organs.

On the relationship between language and other cognitive systems, their writings conflict. Lévi-Strauss considers language to be the preeminent symbol system, one that can serve as a model for all other manner of sign systems, including (as we have seen) ritual masks. It is in fact this belief that accounts for the close ties between Lévi-Straussian structuralism and the semiotic movement that has engulfed much of literary and ethnographic analysis. Chomsky, on the other hand, is extremely skeptical of such semiotic analyses and would not acknowledge "nontrivial" parallels between language and other sign systems.

Lévi-Strauss is more willing than Piaget to comment on political and societal issues. In general, he has a traditionally conservative, deeply melancholy view of human nature, a desire for return to a simpler, more primitive, and better balanced kind of existence. There are strains of this romanticism in Chomsky's political writing, but the pose is married to a radical, left-wing political stance that would be inimical to both Piaget and Lévi-Strauss. This suggests to me, however, a possible connecting link between the three individuals—not Descartes and Kant, as I thought some years ago, but rather the contradictory person of Jean-Jacques Rousseau.

In the case of Lévi-Strauss, the ties to Rousseau are most apparent. He has eulogized Rousseau as his master and as the founder of social sciences; beyond question, Levi-Strauss's search for the nature of man has deep affinity with Rousseau's own design. Piaget, in many ways, is a figure very different in temperament and sensibility from his Genevan forebear. Yet even in his earliest writings, Piaget paid homage to Rousseau: one of the stanzas of his adolescent prose-poem "La mission de l'idée" contains the line "the revolution was made in Rousseau's contemplative walks." Moreover, Piaget spent his working life at the Institute of Jean-Jacques Rousseau, and his interest in the development of the child and the stages through which each child passes has its unmistakable origins in the pioneering writings of Rousseau, particularly *Émile*. Rousseau's contribution to Piaget's views on sociology and moral judgment also should not be underestimated.

I had thought that any ties between Chomsky and Rousseau would be implicit and that in suggesting such ties, I would be going beyond the data; but, in fact, in two essays written in the early 1970's, Chomsky reveals his own attraction to Rousseau (or, as he puts it, "some of the several Rousseaus"). Chomsky singles out for special attention Rousseau's search for man's essential nature; his belief that it is reason, language, and self-perception that set men apart from other animals; his linking of language with the possibility of free thought and self-expression; and his associated criticisms of authoritarian institutions.

As I see it, Chomsky has been seeking, in his own life as much as in his work, to effect a bridge between rationality, logic, and hard science on the one hand, and human nature, human experience, and a "just society" on the other. This dialectic accounts for much of the appeal of Chomsky as a contemporary intellectual figure, even as it explains many of the apparent contradictions between his professed views about biology (severely constraining) and his views about society (potentially free and unencumbered). Rousseau was among the first to raise many of the issues that Chomsky has been pondering— the origins of inequality among men, the nature of the social contract, the notion of an individual apart from any culture, the damaging effects of one's culture—and Rousseau's unflinching stand in defense of his beliefs against those who would dilute them is reminiscent of Chomsky's own role with respect to many social issues today. I see the recent "more public" Chomsky as addressing much of Rousseau's agenda, though of course he is doing so in the light of mathematical and scientific insights unavailable to Rousseau two centuries ago.

Whatever their differences in beliefs and style, Lévi-Strauss, Chomsky, and Piaget share the quest described in the title of this book and partake of it with the kind of singlemindedness that continues to make them unique in the social sciences of our time. From my present vantage point, I see Piaget as preoccupied with one type of mind, the mind of the scientist, and Lévi-Strauss as occupied with an opposing type, the mind of the artist, which includes in its broadest sense, the painter, the poet, the musician, the myth-maker, the individual trying to understand and vivify the sensible qualities in his society. In this vein, Piaget and Lévi-Strauss serve as complements to one another, focusing as they do on the two most important and pervasive aspects of human cognition.

Because of his interest in language, Chomsky falls somewhere between Piaget and Lévi-Strauss. Language is certainly a field for artistic exploration, but it participates as well in the work of the scientist. Indeed, in his own writings, Chomsky has focused on what one might call the precise and mundane uses of language, while deliberately neglecting its more poetic aspects. But it is equally important to note that Chomsky has a more pluralistic notion of mind than his two colleagues. He sees the mind as composed of different mental organs, and so he would regard language, logical thinking, and art as perhaps different domains of mind, each operating by its own rules. This view of mind, which may include still other forms of rational and social intelligence, is one with which I myself have fallen into sympathy during the past several years. Note that this view makes room for the contributions of all three men. Though both Piaget and Lévi-Strauss may have thought they were describing all of mind, or at least its deepest aspects, the fact that they were describing only part of human mentation hardly makes their work irrelevant or misleading. And the kind of rich portrait they have provided of scientific and artistic thought will be needed if Chomsky's multifaceted program is ever to become a reality.

Every program of research has its limitations, and I continue to see certain problems and areas of relative neglect in structuralism as it has been carried out by these three seminal thinkers. A first area involves the limited potential of their respective systems to handle creative thought—innovations of the sort associated with major artists, scientists, and humanistic thinkers. All three of the structuralists have of course discussed this issue: Chomsky, by calling attention to the creativity entailed in ordinary language; Piaget, by looking for the roots of invention in elementary biological and equilibrative processes; and Lévi-Strauss, by challenging in a deep way the whole concept of original invention. But there is something about their closed systems of explanation, their delimited view of the routes that the mind can follow, which makes it difficult to envision how one could ever account within structuralist social science for the innovative work of an Einstein, a Shakespeare, or a Freud.

Another area of relative neglect concerns the "formative" effects of culture. This criticism is certainly reasonable in the cases of Piaget, who deliberately focused on what is universal in the thought processes of human beings, and Chomsky, who considers differences among languages, cultures, and other domains of cognition to be of secondary importance in his own work. It is more curious to level this criticism against Lévi-Strauss, who has devoted a considerable portion of his work to explicating the differences among cultures. But Lévi-Strauss believes that the actual units of culture are finite, that they are in a sense present from the beginning, and that individual human cultures simply choose one or another combination from among them. Absent from all of their views is an acknowledgment of the innovative aspects of culture—the claim (which I would defend) that it is the invention and amplification of new systems of meanings (for example, literacy, science, mathematics, new forms of art) that make possible progress in various areas of human knowledge and that make various human cultures across time and space, at least in part, incommensurate with one another. There is insufficient room in a structuralistist system of thinking for an evolutionary and innovative view of human culture.

5. THE COGNITIVE SCIENCES: THE "NEW" QUEST FOR MIND

The major change in the cognitively oriented social sciences over the past decade has been a subtle but extremely important one. Though the area still features individual researchers and teams organized into cliques and schools, the role of the individual charismatic figure has to some extent faded. There is increasing (and welcome) evidence of an emerging consensus that extends beyond such central figures.

This convergence is represented by, though it is by no means restricted to, a movement known as the cognitive sciences. Centering on work in computer simulation of intelligence but extending to a variety of disciplines, including psychology, linguistics, anthropology, neurobiology, and philosophy, the cognitive sciences seek to develop models of mental processes and representations that are biologically founded, logically justifiable, psychologically real, and capable of being programmed on a computer.

There is, as yet, no single text that joins together the various parts of the cognitive scientific puzzle and provides an overview of the whole. Such a text may, in fact, be premature. However, an excellent glimpse of the kind of issues being confronted by the cognitive sciences, and the kind of dialogue in which cognitive scientists now engage can be found in the pages of an open peer review journal, *The Behavioral and Brain Sciences*, issued by Cambridge University Press. Here one encounters an atmosphere that, I believe, would delight all three of our structuralists: major figures from aforementioned disciplines engaging in heated debate on such topics as the nature of intelligence, rules and representation in language, the validity of the stage concept, and the merits of sociobiology. There are, of course, factions and schools, including ones which do not speak to each other, or speak right past one another, but for those who can step somewhat outside the fray, there exists considerable agreement about *which* issues are important, which approaches developed over the past several decades are worth taking seriously.

Scholars differ among one another regarding the exact definition or delimitation of the cognitive sciences. In my own view, the cognitive sciences can be instructively viewed as a contemporary, empirically based attempt to address some longstanding questions in the area of philosophy. Philosophers have debated for centuries about the nature of mental representation, the status of mind and body, the relationship between language and thought, the source of novel ideas; of late, the contributions of empirical research to these issues have begun to be recognized by philosophers. However, it is only in the past few decades, I think, that a critical mass of work has accumulated such that one can begin an assessment of which of the original philosophical questions have already been answered by science, which cannot in principle be answered, and which, while answerable in principle, have yet to be illuminated by empirical science. It is because I find Piaget, Lévi-Strauss, and Chomsky particularly sensitive to this program, admirably alert to important philosophical questions and to the kind of evidence which might lead to their resolution, that I believe they continue to assume—and to merit—a central role in any examination of the social sciences today.

Appendix,
Notes,
and Index

Genesis

CHAPTER 1

In the beginning God created the heaven and the earth.

2 And the earth was without form, and void; and darkness *was* upon the face of the deep. And the Spirit of God moved upon the face of the waters.

3 And God said, Let there be light: and there was light.

4 And God saw the light, that *it was* good: and God divided the light from the darkness.

5 And God called the light Day, and the darkness he called Night. And the evening and the morning were the first day.

6 ❡ And God said, Let there be a firmament in the midst of the waters, and let it divide the waters from the waters.

7 And God made the firmament, and divided the waters which *were* under the firmament from the waters which *were* above the firmament: and it was so.

8 And God called the firmament Heaven. And the evening and the morning were the second day.

9 ❡ And God said, Let the waters under the heaven be gathered unto one place, and let the dry *land* appear: and it was so.

10 And God called the dry *land* Earth; and the gathering together of the waters called he Seas: and God saw that *it was* good.

11 And God said, Let the earth bring forth grass, the herb yielding seed, *and* the fruit tree yielding fruit after his kind, whose seed *is* in itself, upon the earth: and it was so.

12 And the earth brought forth grass, *and* herb yielding seed after his kind, and the tree yielding fruit, whose seed *was* in itself, after his kind: and God saw that *it was* good.

13 And the evening and the morning were the third day.

14 ❡ And God said, Let there be lights in the firmament of the heaven to divide the day from the night; and let them be for signs, and for seasons, and for days, and years:

15 And let them be for lights in the firmament of the heaven to give light upon the earth: and it was so.

16 And God made two great lights; the greater light to rule the day, and the lesser light to rule the night: *he made* the stars also.

17 And God set them in the firmament of the heaven to give light upon the earth,

18 And to rule over the day and over the night, and to divide the light from the darkness: and God saw that *it was* good.

19 And the evening and the morning were the fourth day.

20 And God said, Let the waters bring forth abundantly the moving creature that hath life, and fowl *that* may fly above the earth in the open firmament of heaven.

21 And God created great whales, and every living creature that moveth, which the waters brought forth abundantly, after their kind, and every winged fowl after his kind: and God saw that *it was* good.

22 And God blessed them, saying, Be fruitful, and multiply, and fill the waters in the seas, and let fowl multiply in the earth.

23 And the evening and the morning were the fifth day.

24 ¶ And God said. Let the earth bring forth the living creature after his kind, cattle, and creeping thing, and beast of the earth after his kind: and it was so.

25 And God made the beast of the earth after his kind, and cattle after their kind, and every thing that creepeth upon the earth after his kind: and God saw that *it was* good.

26 ¶ And God said, Let us make man in our image, after our likeness: and let them have dominion over the fish of the sea, and over the fowl of the air, and over the cattle, and over all the earth,

and over every creeping thing that creepeth upon the earth.

27 So God created man in his *own* image, in the image of God created he him; male and female created he them.

28 And God blessed them, and God said unto them, Be fruitful, and multiply, and replenish the earth, and subdue it: and have dominion over the fish of the sea, and over the fowl of the air, and over every living thing that moveth upon the earth.

29 ¶ And God said, Behold, I have given you every herb bearing seed, which *is* upon the face of all the earth, and every tree, in the which *is* the fruit of a tree yielding seed; to you it shall be for meat.

30 And to every beast of the earth, and to every fowl of the air, and to every thing that creepeth upon the earth, wherein *there is* life, *I have given* every green herb for meat: and it was so.

31 And God saw every thing that he had made, and, behold, *it was* very good. And the evening and the morning were the sixth day.

CHAPTER 2

Thus the heavens and the earth were finished, and all the host of them.

2 And on the seventh day God ended his work which he had made; and he rested on the seventh day from all his work which he had made.

3 And God blessed the seventh day, and sanctified it: because that in it he had rested from all his work which God created and made.

4 ❡ These *are* the generations ot the heavens and of the earth when they were created, in the day that the LORD God made the earth and the heavens,

5 And every plant of the field before it was in the earth, and every herb of the field before it grew: for the LORD God had not caused it to rain upon the earth, and *there was* not a man to till the ground.

6 But there went up a mist from the earth, and watered the whole face of the ground.

7 And the LORD God formed man *of* the dust of the ground, and breathed into his nostrils the breath of life; and man became a living soul.

8 ❡ And the LORD God planted a garden eastward in E'den; and there he put the man whom he had formed.

9 And out of the ground made the LORD God to grow every tree that is pleasant to the sight, and good for food; the tree of life also in the midst of the garden, and the tree of knowledge of good and evil.

10 And a river went out of E'den to water the garden; and from thence it was parted, and became into four heads.

11 The name of the first *is* Pi'son: that *is* it which compasseth the whole land of Hav'i-läh, where *there is* gold;

12 And the gold of that land *is* good: there *is* bdellium and the onyx stone.

13 And the name of the second river *is* Gi'hŏn: the same *is* it that compasseth the whole land of Ethiopia.

14 And the name of the third river is Hid'de-kel: that *is* it which goeth toward the east of Assyria.

And the fourth river *is* Eu-phra'tes.

15 And the LORD God took the man, and put him into the garden of E'den to dress it and to keep it.

16 And the LORD God commanded the man, saying, Of every tree of the garden thou mayest freely eat:

17 But of the tree of the knowledge of good and evil, thou shalt not eat of it: for in the day that thou eatest thereof thou shalt surely die.

18 ❡ And the LORD God said, *It is* not good that the man should be alone; I will make him a help meet for him.

19 And out of the ground the LORD God formed every beast of the field, and every fowl of the air; and brought *them* unto Adam to see what he would call them: and whatsoever Adam called every living creature, that *was* the name thereof.

20 And Adam gave names to all cattle, and to the fowl of the air, and to every beast of the field; but for Adam there was not found a help meet for him.

21 And the LORD God caused a deep sleep to fall upon Adam, and he slept; and he took one of his ribs, and closed up the flesh instead thereof.

22 And the rib, which the LORD God had taken from man, made he a woman, and brought her unto the man.

23 And Adam said, This *is* now bone of my bones, and flesh of my flesh: she shall be called Woman, because she was taken out of man.

24 Therefore shall a man leave nis father and his mother, and shall cleave unto his wife: and they shall be one flesh.

25 And they were both naked, the man and his wife, and were not ashamed.

CHAPTER 3

Now the serpent was more subtile than any beast of the field which the Lord God had made. And he said unto the woman, Yea, hath God said, Ye shall not eat of every tree of the garden?

2 And the woman said unto the serpent, We may eat of the fruit of the trees of the garden:

3 But of the fruit of the tree which is in the midst of the garden, God hath said, Ye shall not eat of it, neither shall ye touch it, lest ye die.

4 And the serpent said unto the woman, Ye shall not surely die:

5 For God doth know that in the day ye eat thereof, then your eyes shall be opened, and ye shall be as gods, knowing good and evil.

6 And when the woman saw that the tree was good for food, and that it was pleasant to the eyes, and a tree to be desired to make one wise, she took of the fruit thereof, and did eat, and gave also unto her husband with her; and he did eat.

7 And the eyes of them both were opened, and they knew that they were naked; and they sewed fig leaves together, and made themselves aprons.

8 And they heard the voice of the Lord God walking in the garden in the cool of the day: and Adam and his wife hid themselves from the presence of the Lord God amongst the trees of the garden.

9 And the Lord God called unto Adam, and said unto him, Where art thou?

10 And he said, I heard thy voice in the garden, and I was afraid, because I was naked; and I hid myself.

11 And he said, Who told thee that thou wast naked? Hast thou eaten of the tree, whereof I commanded thee that thou shouldest not eat?

12 And the man said, The woman whom thou gavest to be with me, she gave me of the tree, and I did eat.

13 And the Lord God said unto the woman, What is this that thou hast done? And the woman said, The serpent beguiled me, and I did eat.

14 And the Lord God said unto the serpent, Because thou hast done this, thou art cursed above all cattle, and above every beast of the field; upon thy belly shalt thou go, and dust shalt thou eat all the days of thy life:

15 And I will put enmity between thee and the woman, and between thy seed and her seed; it shall bruise thy head, and thou shalt bruise his heel.

16 Unto the woman he said, I will greatly multiply thy sorrow and thy conception; in sorrow thou shalt bring forth children; and thy desire shall be to thy husband, and he shall rule over thee.

17 And unto Adam he said, Because thou hast hearkened unto the voice of thy wife, and hast eaten of the tree, of which I commanded thee, saying, Thou shalt not eat of it: cursed is the ground for thy sake; in sorrow shalt thou eat of it all the days of thy life;

18 Thorns also and thistles shall it bring forth to thee; and thou shalt eat the herb of the field:

19 In the sweat of thy face shalt thou eat bread, till thou return

unto the ground; for out of it wast thou taken: for dust thou *art,* and unto dust shalt thou return.

20 And Adam called his wife's name Eve; because she was the mother of all living.

21 Unto Adam also and to his wife did the Lord God make coats of skins, and clothed them.

22 ¶ And the Lord God said, Behold, the man is become as one of us, to know good and evil: and now, lest he put forth his hand, and take also of the tree of life, and eat, and live for ever:

23 Therefore the Lord God sent him forth from the garden of E'den, to till the ground from whence he was taken.

24 So he drove out the man: and he placed at the east of the garden of E'den cherubim, and a flaming sword which turned every way, to keep the way of the tree of life.

CHAPTER 4

And Adam knew Eve his wife; and she conceived, and bare Cain, and said, I have gotten a man from the Lord.

2 And she again bare his brother Abel. And Abel was a keeper of sheep, but Cain was a tiller of the ground.

3 And in process of time it came to pass, that Cain brought of the fruit of the ground an offering unto the Lord.

4 And Abel, he also brought of the firstlings of his flock and of the fat thereof. And the Lord had respect unto Abel and to his offering:

5 But unto Cain and to his offering he had not respect. And Cain was very wroth, and his countenance fell.

6 And the Lord said unto Cain, Why art thou wroth? and why is thy countenance fallen?

7 If thou doest well, shalt thou not be accepted? and if thou doest not well, sin lieth at the door. And unto thee shall be his desire, and thou shalt rule over him.

8 And Cain talked with Abel his brother: and it came to pass, when they were in the field, that Cain rose up against Abel his brother, and slew him.

9 ¶ And the Lord said unto Cain, Where is Abel thy brother? And he said, I know not: Am I my brother's keeper?

10 And he said, What hast thou done? the voice of thy brother's blood crieth unto me from the ground.

11 And now art thou cursed from the earth, which hath opened her mouth to receive thy brother's blood from thy hand;

12 When thou tillest the ground, it shall not henceforth yield unto thee her strength; a fugitive and a vagabond shalt thou be in the earth.

13 And Cain said unto the Lord, My punishment is greater than I can bear.

14 Behold, thou hast driven me out this day from the face of the earth; and from thy face shall I be hid; and I shall be a fugitive and a vagabond in the earth; and it shall come to pass, that every one that findeth me shall slay me.

15 And the Lord said unto him, Therefore whosoever slayeth Cain, vengeance shall be taken on him sevenfold. And the Lord set a mark upon Cain, lest any finding him should kill him.

16 ¶ And Cain went out from the presence of the Lord, and dwelt in the land of Nod, on the east of Eden.

17 And Cain knew his wife; and she conceived, and bare Enoch: and he builded a city, and called the name of the city, after the name of his son, Enoch.

18 And unto Enoch was born Irad: and Irad begat Me-hu'-jael: and Me-hu'-jael begat Me-thu'-sa-el: and Me-thu'-sa-el begat La'-mech.

19 ¶ And La'-mech took unto him two wives: the name of the one was Adah, and the name of the other Zil'-lah.

20 And Adah bare Ja'-bal: he was the father of such as dwell in tents, and of such as have cattle.

21 And his brother's name was Ju'-bal: he was the father of all such as handle the harp and organ.

22 And Zil'-lah, she also bare Tubal-cain, an instructor of every artificer in brass and iron: and the sister of Tubal-cain was Na'-a-mah.

23 And La'mech said unto his wives, Adah and Zil'lah, Hear my voice; ye wives of La'-mech, hearken unto my speech: for I have slain a man to my wounding, and a young man to my hurt.

24 If Cain shall be avenged sevenfold, truly La'-mech seventy and sevenfold.

25 ¶ And Adam knew his wife again; and she bare a son, and called his name Seth: For God, said she, hath appointed me another seed instead of Abel, whom Cain slew.

26 And to Seth, to him also there was born a son; and he called his name Enos: then began men to call upon the name of the LORD.

Notes

The recent publication of several excellent collections and bibliographies on structuralism makes superfluous the inclusion of a separate list of recommended readings here. Readers who want to pursue particular themes should consult the notes to the pages where the topics are first introduced. Certain works which are particularly useful are listed directly below, with the abbreviations by which they are referred to in the Notes.

CCN: J. Piaget *et al.*, *The Child's Conception of Number* (New York: Norton, 1965).

CCW: J. Piaget, *The Child's Conception of the World* (Totowa, N.J.: Littlefield Adams, 1965).

C L-S: E. N. Hayes and T. Hayes (eds.), *Claude Lévi-Strauss: The Anthropologist as Hero* (Cambridge, Mass.: MIT Press, 1970).

CR: J. Piaget, *The Construction of Reality in the Child* (New York: Basic Books, 1954).

EGLT: B. Inhelder and J. Piaget, *The Early Growth of Logic in the Child* (New York: Norton, 1964).

ESK: C. Lévi-Strauss, *The Elementary Structures of Kinship* (Boston: Beacon Press, 1969).

GLT: B. Inhelder and J. Piaget, *The Growth of Logical Thinking from Childhood to Adolescence* (New York: Basic Books, 1958).

IS: M. Lane (ed.), *Introduction to Structuralism* (New York: Basic Books, 1970).

JR: J. Piaget, *Judgment and Reasoning in the Child* (Paterson, N.J.: Littlefield Adams, 1964).

L-S: E. Leach, *Lévi-Strauss* (London: Fontana Books, 1970).

LT: J. Piaget, *The Language and Thought of the Child* (Cleveland: Meridian, 1963).

OI: J. Piaget, *The Origins of Intelligence in Children* (New York: Norton, 1963).

S: J. Piaget, *Structuralism* (New York: Basic Books, 1970).

SA: C. Lévi-Strauss, *Structural Anthropology* (New York: Basic Books, 1963).

SM: C. Lévi-Strauss, *The Savage Mind* (Chicago: Univ. of Chicago Press, 1966).

SPS: J. Piaget, *Six Psychological Studies* (D. Elkind, ed.) (New York: Random House, 1968).

T: C. Lévi-Strauss, *Totemism* (Boston: Beacon Press, 1963).

TT: C. Lévi-Strauss, *Tristes Tropiques* (New York: Atheneum, 1964).

CHAPTER 1

p. 3 The epigraph comes from Balzac's *Louis Lambert* (Boston: Little, Brown, 1888), p. 63.

p. 4 the most innovative group: Some of the better introductions to structuralism are *IS, S,* and R. Bastide (ed.), *Sens et usage du terme 'structure' dans les sciences humaines* (The Hague: Morton, 1962). Thorough descriptive works on Piaget and Lévi-Strauss are: J. Flavell, *The Developmental Psychology of Jean Piaget* (Princeton: Van Nostrand, 1963); and Y. Simonis, *Claude Lévi-Strauss, ou la "passion de l'inceste"* (Paris: Aubier-Montaigne, 1968). The best critical introductions are H. Furth, *Piaget and Knowledge* (Englewood Cliffs, N.J.: Prentice-Hall, 1968), and *L-S.*

p. 4 Paragraph (1): Piaget's research on conservation of substance was reported in J. Piaget and B. Inhelder, *Le Développement des quantités chez l'enfant* (Neuchâtel: Delachaux et Niestlé, 1941). A considerable amount of research on conservation has tended to confirm Piaget's findings. For some of the better studies, see I. Sigel and F. Hooper (eds.), *Logical Thinking in Young Children* (New York: Holt, Rinehart and Winston, 1968).

p. 5 Paragraph (2): Jakobson's work is described in his monograph *Child Language Aphasia and Phonological Universals* (The Hague: Mouton, 1968) and in his essay "Why Mama and Papa," reprinted in *Selected Writings*, Vol. I (The Hague: Mouton, 1962), pp. 538–45. There has been little empirical research relevant to Jakobson's claim.

p. 5 Paragraph (3): Lévi-Strauss's hypothesis about the sources of animal names is reported in *SM*, pp. 204 ff.

p. 5 Paragraph (4): Leach's structuralist account of Genesis appears in "Lévi-Strauss in the Garden of Eden: An Examination of Some Recent Developments in the Analysis of Myth," in *C L-S*, pp. 47–60.

p. 11 In their lives and works, these men . . .: I have written a number of papers which seek to compare the two men: "Piaget and Lévi-Strauss:

The Quest for Mind," *Social Research* Vol. 37 (1970), 348–65; "The Structural Analysis of Myths and Protocols," *Semiotica,* Vol. 5 (1972), 31–57; "Structure and Development," *The Human Context,* 1972, in press.

CHAPTER 2

p. 15 The first quotation from Descartes is found in his *Discourse on Method* (New York: Dutton, 1951), p. 66, the second comes from his sixth meditation in *Meditations on Philosophy* (New York: Liberal Arts Press, 1960), p. 79.

p. 15 The "articles of faith" held by most Americans have been specified by various commentators, including A. de Tocqueville, *Democracy in America* (New York: Vintage, 1954); R. Williams, *American Society* (New York: Knopf, 1956); M. Lerner, *America as a Civilization* (New York: Simon and Schuster, 1957). More recently, interest has centered on the gap between the ideals expressed by most Americans and the reality of contemporary life. See, for example, C. W. Mills, *White Collar* (New York: Oxford Univ. Press, 1951); H. Marcuse, *One Dimensional Man* (Boston: Beacon Press, 1964); M. Harrington, *The Other America* (New York: Macmillan, 1962).

p. 16 man is best viewed: For an extreme statement of the environmentalist position, see B. F. Skinner, *Beyond Freedom and Dignity* (New York: Knopf, 1971).

p. 16 the traditions of their society: Many aspects of traditional French society are described in S. Hoffman *et al., In Search of France* (Cambridge, Mass.: Harvard Univ. Press, 1963).

p. 17 the most influential philosopher: Descartes' principal ideas are put forth in his *Discourse on Method* (New York: Dutton, 1951) and in his *Meditation on First Philosophy* (New York: Liberal Arts Press, 1960).

p. 18 only one other figure: Rousseau's major works include *The Social Contract* (New York: Hafner, 1947); *The First and Second Discourses* (New York: St. Martin's Press, 1964); and *Émile* (New York: Dutton, 1962). His model of the state of nature is put forth in *The Social Contract,* from which the brief quotation is taken. Lévi-Strauss has already written one essay on Rousseau in *Jean-Jacques Rousseau* (Neuchâtel Baconnière, 1962) and is presently working on a lengthier homage.

p. 21 Comte's boast is found in M. Harris, *The Rise of Anthropological Theory* (New York: Crowell, 1968), p. 61. This book provides a useful, if somewhat doctrinaire, introduction to the early history of social-scientific thought.

p. 21 Of the early social thinkers, Durkheim has, deservedly, been the most carefully studied. Excellent essays by a variety of authors appear in K. Wolff (ed.), *Émile Durkheim* (Columbus: Ohio State Univ. Press, 1960). Other studies include H. S. Hughes, *Consciousness and Society* (New York: Vintage, 1961), and T. Parsons, *The Structure of Social Action* (New York:

McGraw-Hill, 1937). Durkheim's most important works are *The Elementary Forms of Religious Life* (New York: Free Press, 1965), *Suicide* (New York: Free Press, 1951), and *The Division of Labor in Society* (New York: Free Press, 1964).

p. 22 the flux and flow of reality: Bergson's examination of the experiential flux is found in *An Introduction to Metaphysics* (Totowa, N.J.: Littlefield Adams, 1965), p. 16. His other philosophical works include *Creative Evolution* (New York: Holt, 1911) and *Matter and Memory* (New York: Macmillan, 1912). A helpful introduction to Bergson's orientation can be found in H. S. Hughes, *Consciousness and Society* (New York: Vintage, 1961), pp. 113–24.

p. 24 The structural analyst . . .: The terminology used in this preliminary structural analysis comes from linguistic study, in particular from the works of Ferdinand de Saussure, *Course in General Linguistics* (New York: McGraw-Hill, 1966), R. Jakobson, *Selected Writings*, Vol. 1 (The Hague: Mouton, 1962), and N. Troubetzkoy, *Grundzüge der Phonologie* (Prague: 1939). It has been appropriated by Lévi-Strauss and others who seek to apply the methods of structural linguistics to other areas of study.

p. 24 table: Such a scheme has many weaknesses, of course. One risks leaving out important figures, forces, or counterforces, oversimplifying the complexity of a man's thought, ignoring factors which have both reversible and irreversible facets. Conversely, as further subtleties are introduced into the scheme, its economy and simplicity are threatened.

p. 26 The history of scientific disciplines: For pioneering investigations of the development of scientific thought, see: J. Piaget, *Introduction à l'épistémologie génétique* (Paris: Presses Univ. de France, 1950), T. Kuhn, *The Structure of Scientific Revolutions* (Chicago: Univ. of Chicago Press, 1962), M. Foucault, *The Order of Things* (New York: Pantheon, 1970). Some of the articles and general histories of social science on which the present account draws are: G. Allport, "The Historical Background of Modern Social Psychology," in G. Lindzey (ed.), *Handbook of Social Psychology*, Vol. 1 (Reading, Mass.: Addison-Wesley, 1954), pp. 3–56; A. Kardiner and E. Preble, *They Studied Man* (New York: Mentor, 1962); M. Harris, *The Rise of Anthropological Theory* (New York: Crowell, 1968); E. Boring, *A History of Experimental Psychology* (New York: Appleton-Century-Crofts, 1950); H. S. Hughes, *Consciousness and Society* (New York: Vintage, 1961); D. Sills (ed.), various biographical articles in *The International Encyclopedia of the Social Sciences* (New York: Macmillan, 1968); L. Bramson, *The Political Context of Sociology* (Princeton: Princeton Univ. Press, 1961); E. Boring, *Sensation and Perception in the History of Experimental Psychology* (New York: Appleton-Century-Crofts, 1942).

p. 29 John Watson's environmentalist claim appeared in *Behaviorism* (New York: Norton, 1930), p. 104. A useful introduction to the theory and methodology of behaviorism is H. Rachlin, *Introduction to Modern Behaviorism* (San Francisco: Freeman, 1970). Discussions of the pros and cons of behaviorism appear in N. Wann (ed.), *Behaviorism and Phenomenology* (Chicago: Univ. of Chicago Press, 1964).

p. 29 Gestalt psychology is effectively presented in W. Köhler, *Gestalt Psychology* (New York: Mentor, 1947), and an exhaustive account of its postulates appears in Kurt Koffka's classic text *Principles of Gestalt Psychology* (New York: Harcourt, 1935). A sympathetic critique of this school appears in J. Piaget, *The Psychology of Intelligence* (Paterson, N.J.: Littlefield Adams, 1963), Chapter 3.

p. 31 Freud's individual works are too familiar and too numerous to mention. The standard biography is E. Jones, *The Life and Work of Sigmund Freud* (New York: Basic Books, 1953). Two excellent critical introductions are P. Rieff, *Freud: The Mind of the Moralist* (New York: Anchor Books, 1961) and P. Roazen, *Freud: Political and Social Thought* (New York: Knopf, 1968).

p. 32 Yet neither the Gestaltists nor the psychoanalysts . . .: This judgment is perhaps unduly harsh, in view of the fact that contemporary psychology has yet to resolve most of the issues involved. Yet it seems fair to credit the structuralist school with a greater sensitivity to these problems and, perhaps, with genuine progress toward their resolution.

p. 33 Boas's ideas and influence can be gleaned from his monumental *General Anthropology* (Boston: Heath, 1938). See also A. L. Kroeber *et al.*, *Franz Boas 1858–1942*, American Anthropological Association Memoir Series, 1943, no. 61.

p. 34 Malinowski's approach is conveyed in a number of monographs, among them *The Argonauts of the Western Pacific* (New York: Dutton, 1964); *Crime and Custom in Savage Society* (New York: Harcourt Brace, 1926); *The Sexual Life of Savages in Northwestern Melanesia* (New York: Harcourt Brace, 1929). Malinowski's description of the ethnographer's goals is found in *Argonauts of the Western Pacific*, p. 25.

p. 36 The quotation from Mauss comes from *The Gift* (New York: Norton, 1967), pp. 78–9. His essays are collected in *Sociologie et anthropologie* (Paris: Presses Univ. de France, 1950), which has a lengthy and perspicacious introduction by his follower, Claude Lévi-Strauss. A. R. Radcliffe-Brown's views on social structure are found in *Structure and Function in Primitive Society* (Glencoe, Ill.: Free Press, 1952).

p. 39 Our developmental analysis has revealed . . .: A caveat to be entered here is that the determination of stages and transitional points in a developmental analysis is a delicate problem. What from one point of view is a new stage may, when examined more closely, be only an elaboration of a previous stage, or a transitional phase. What is needed is an independent definition of stages and transitions; yet this is difficult to achieve, since every observer brings to the task his own peculiar perspective. No doubt, later histories of this period, even if they recognize the importance of the structuralist movement, will see it as an imperfect and transitional phase, rather than as a high point of social-scientific thought.

p. 42 The example of a model expressed in purely formal language is a trivially simple one, but there is no reason why a model of great complexity cannot be developed. Naturally the analyst attempts to devise the simplest model consistent with all the relevant empirical and logical considerations.

p. 42 Husserl's most influential work is his *Logical Investigations*

(New York: Humanities Press, 1970). Merleau-Ponty, a contemporary of Piaget and Lévi-Strauss, wrote *The Phenomenology of Perception* (London: Routledge and Kegan Paul, 1965), and *The Structure of Behavior* (Boston: Beacon Press, 1963).

p. 43 Lévi-Strauss's critical remarks concerning philosophy appear in an interview with R. Bellour, in *Les Lettres françaises*, no. 1165 (1967). See also his assessment of existentialism in .S. de Gramont, "There Are No Superior Societies," in *C L-S*, p. 21.

p. 44 the pioneering work: Saussure's lectures were published posthumously in *Course in General Linguistics* (New York: McGraw-Hill, 1966). Jakobson's writings are now appearing in a standard edition, *Selected Writings* (The Hague: Mouton, 1962). The best introduction to his work is *Essais de linguistique generale* (Paris: Éditions de Minuit, 1963).

p. 45 Jakobson and his associates . . .: The theory of distinctive features had to overcome considerable resistance from the older schools of linguists before it finally won broad acceptance. Even as linguistics was the first structuralist science, however, its structuralist tenets are now being challenged by a newer, more "dynamic," school of investigation.

p. 46 Interest in these "semiotic" questions: Among the most notable studies of symbols and symbol systems are: S. Langer, *Philosophy in a New Key* (Cambridge, Mass.: Harvard Univ. Press, 1942); E. Cassirer, *Philosophy of Symbolic Forms* (New Haven, Conn.: Yale Univ. Press, 1953); B. Whorf, *Language, Thought and Reality* (New York: Wiley, 1956); N. Goodman, *Languages of Art* (Indianapolis: Bobbs-Merrill, 1968); C. Peirce, *Philosophical Writings* (J. Buchler, ed.) (New York: Dover, 1955); C. Morris, *Signs, Language and Behavior* (New York: Prentice-Hall, 1946).

p. 46 they were sufficiently impressed . . .: Lévi-Strauss's debt to linguistics is spelled out explicitly in several essays—for example, "Language and the Analysis of Social Laws" and "Linguistics and Anthropology," both reprinted in *SA*, Part I. Piaget's debt to linguistics is less often articulated; but see his *Play, Dreams and Imitation* (New York: Norton, 1951), and his address "Psychology, Interdisciplinary Relations, and the System of Sciences," delivered at the XVIIIth Meeting of the International Congress of Psychology, Moscow, 1966, in which he remarked (p. 27) that "Linguistics is undoubtedly the most advanced of the social sciences, both by virtue of its theoretical structures and by the precision of its knowledge."

CHAPTER 3

p. 51 The Bergson quotation appears in *An Introduction to Metaphysics: The Creative Mind* (Totowa, N.J.: Littlefield Adams, 1965), p. 188.

p. 51 The quotation from Piaget is cited by J. de Aguriaguerra and R. Tissot in "The Apraxias," in *Handbook of Clinical Neurology*, Vol. IV (P. Winken and G. Bryn, eds.) (Amsterdam: North Holland Pub. Co., 1969), p. 59.

p. 52 The novel from which this quotation is taken is no longer readily available, a state of affairs with which Piaget seems quite satisfied. The reference is *Recherche* (Lausanne: Edition la Concorde, 1918), p. 249. No doubt a publisher will eventually reissue this work, if only to cash in on a famous name. Piaget's subsequently cited recollections, including the brief quotations, come primarily from his autobiographical essay which appears in E. Boring *et al.* (eds.), *A History of Psychology in Autobiography* (Barre, Mass.: Clark Univ. Press, 1952), pp. 237–56; this work focuses on his intellectual development rather than his personal life. However, Piaget's preferences and prejudices, as well as references to pivotal personal events, occasionally come through in his scholarly writings, particularly of late.

p. 55 He took courses . . .: It is interesting, and perhaps not entirely accidental, that Freud undertook postdoctoral studies quite similar to those of Piaget.

p. 56 Piaget's first articles appeared in French and Swiss journals and have not been translated. On the other hand, each of his first five books was quickly translated into several languages and made his name familiar to English-speaking audiences in the 1920's. The books were *The Language and Thought of the Child* (New York: Harcourt Brace, 1926); *Judgment and Reasoning in the Child* (New York: Harcourt Brace, 1928); *The Child's Conception of the World* (New York: Harcourt Brace, 1929); *The Child's Conception of Physical Causality* (London: Kegan Paul, 1930); *The Moral Judgment of the Child* (London: Kegan Paul, 1932).

p. 57 this vast output: The Jean Piaget Society, recently organized at Temple University, plans to collect all of Piaget's writings, and may eventually issue a standard edition.

p. 59 Darwin's account . . . was too simple: The affinities and contrasts between Piaget's views of evolution and those of the discredited Lamarck and Lysenko schools are too complex to permit review here. It is perhaps most useful to note that a few eminent geneticists, among them C. H. Waddington of Edinburgh, share some of Piaget's views on genetics and development, but that most workers in the field greet Piaget's evolutionary speculations with healthy though respectful skepticism. For a detailed statement of Piaget's views, see his *Biologie et connaissance* (Paris: Gallimard, 1967). Waddington's views are put forth in an article which appeared in A. Koestler (ed.), *Beyond Reductionism* (New York: Macmillan, 1970); for a useful summary, see G. Steiner's review of this book in *The New Yorker*, March 6, 1971, pp. 108–10.

p. 59 an organism's intelligence was embodied . . .: The best brief introduction to Piaget's theory will be found in his little book (with B. Inhelder) *The Psychology of the Child* (New York: Basic Books, 1969), and his chapter, "Piaget's Theory," in *Carmichael's Handbook of Child Psychology* (P. Mussen, ed.) (New York: Wiley, 1970), pp. 703–32.

p. 63 The young child is . . .: Piaget now regrets his introduction of the term "egocentrism," because it has been so widely misinterpreted. However, it is unlikely that a more neutral term can be successfully substituted at this late date.

p. 66 The sample story and Gio's paraphrase appear in *LT*, pp. 99, 116.

p. 66 The different uses of the word "because" are presented in *JR*, p. 17.

p. 68 The child's notion of thought processes is described in *CCW*, p. 37. Specific examples quoted are found on pp. 39, 45, 53, 100, 92, 119.

p. 71 Piaget . . . has perceived a relationship: Today Piaget is less likely to draw parallels between primitives and children than he was in the 1920's. See Chapter 5 of this book.

p. 72 "La première année de l'enfant," *British Journal of Psychology*, Vol. 18 (1927), 97–120, contains Piaget's initial assessment of his observations of infants.

p. 75 Piaget's definitions of scheme, accommodation, and assimilation are difficult to pinpoint and to summarize, particularly since he often shifts terminology without warning. Imposed upon this is a language problem, with some translators speaking exclusively of schemes, others only of schemas, still others employing both terms indiscriminately or in different contexts. Here we will reserve the terms "assimilation" and "accommodation" for the inseparable biological counterparts of all organic activity. The assimilatory pole emphasizes an environmental interaction in which the organism does not make significant adjustments in its behavioral repertoire, while the accommodatory pole stresses an interaction in which the organism adjusts its repertoire so as to match the form and structure of the environmental object. Note that it is necessary to postulate a separate environmental object, even though Piaget claims that in a strict sense one cannot conceive of an object apart from a constructing individual. The scheme is the underlying pattern which allows the performance of a variety of acts, all of which have a similar structure.

p. 76 The description of a circular reaction appears in *OI*, pp. 91–2.

p. 77 Laurent's experimentation with the tin box is described on p. 201.

p. 78 Jacqueline's exploration of new objects is described on p. 253.

p. 79 Jacqueline's discovery with the box is described on p. 272.

p. 79 Laurent's initial attempt to reach the watch is described on p. 283.

p. 80 Laurent's successful strategy is described on p. 283.

p. 81 Jacqueline's adventures at the door are described on p. 339.

p. 81 The renowned example of the opening of the matchbox is described on p. 338.

p. 84 Piaget's description of the object concept occupies the first part of his *tour de force*, *CR*. In this work he traces the early genesis of such epistemological categories as space, time, and causality.

p. 85 The description of Laurent playing with the box is found on p. 45; that of Jacqueline on the mattress, on p. 51.

p. 86 This attraction to A: The so-called "A, not B" phenomenon has been much studied of late, in an effort to unravel the underlying mechanisms. Much useful work has been done by Gerald Gratch; see, for example, G. Gratch and W. Landers, "Stage IV of Piaget's Theory of Infant Object Concepts: A Longitudinal Study," *Child Development*, Vol. 42 (1971), 359–72.

p. 87 Lucienne's search for the watch is described in *CR*, p. 51; Jacqueline's search for the coin, p. 79.

p. 88 Poincaré's hypotheses about the mathematics of space perception are put forth in his book *The Value of Science* (New York: Dover, 1958). Piaget's speculations about the spatial group are found in *CR*, Chapter 2.

p. 91 Conservation studies are reported in J. Piaget and B. Inhelder, *Le Développement des quantités chez l'enfant* (Neuchâtel: Delachaux et Niestlé, 1941). It has sometimes been argued that Piaget is not testing the child's understanding of physical laws, but simply his grasp of the terms "same," "more," and "less." Although this criticism may well be logically unassailable, it is, in my view, beside the point. The child has heard the words "same" and "more" frequently since early childhood, and if he does not have an adult understanding of these terms, it is because he does not understand the underlying concepts. Once he comprehends what "same" means on a nonlinguistic level, his performance on conservation tasks and his understanding of the verbal interrogation will improve accordingly. A demonstration that conservation tasks are more than a simple verbal game comes from studies in which language is not employed: it has been shown that physiological reactions are heightened when conservation of quantity is violated by means of a special apparatus which covertly alters the amount of fluid. Cf. T. Achenbach, "Surprise and GST as Indicators of Conservation," *Proceedings of the American Psychological Association*, Vol. 5, 1970, 281–2.

p. 92 Most of Piaget's conservation studies, including the first ones, were conducted with Bärbel Inhelder, his collaborator of many years. In what follows, Piaget's name alone will often be used in referring to work done in conjunction with Inhelder and other members of the Genevan research group.

pp. 92–3 Classification tasks are described in *EGLT*. Conservation of number is treated in *CCN*.

p. 94 Piaget's research on concrete operations is usefully summarized in two books written with Inhelder: *GLT* and *EGLT*.

p. 96 It is not as yet possible to verify: For a critical review of Piaget's claims, see J. S. Bruner, "Review of *The Growth of Logical Thinking*," *British Journal of Psychology*, 1959, 50, 363–70, and J. S. Bruner *et al.*, *Studies in Cognitive Growth* (New York: Wiley, 1966). Piaget's response to these criticisms is contained in his lectures published as *On the Development of Identity and Memory* (Barre, Mass.: Clark Univ. Press, 1968).

p. 99 A detailed account of the stages involved in solving the billiards problem can be found in *GLT*, pp. 4–19.

p. 99 Testimony of the eight- to nine-year-olds is found on p. 8.

p. 99 Explanations in terms of necessity appear on pp. 13–14.

p. 101 Mam's account is given on p. 110.

p. 103 The claim that the adolescent reasons like a formal logician can be taken to mean that he has constructed for himself the opening lessons of a modern treatise on logic. He is able to appreciate all the possible relationships between two propositions, p and q, ranging from implication (p implies q) to disjunction (either p and q, or not p and q, or p and not *q*, or not *p* and not *q*). Naturally he need not be aware of the propositional calculus, which was not even formalized until recent decades. Rather, when faced with a verbal problem or a scientific experiment, his reasoning appears to draw upon the cognitive machinery necessary for an explicit knowledge of the propositional calculus. Of course, implicit and explicit knowledge of these postulates need not be equivalent, but Piaget does not speculate on the differences, if any.

p. 103 It has been proposed that formal operations first emerged in societies where the majority of people were essentially at the stage of concrete operations, but where those whose thought was slightly more advanced were valued and rewarded. Drawing upon this argument, some commentators have suggested that in a society where the capacity for formal operations is widespread, thought levels aspire to a still-higher stage, which may be expected gradually to emerge. While this idea is appealing, and consistent with Piagetian developmental theory, I can see no way of assessing its plausibility.

p. 104 Piaget has written one monograph on equilibration and is reportedly completing another one. He considers this topic so important that he has lectured on it repeatedly in the last twenty years and selected it as his major topic at a conference of specialists on child development and at the first meetings of the Jean Piaget Society. An accessible, though far from simple, account of his views on equilibrium some years ago can be found in his essay "Logique et équilibre dans les comportements du sujet," in *Études d'épistémologie génétique. II* (Paris: Presses Universitaires de France, 1956), pp. 27–118, and in his paper "The Role of the Concept of Equilibrium in Psychological Explanation," in SPS, pp. 110–15. The present quotation is from *GLT*, p. 243.

p. 105 To supply references for Piaget's varied pursuits would take many pages. Some of his most important books in areas other than child development are: *The Mechanisms of Perception* (New York: Basic Books, 1969); *Genetic Epistemology* (New York: Columbia Univ. Press, 1970); *Introduction à l'épistémologie génétique* (Paris: Presses Univ. de France, 1950); *The Science of Education and the Psychology of the Child* (New York: Orion, 1970); *Études sociologiques* (Geneva: Droz, 1965); *Biologie et connaissance* (Paris: Gallimard, 1967).

p. 105 His overall conclusion . . .: Even as the respiratory, digestive, and excretory systems function in an integrated manner, thereby achieving physiological equilibrium, the cognitive systems of the child are so constituted as to maintain maximum intellectual equilibrium consistent with their growth.

p. 107 he places a premium in this regard . . .: Some thirty years ago, McCulloch and Pitts proposed a mathematical model of the nervous system, and their pioneering work has proved enormously influential in biological and artificial-intelligence circles. Cf. W. S. McCulloch and W. H. Pitts, "A Logical Calculus of the Ideas Immanent in Nervous Activity," *Bulletin of Mathematical Biophysics*, Vol. 5 (Chicago: Univ. of Chicago Press, 1943), 115–33.

p. 107 Piaget makes a key distinction . . .: Piaget's recent thoughts on philosophy's relationship to science appear in his introductory essay in *Logique et connaissance scientifique* (Paris: Gallimard, 1967) and in a lively volume called *Sagesse et illusion de la philosophie* (Paris: Presses Univ. de France, 1965).

p. 109 Elkind's account of Piaget's visit appeared in "Giant in the Nursery Room," *The New York Times Magazine*, May 26, 1968, p. 25. Piaget's lectures were published as *On the Development of Identity and Memory* (Barre, Mass.: Clark Univ. Press, 1968).

p. 110 H. Stuart Hughes relates this anecdote about Freud and James in his *Consciousness and Society* (New York: Vintage, 1963), p. 113.

Chapter 4

p. 111 The quotation from Rousseau is taken from *Émile* (New York: Dutton, 1962); that from Tylor is found in *Primitive Culture* (London: J. Murray, 1871), p. 22.

p. 111 Lévi-Strauss's play is described in *TT*, pp. 376–80.

p. 113 Most of the account here of Lévi-Strauss's early life is gleaned from his autobiography; *L-S* includes a few more facts, and Lévi-Strauss himself provides scattered additional information throughout his writings.

p. 114 Lévi-Strauss's enthusiastic remarks about geology are found on p. 60 of his autobiography.

p. 114 His encounter with Marxism is described on p. 61.

p. 115 His description of reading Lowie is found on p. 63.

p. 116 His encounter with the Nambikwara is described in *TT*, p. 310.

p. 118 The characterization of "a people's customs" is found on p. 60 of *TT*.

p. 119 Lévi-Strauss's anthropological "manifesto" is presented in his essay "Structural Analysis in Linguistics and in Anthropology," in *SA*, p. 35.

p. 119 Linguistic systems dealt with symbols or signs . . .: Defining the terms "sign," "symbol," and others in the area of denotation and meaning is a major undertaking, which has inspired the new scientific field of semiotics. Piaget, for example, uses "sign" and "symbol" in a way directly opposite to that of other specialists, and any resolution of the inconsistency would be rather arbitrary. In the present discussion, therefore, both these terms will be used to refer to arbitrary elements; units which are not totally arbitrary (such as the words "twenty-one" or "blackboard") will be so designated.

p. 122 Lévi-Strauss discusses his solution of the avunculate problem on pp. 41–50 of his essay "Structural Analysis in Linguistics and in Anthropology," in *SA*. (Part I of this book also contains other early articles on the same subject.) In order to clarify this solution, however, I have made some assumptions not spelled out in the original. Lévi-Strauss does not indicate whether one has to know one or two of the four possible relationships, nor does he indicate which two of the possible relationships are necessary or whether any two will suffice. Brief consideration reveals that his hypothesis varies in its force, depending on whether one interprets it weakly (knowledge that two units have opposite signs will tell you only that the other units will also have opposite signs) or in a strong form (knowledge of the sign of the first member will tell you the sign of the third member; knowledge of the sign of the second member will tell you the sign of the fourth member). I have interpreted his thesis as follows: if one knows that two relations have the same sign, one can infer that the other two will have opposite signs. Almost no one, perhaps not even Lévi-Strauss himself, maintains that his original formulation is adequate; and a fair case can be made that either he is clearly wrong or his point is trivial and uninteresting. Why, then, even introduce this example? In the first place, most other examples of the structural analysis of kinship are simply too complex and technical to introduce in a book of this sort. Second, even if the facts do not fully support the claim, the present example does provide valuable clues to what an effective structural analysis might be like. The simplicity which renders it vulnerable constitutes at the same time its scientific (and aesthetic) appeal.

p. 123 The "sympathetic critic" was R. H. Lowie, the distinguished American anthropologist whose book on primitive society had originally attracted Lévi-Strauss to the field.

p. 124 Lévi-Strauss's assessment of Mauss's work is found in a long introductory essay to the collected papers of Mauss, *Sociologie et anthropologie* (Paris: Univ. de France, 1950). His own initial encounter with *The Gift* (Glencoe, Ill.: Free Press, 1954) is described on p. 33 of that essay.

p. 125 The vignette appears in Margaret Mead, *Sex and Temperament in Three Primitive Societies* (New York: Morrow, 1935).

p. 126 Lévi-Strauss's comment on theoretical exchange of men by women appears on p. 144 of *ESK*.

p. 127 language tended to "impoverish perception": This lament appears in *ESK*, p. 496.

p. 130 Lévi-Strauss analyzes the roles of the shaman and the psychoanalyst in two essays, both reprinted in *SA*: "The Sorcerer and His Magic" (pp. 167–85) and "The Effectiveness of Symbols" (pp. 186–205).

p. 131 The discussion of split representation appears in the essay "Split Representation in the Art of Asia and Africa," in *SA*, pp. 245–68.

p. 133 the "uninvited guest": Cf. Lévi-Strauss's remark to an interviewer, quoted in *The New York Times*, January 21, 1972, p. 47: "These experiments, represented by societies unlike our own, described and analyzed by anthropologists, provide one of the purest ways to understand what happens in the human mind and how it operates. That's what anthropology is good for in the most general way and what we can expect from it in the long run."

p. 135 Lévi-Strauss's "succinct formula," as well as his expatiation on totemism, is found in his little tome, *T*.

p. 136 the perceiving of associations is *the way*: Lévi-Strauss's theory of the brain appears in *T*.

p. 137 Hanunóo activities described on p. 4 of *SM*.

p. 138 The similarity between the churinga and modern archives is discussed in *SM*, p. 238.

p. 138 Both primitives and scientists . . .: On the centrality of classification, see G. Simpson, *Principles of Animal Taxonomy* (New York: Columbia Univ. Press, 1961).

p. 139 The *bricoleur*'s activities are described on pp. 16–22 of *SM*.

p. 142 Naming practices are discussed on pp. 204–10 of *SM*. The extract here is taken from p. 207.

p. 144 Lévi-Strauss's remarks about his own work were made in a personal communication to the author.

p. 144 One well-known anthropologist: David Maybury-Lewis.

p. 146 an (admittedly obscure) formula: Presented by Lévi-Strauss in his essay "The Structural Study of Myth," in *SA*, p. 288, and again in *Du miel aux cendres* (Paris: Plon, 1966), p. 212. It reads: $Fx(a) : Fy(b) \simeq Fx(b) : Fa-1(y)$. I have been unable to make sense of this formula, and no other commentators seem to have been able to shed light on it, either.

p. 146 various kinds of orderly transformation: The transformational aspect of music brings it close to the kinds of cognitive systems described by Piaget. These similarities have recently been examined by M. Pflederer, "Conservation and the Development of Musical Intelligence," *Journal of Research in Music Education*, Vol. 15 (1967), 215–23.

pp. 147–8 References for the *Mythologiques* are: *The Raw and the Cooked* (New York: Harper and Row, 1969); *Du miel aux cendres* (Paris: Plon, 1966); *L'Origine des manières de la table* (Paris: Plon, 1968); *L'Homme nu* (Paris: Plon, 1971).

p. 149 Lévi-Strauss's remarks concerning the underlying affinities among the Mind, Culture, and Nature have appeared frequently in recent interviews and writing. See, for example, the Introduction to *ESK*, p. xxix.

p. 151 Leach's structural analysis of Judges and Genesis is found in M. Lane (ed.), *Introduction to Structuralism* (New York: Basic Books, 1970), pp. 248–92.

p. 152–7 Leach's version of Genesis is presented in his essay "Lévi-Strauss in the Garden of Eden," in *CL-S*, pp. 47–60. His characterization of his own exercise appears on pp. 59–60.

p. 160 Lévi-Strauss's remarks on the mission of anthropology were made in an address on the occasion of the two-hundredth anniversary of the birth of James Smithson, founder of the Smithsonian Institution. The address, entitled "Anthropology: Its Achievements and Future," was subsequently published in *Knowledge Among Men* (New York: Simon and Schuster, 1966). The passage cited here appears on p. 122.

CHAPTER 5

p. 165 Piaget's remark on psychological explanation appears in *The Psychology of Intelligence* (Paterson, N.J.: Littlefield Adams, 1963), p. 3.

p. 172   structuralists . . . new mathematical tools: Piaget believes that a metatheory of structures will be forthcoming, and looks to the newer branches of mathematics for clues regarding its form. His Center for Genetic Epistemology seeks to translate this vision into a reality.

p. 172   D'Arcy Thompson's most distinguished work in his two-volume essay *On Growth and Form* (Cambridge, Mass.: Harvard Univ. Press, 1942), a careful study of the mathematical properties of naturally occurring forms.

p. 177   all thought is . . . a reflection of language: A defense of the determining role of language in thought can be found in the writings of Benjamin Lee Whorf. See his *Language, Thought and Reality* (Cambridge: MIT Press, 1956). The opposite view is insistently expressed in J. Hadamarad, *The Psychology of Invention in the Mathematical Field* (Princeton: Princeton Univ. Press, 1945).

p. 178   Studies on thought in the deaf include H. Furth, *Thinking Without Language: Psychological Implications of Deafness* (New York: Free Press, 1966); M. Vincent-Borelli, "La Naissance des opérations logiques chez les sourds-muets," *Enfance*, Vol. 4 (1951), 222–38; H. Sinclair-de-Zwart, *Langage et opérations: Sous-systèmes linguistiques et opérations concrètes* (Paris; Dunod, 1967). Piaget's reference to the "prelogic inherent in speech" is found in his *Biologie et connaissance* (Paris: Gallimard, 1967), p. 191.

p. 179   Lévi-Strauss . . . attributes to language a determining role: Lévi-Strauss's respect for language is apparent throughout his writings. The remark quoted here comes from p. 252 of *SM*.

p. 180   Piaget concedes . . .: Piaget's remarks on formal operations are found in *GLT, passim*.

p. 181   Lévi-Strauss's own thought processes are the subject of comment in J. Hadamarad, *The Psychology of Invention in the Mathematical Field* (Princeton: Princeton Univ. Press, 1945), p. 90.

p. 182   Piaget's comments on primitive thought and childhood thought are found in *CCW*. Lévi-Strauss answered this analogy in his chapter on "The Archaic Illusion," in *ESK*, pp. 84–97.

p. 183   both men have modified their positions: Lévi-Strauss's altered views on primitive and modern thought appear in the opening chapters of *SM*; Piaget's most recent remarks on primitive thought appear in his book *S*, p. 117, and in "Nécessité et signification des recherches comparatives en psychologie génétique," *International Journal of Psychology*, Vol. I (1966), 3–13.

p. 184   The myths, however, are the products . . .: I do not mean to suggest that mythmaking is a passive process, consisting primarily of repetition. There is ample room for inventiveness, development of intricate skills, evolution of new thematic material or stylistic techniques. Cf. A. B. Lord, *The Singer of Tales* (Cambridge, Mass.: Harvard Univ. Press, 1960). The difficulty in assessing the intellectual operations underlying mythopoetic activity stems from the near-impossibility of ascertaining which portions of a myth originate with the teller and which are slight modifications of earlier versions. It is as if individuals in our culture were taught the laws of physics in a rote manner as young children, and were later asked in the same terms learned earlier to describe what was happening in a laboratory experiment.

p. 184 Piaget has a stronger case: Cross-cultural studies of Piagetian tasks are reported in J. S. Bruner *et al., Studies in Cognitive Growth* (New York: Wiley, 1966), D. Elkind and J. Flavell (eds.) *Studies in Cognitive Development* (New York: Oxford Univ. Press, 1969), and recent volumes of the *International Journal of Psychology.*

p. 188 Piaget's remarks on Lévi-Strauss's structuralism are found in his book *S,* Chapter VI .

p. 189 Lévi-Strauss vacillates in his attitudes toward history. He makes sympathetic comments in his inaugural lecture at the College de France (*The Scope of Anthropology* [London: Jonathan Cape, 1967]), yet is openly critical of the craft in *The Savage Mind,* published shortly afterwards.

p. 189 For Lévi-Strauss's views on genetic studies, see his essays "Structure and Dialectics" in *Structural Anthropology* (New York: Basic Books, 1963), pp. 232–44, and his graceful study "The Story of Asdiwal" in E. Leach (ed.), *The Structural Study of Myth and Totemism* (London: Tavistock, 1967).

p. 190 For Lévi-Strauss's remarks on hot and cold societies, see *The Scope of Anthropology* (London: Jonathan Cape, 1967); that this dichotomy is a vast oversimplification is demonstrated by such so-called "primitive" societies as the Manus, studied by Margaret Mead, which adapt to change more readily than many "modern" societies.

p. 191 adolescents often progress . . . only to fall back: Findings of regression in the thought of adolescents living in a concrete-operational society are reported by L. Kohlberg; see his "Stage and Sequence: The Cognitive Developmental Approach to Socialization," in D. Goslin (ed.), *Handbook of Socialization: Theory and Research* (New York: Rand McNally, 1969), pp. 347–380.

p. 192 The description of root metaphors in cosmic theories has been introduced by S. Pepper in his book *World Hypotheses* (Berkeley: Univ. of Calif. Press, 1948).

p. 193 Lévi-Strauss's remarks on South American Indians and his own thought processes appear in the overture to *The Raw and the Cooked,* p. 13.

p. 193 His views on how myths operate are given on p. 12.

p. 194 Piaget's remarks on the creative imagination are found in his book *L'Image mentale chez l'enfant* (Paris: Presses Univ. de France, 1966), p. vii.

p. 194 Lévi-Strauss's allusions to the character of primitive thought are found in *TT* and *The Scope of Anthropology* (London: Jonathan Cape, 1967).

p. 195 The contrast between Piagetian and Lévi-Straussian analysis outlined in the pages that follow is amplified in my article "The Structural Analysis of Myths and Protocols," *Semiotica,* Vol. 5 (1971), 31–57.

p. 195 The *Viergruppe,* composed of the operations of identity, negation, reciprocity, and correlation, is described in *Traité de Logique* (Paris:

Colin, 1949) and applied to the analysis of adolescent thought processes in *GLT*.

p. 198   Jakobson's book was translated in 1968 (The Hague: Mouton).

p. 199   Jakobson's notes on solidarity appear on p. 51; his remarks on development, on p. 65.

p. 200   Relations between color instinct and phonological systems are characterized on pp. 73 ff.

p. 201   The scientist making the "bold claim" was D. I. Mason, cited by Lévi-Strauss in *SA*, p. 92.

p. 201   Presentation of Jakobson's ideas, and their relevance for our efforts at synthesizing the developmental and structural approaches, is undertaken at greater length in my article "Structure and Development," in *The Human Context* (in press, 1972).

p. 202   Jakobson's discussion of the six forms of verbal communication is found in "Closing Statement: Linguistics and Poetics," in T. Sebeok (ed.), *Style and Language* (Cambridge, Mass.: MIT Press 1960), pp. 350–77. His developmental analysis has been presented in various lectures, including an unpublished series delivered at Harvard University in 1968–9.

p. 206   For an extended discussion of the notion of the mode, see my article "From Mode to Symbol," *British Journal of Aesthetics*, Vol. 10 (1970), 359–75.

p. 209   For considerations pertinent to a psychology of the artist, see my forthcoming book, *Art and Human Development* (New York: Wiley, in press), Chap. 3, and my essays "Problem Solving in the Arts," *Journal of Aesthetic Education*, Vol. 5 (1971), 93–114; "The Development of Sensitivity to Artistic Styles," *Journal of Aesthetics and Art Criticism*, Vol. 29 (1971), 515–27; "From Mode to Symbol: Thoughts on the Genesis of the Arts," *British Journal of Aesthetics*, Vol. 10 (1970), 259–75.

p. 210   Both of our thinkers . . .: Lévi-Strauss's cosmic views have emerged in various interviews he has recently granted: G. Charbonier (ed.), *Entretiens avec Claude Lévi-Strauss* (Paris: Plon-Julliard, 1961); S. de Gramont, "There Are No Superior Societies," in *CL-S*, pp. 3–21; "A contre-courant," *Le Nouvel Observateur* (January 25, 1967), pp. 30–2, as well as in numerous asides in his *Mythologiques*. Piaget's search for universal structures is most fully explicated in his book on structuralism.

p. 211   Not only do structures . . .: The relationship between physical and operational structures is described in *S*, pp. 37–51. The quotation actually represents two separate extracts, from pp. 41 and 45, respectively. Piaget quoted the remark by Niels Bohr in a personal conversation with the author.

CHAPTER 6

p. 213   The epigraph is taken from S. de Gramont, "There Are No Superior Societies," in *C L-S*, p. 17.

p. 213   Among accounts of the student uprising in France are R. Aron, *The Elusive Revolution* (New York: Praeger, 1969); A. Touraine, *The May*

Movement: Reform and Revolution (New York: Random House, 1971); Épistémon, *Ces idées qui ont ébranlé la France* (Paris, Fayard, 1968).

p. 214 Lacan and Foucault are not well known in this country, but have enthusiastic followings in France. Lacan, a maverick psychoanalyst whose oral presentations are as magnetic as were Wittgenstein's, has one major work in translation, *The Language of the Self* (Baltimore: Johns Hopkins Univ. Press, 1968). Foucault, a historian or "archaeologist" of the social sciences, is best known for his works *Madness and Civilization* (New York: Pantheon, 1965) and *The Order of Things* (New York: Pantheon, 1970). He rejects the label "structuralist," but has nonetheless been labeled in this way by most commentators.

p. 214 Daniel Cohn-Bendit's interpretation of the events which he helped precipitate can be found in the book *Obsolete Communism* (with G. Cohn-Bendit) (New York: McGraw-Hill, 1969).

p. 215 the French university was like structuralism: This negative evaluation is found in an anonymous account of the events of May: Epistémon, *Ces idées qui ont ébranlé la France* (Paris: Fayard, 1968).

p. 216 For symposia on the work of Piaget, see R. Ripple and V. Rockcastle (eds.), *Piaget Rediscovered* (Ithaca, N.Y.: Cornell Univ. Press, 1964); W. Kessen and C. Kuhlmann (eds.), "Thought in the Young Child," *Monograph Soc. Res. Ch. Develp.*, Vol. 27 (1962).

p. 216 Bruner's criticisms of Piaget are voiced in his book *Studies in Cognitive Growth* (New York: Wiley, 1966). Bever and Mehler's research was reported in "The Study of Competence in Cognitive Psychology," *International Journal of Psychology*, Vol. III (1968), 273–80.

p. 216 The discussion of scientific movements in terms of new paradigms is based on the work of the historian of science T. Kuhn. See his *Structure of Scientific Revolutions* (Chicago: Univ. of Chicago Press, 1962).

p. 217 some valiant attempts: For a neo-behaviorist attempt to translate Piaget into stimuli and responses, see D. Berlynés' thoughtful book *Structure and Direction in Thinking* (New York: Wiley, 1965). Discussion of the irreconcilability of the behaviorist and Piagetian perspectives can be found in H. Furth, *Piaget and Knowledge* (Englewood Cliffs, N.J.: Prentice-Hall, 1968).

p. 217 Some of the more responsible critiques of Lévi-Strauss's work include D. Maybury-Lewis, "Science or Bricolage?" in *C L-S*, 150–63; R. Zimmerman, "Lévi-Strauss and the Primitive," also in *C L-S*, pp. 216–34; E. Leach, *Lévi-Strauss* (London: Fontana, 1970); M. Douglas, "The Meaning of Myth, with Special Reference to *La Geste d'Asdiwal*," in E. Leach (ed.), *The Structural Study of Myth and Totemism* (London: Tavistock, 1967). Those critics who generate more heat than light are better left uncited.

p. 218 Comprehensive introductions to ethnoscience are found in A. K. Romney and R. D. Andrade (eds.), "Transcultural Studies in Cognition," *American Anthropologist*, Vol. 66 (1964), No. 3, part 2, and in S. Tyler (ed.), *Cognitive Anthropology* (New York: Holt, 1969).

p. 220 Intelligent critical analyses of structuralism are found in such collections as R. Bastide, *Sens et usage du terme 'structure' dans les sciences humaines* (The Hague: Mouton, 1962); J. Tanner and B. Inhelder (eds.) *Discussions in Child Development* (New York: International Univ. Press 1956–60); P. Ricoeur, "Structure et hermeneutique," *L'Esprit*, Vol. 322 (November 1963), pp. 598–627. It is perhaps significant that the more probing critiques of structuralism have come from Continental scholars, who seem more attuned to what Piaget, Lévi-Strauss, and their compeers are trying to do. All too often, Anglo-Saxon commentators appear to me to have missed the point. For a similar view, see B. Scholte, "Epistemic Paradigms: Some Problems in Cultural Research in Social Anthropological History and Theory," in *C L-S,* pp. 108–22.

p. 222 Sartre's book has not yet been translated into English. See *Critique de la raison dialectique* (Paris: Gallimard, 1960).

p. 223 Lévi-Strauss's principal response to Sartre appears in *SM,* Chapter 9. Also note his denial of the political bias of structuralism in S. de Gramont, "There Are No Superior Societies," in *C L-S,* p. 19, and in G. Charbonnier (ed.), *Entretiens avec Claude Lévi-Strauss* (Paris: Plon, 1961), p. 16.

p. 225 Piaget's remarks on teaching can be found in an address, to a group of educators, included in R. Ripple and V. Rockcastle (eds.), *Piaget Rediscovered* (Ithaca, N.Y.: Cornell Univ. Press, 1964) and in an interview in *Psychology Today* (May 1970), pp. 25–32.

p. 226 On the object concept in cats, see H. Gruber *et al.,* "The Development of Object Permanence in the Cat," *Developmental Psychology,* Vol. 4 (1971), 9–15.

p. 226 For Piaget's remarks on behaviorism and reflexology, see his review of J. S. Bruner's *Studies in Cognitive Growth,* in *Contemporary Psychology,* Vol. 12 (1967), 532–3.

p. 227 the great emphasis . . . on the primacy of intellect: Signs of the revolt against intellect can be found everywhere, but it is difficult to determine whether the present period is especially marked by this trend. Some works which would defend this proposition are S. Sontag, *Against Interpretation* (New York: Delta, 1967); T. Roszak, *The Making of a Counter-Culture* (New York: Doubleday, 1968); C. Reich, *The Greening of America* (New York: Random House, 1970). Social-scientific works which focus on the affective dimensions of experience include E. Erikson, *Identity, Youth and Crisis* (New York: Norton, 1968); Rollo May, *Love and Will* (New York: Norton, 1969); E. Goffman, *The Presentation of Self in Everyday Life* (Garden City, N.Y.: Doubleday Anchor, 1970); H. Garfinkel, *Studies in Ethnomodology* (Englewood Cliffs, N.J.: Prentice-Hall, 1967); E. Hall, *The Silent Language* (Greenwich, Conn.: Fawcett, 1959).

p. 228 De Gramont's account of the structuralist vogue and Lévi-Strauss's petulance toward faddists appears in "There Are No Superior Societies," in *C L-S,* pp. 2–21. See the other articles in this book for further examples of the impact of structuralism.

p. 229 Notable efforts to apply structuralist analysis to literature include R. Jakobson and L. Jones, *Shakespeare's Verbal Art in "Th' Expence of Spirit";* (The Hague: Mouton, 1970), H. Ehrmann, "Structures of Exchange in *Cinna,*" in "Structuralism," *Yale French Studies,* Vol. 37, (1966), pp. 148–

68; R. Barthes, *Le Degré zéro de l'écriture* (Paris: Editions Gonthier, 1964); R. Barthes, *Sur Racine* (Paris: Seuil, 1957); R. Jakobson and C. Lévi-Strauss, "Les Chats de Charles Baudelaire," *L'Homme*, Vol. 2 (1962), 5–21.

p. 230 Barthes' half-serious analysis of the structural properties of furniture, food, and clothing appears in *Elements of Semiology* (London: Jonathan Cape, 1967); see also Leach's summary of this analysis in *L-S*, pp. 46–8.

p. 230 Lévi-Strauss's discussion of meals and their constituents is found in the closing pages of *L'Origine des manières de la table* (Paris: Plon, 1968), and in his essay "The Culinary Triangle," *Partisan Review*, Vol. 32 (1966), 86–95.

p. 231 Barthes' analysis of different kinds of scientific and literary languages is found in his essay "Sciences vs. Literature," reprinted in M. Lane (ed.), *Introduction to Structuralism* (New York: Basic Books, 1970), pp. 410–16.

p. 232 For Lévi-Strauss's view on the relationship between structuralism and art, see the Overture in *The Raw and the Cooked* (New York: Harper and Row, 1969), pp. 1–32; G. Charbonnier (ed.), *Entretiens avec Claude Lévi-Strauss* (Paris: Plon-Julliard, 1961), *passim; L'Homme nu,* "Finale" (Paris: Plon, 1971).

p. 236 Piaget's efforts in genetic epistemology have been reported in a number of essays and books, among them *Genetic Epistemology* (New York: Columbia Univ. Press, 1970), and the encyclopedia *Logique et connaissance scientifique* (Paris: Gallimard, 1967). He is also editor and chief contributor to the series *Études d'épistémologie génétique,* of which over two dozen volumes have already appeared.

p. 236 The differences between geometrical thinking as it develops in the child and in the culture are described in Inhelder and Piaget's book *The Child's Conception of Space* (New York: Norton, 1967).

p. 237 The recent writings on the circle of sciences include an address, "Psychology, Interdisciplinary Relations, and the System of Sciences," delivered at the XVIIIth International Congress of Psychology, Moscow, 1966. The quotation comes from p. 27. The topic is discussed further in the polemical work *Sagesse et illusion de la philosophie* (Paris: Presses Univ. de France, 1965).

p. 237 *Biology and Knowledge: Biologie et connaissance* (Paris: Gallimard, 1967).

p. 238 The transcript of the television program "Vivre et parler" appeared in *Les Lettres Françaises,* (February 19, 1968), no. 1221–2.

p. 238 On the relationship between DNA and language, see R. Masters, "Genes, Language and Evolution," *Semiotica*, Vol. 2 (1970), 295–320; and R. Jakobson, "Linguistics in Relation to the Other Sciences," in *Main Trends in Social Research,* in press.

p. 240 Chomsky's most important writings are *Syntactic Structures* (The Hague: Mouton, 1967); *Aspects of the Theory of Syntax* (Cambridge: MIT Press, 1965); *Language and Mind* (New York: Harcourt, Brace, and World, 1968); *Cartesian Linguistics* (New York: Harper and Row, 1966); and (with M. Halle) *The Sound Pattern of English* (New York: Harper and Row, 1968). Excellent discussions of Chomsky's ideas about early language acquisition appear in F. Smith and G. Miller, *The Genesis of Language* (Cambridge, Mass: MIT Press, 1966). A good introduction for the uninitiated is J. Lyons, *Noam Chomsky* (New York: Viking, 1970).

p. 240 Chomsky has argued that linguistic capacity . . .: Traditional views of language learning, diametrically opposed to Chomsky's theory, are set forth by C. Osgood, "A Behavioristic Analysis of Perception and Language as Cognitive Phenomena," in H. Gruber *et al.* (eds.), *Contemporary Approaches to Cognition* (Cambridge, Mass.: Harvard Univ. Press, 1957), pp. 75–118; and by Chomsky's archantagonist B. F. Skinner, *Verbal Behavior* (New York: Appleton-Century-Crofts, 1957). An intelligent critical discussion of Chomsky's general position can be found in the essays collected by S. Hook (ed.), *Language and Philosophy* (New York: New York University Press, 1969).

p. 242 Piaget's comments on Chomsky and Lévi-Strauss are found in his book *S*, Chapters V and VI; Chomsky's comments on Lévi-Strauss and Piaget are found in his essay *Language and Mind* (New York: Harcourt, Brace, and World, 1968). Lévi-Strauss has indicated his admiration for Piaget's later work and his reservations about the philosophical implications of Chomsky's work, in a personal communication to me, and in his latest writings (*L'Homme nu,* "Finale" [Paris: Plon, 1971]).

p. 243 It is possible to mention here only a few random works by scholars who have undertaken studies of the mind: I. Eibl-Eibesfeldt, *Ethology* (New York: Holt, Reinhart and Winton, 1970); P. Wolff, "The Causes, Controls and Organization of Behavior in the Neonate," *Psychological Issues,* Vol. VI (1966); W. McCulloch, *Embodiments of Mind* (Cambridge, Mass.: MIT Press, 1965); J. Bowlby, *Attachment* (New York: Basic Books, 1969); H. Simon, *Models of Man* (New York: Wiley, 1961); R. Gardner and B. Gardner, "Teaching Sign Language to a Chimpanzee," *Science,* Vol. 165 (1969), 664–72; D. Premack, "A Functional Analysis of Language," *J. Exp. Anal. Behavior,* Vol. 14 (1970), 107–25; A. R. Luria, *The Higher Cortical Functions in Man* (New York: Basic Books, 1966); N. Geschwind, "Disconnection Syndromes in Animals and Man," *Brain,* Vol. 88 (1965), 237–94, 585–644; J. Lettvin, H. Maturana, W. McCulloch, and W. Pitts, "What the Frog's Eye Tells the Frog's Brain," *Proc. Inst. Radio Engnrs.,* Vol. 47 (1959), 1940–51; D. Hubel and T. Wiesel, "The Visual Cortex of the Brain," *Scientific American,* Vol. 209 (1963), 54–62; C. Trevarthen, "Experimental Evidence for a Brain-Stem Contribution to Visual Perception in Man," unpublished paper, 1971; M. Critchley, *The Parietal Lobes* (London: E. J. Arnold, 1953); J. Flynn *et al.,* "Changes in Sensory and Motor Systems During Centrally Elicited Attack," *Behavior Science,* Vol. 16 (1971), 1–19; P. Eimas, "Speech Perception in Infants," *Science,* Vol. 171 (1971), 303–6.

AFTERWORD

p.250 On the cognitive sciences movement: See my introductory essay "Cognition Comes of Age," in M. Piatelli-Palmarini (ed.), *On Language and Learning* (Cambridge: Harvard University Press, 1980).

p.250 For excellent overviews of recent work by Piaget not covered in *The Quest for Mind*, see M. Boden, *Piaget* (New York: Penguin, 1980), and H. Gruber and J. Vonèche (eds.), *The Essential Piaget* (New York: Basic Books, 1978).

p.250 On causality: See, for example, J. Piaget and R. Garcia, *Understanding Causality* (New York: Norton, 1974).

p.251 J. Piaget, *The Grasp of Consciousness* (Cambridge: Harvard University Press, 1976).

p.251 For a partial list of Piaget's recent writings, see the reviews cited earlier and the series *Études d'épistémologie génétique*.

p. 252 Critiques of Piaget: T. G. R. Bower, *Development in Infancy* (San Francisco: W. H. Freeman, 1974); P. Bryant, *Perception and Understanding in Young Children: An Experimental Approach* (New York: Basic Books, 1974); C. Brainerd, *Piaget's Theory of Intelligence* (Englewood Cliffs: Prentice-Hall, 1978); R. Gelman and C. R. Gallistel, *The Child's Understanding of Number* (Cambridge: Harvard University Press, 1978).

p.252 Extensions of Piaget: See L. Kohlberg, "Stage and Sequence: The Cognitive-Developmental Approach to Socialization," in D. Goslin (ed.), *Handbook of Socialization Theory and Research* (Chicago: Rand McNally,1969); H. Gruber, *Darwin on Man*, second edition (Chicago: University of Chicago Press, 1981).

p.253 Piaget's lifelong interest in biology: J. Piaget, *Behavior and Evolution* (New York: Pantheon Books, 1978); *Adaptation vitale et psychologie de l'intelligence: selection organique et phénocopie* (Paris: Hermann, 1974).

pp.253–4 Concept of equilibration: See, in particular, volumes 31–35 of *Études d'épistémologie génétique* (Paris: Presses Universitaires de France, 1974–77).

p.255 Lévi-Strauss's study of masks: *La voie des masques* (Paris: Plon, 1979).

p.257 Lévi-Strauss's address to a French-Japanese circle: "Colloque sur les études franco-japonaises en France," Paris, October, 1979.

p.257 The meaning of the bean: See Lévi-Strauss, "Pythagoras in America," in R.G. Hook (ed.), *Fantasy and Symbol: Studies in Anthropological Interpretation* (New York: Academic Press, 1979).

p.258 Sources on Chomsky's principal ideas: See J. Lyons, *Noam Chomsky* (New York: Viking, 1970), and Chomsky's *Language and Mind* (New York: Harcourt, Brace & Jovanovich, 1972), *Reflections on Language* (New York: Pantheon, 1975), and *Rules and Representations* (New York: Columbia University Press, 1980).

p.258 Debate at Royaumont: See M. Piatelli-Palmarini (ed.), *On Language and Learning* (Cambridge: Harvard University Press, 1980). My views of this debate appear in "The Meeting on the Summit," *Psychology Today*, July, 1979.

p.261 Rousseau's influence on Lévi-Strauss: See *Anthropologie structurale deux* (Paris: Plon, 1973). In a personal communication, Lévi-Strauss has made the tantalizing suggestion that while Rousseau's influence on him has been considerable, it is no stronger than that of Chateaubriand, "his contradictory twin."

pp.262–3 Chomsky on Rousseau: *For Reasons of State* (New York: Pantheon, 1973). I am thankful to Noam Chomsky for calling these essays to my attention.

p.264 Certain problems in structuralism: In a personal communication, Chomsky has pointed out to me that the study of creativity has not advanced very far in any of the social sciences. I agree, but wonder whether structuralist approaches may in principle be inhospitable to this line of study.

Index